£50

SELECTED PAPERS FROM THE FIFTH WORLD CONGRESS OF
CENTRAL AND EAST EUROPEAN STUDIES, WARSAW, 1995

Edited for the International Council for Central and East European
Studies by Ronald J. Hill, Professor of Comparative Government, Trinity
College, University of Dublin, Ireland

Titles include:

Sue Bridger (*editor*)
WOMEN AND POLITICAL CHANGE
Perspectives from East–Central Europe

J. A. Dunn (*editor*)
LANGUAGE AND SOCIETY IN POST-COMMUNIST EUROPE

William E. Ferry and Roger E. Kanet (*editors*)
POST-COMMUNIST STATES IN THE WORLD COMMUNITY

Graeme Gill (*editor*)
ELITES AND LEADERSHIP IN RUSSIAN POLITICS

Paul G. Hare (*editor*)
SYSTEMIC CHANGE IN POST-COMMUNIST ECONOMIES

A. Kemp-Welch (*editor*)
STALINISM IN POLAND, 1944–1956

Stanislav J. Kirschbaum (*editor*)
HISTORICAL REFLECTIONS ON CENTRAL EUROPE

Carol S. Leonard (*editor*)
THE MICROECONOMICS OF POST-COMMUNIST CHANGE

Kevin McDermott and John Morison (*editors*)
POLITICS AND SOCIETY UNDER THE BOLSHEVIKS

John Morison (*editor*)
ETHNIC AND NATIONAL ISSUES IN RUSSIAN AND EAST
EUROPEAN HISTORY

Judith Pallot (*editor*)
TRANSFORMING PEASANTS
Society, State and the Peasantry, 1861–1930

Karen L. Ryan and Barry P. Scherr (*editors*)
TWENTIETH-CENTURY RUSSIAN LITERATURE

Richard Sakwa (*editor*)
THE EXPERIENCE OF DEMOCRATIZATION IN EASTERN
EUROPE

Ray Taras (*editor*)
NATIONAL IDENTITIES AND ETHNIC MINORITIES IN EASTERN
EUROPE

Ian D. Thatcher (*editor*)
REGIME AND SOCIETY IN TWENTIETH-CENTURY RUSSIA

International Council for Central and East European Studies
Series Standing Order ISBN 0–333–71195–5
(*outside North America only*)

You can receive future titles in this series as they are published by placing a standing order.
Please contact your bookseller or, in case of difficulty, write to us at the address below with
your name and address, the title of the series and the ISBN quoted above.

Customer Services Department, Macmillan Distribution Ltd
Houndmills, Basingstoke, Hampshire RG21 6XS, England

Systemic Change in Post-Communist Economies

Selected Papers from the Fifth World Congress of Central and East European Studies, Warsaw, 1995

Edited by

Paul G. Hare
Head, School of Management
Heriot-Watt University
Edinburgh

First published in Great Britain 1999 by
MACMILLAN PRESS LTD
Houndmills, Basingstoke, Hampshire RG21 6XS and London
Companies and representatives throughout the world

A catalogue record for this book is available from the British Library.

ISBN 0–333–69545–3

 First published in the United States of America 1999 by
ST. MARTIN'S PRESS, INC.,
Scholarly and Reference Division,
175 Fifth Avenue, New York, N.Y. 10010

ISBN 0–312–22642–X

Library of Congress Cataloging-in-Publication Data
World Congress of Central and East European Studies (5th : 1995 :
Warsaw, Poland)
Systemic change in post-communist economies : selected papers from
the Fifth World Congress of Central and East European Studies,
Warsaw, 1995 / edited by Paul G. Hare.
     p.   cm. — (Selected papers from the Fifth World Congress of
Central and East European Studies, Warsaw, 1995)
Includes bibliographical references and index.
ISBN 0–312–22642–X (cloth)
1. Post-communism—Economic aspects—Europe, Central—Congresses.
2. Post-communism—Economic aspects—Europe, Eastern—Congresses.
3. Post-communism—Economic aspects—Russia (Federation)–
–Congresses. I. Hare, P. G. II. Title. III. Series.
HC244.W68   1995
338.947—dc21   99–30906
                                                              CIP

This book is printed on paper suitable for recycling and made from fully managed and
sustained forest sources.

10   9   8   7   6   5   4   3   2   1
08   07   06   05   04   03   02   01   00   99

Printed and bound in Great Britain by Antony Rowe Ltd, Chippenham, Wiltshire

Contents

v

General Editor's Introduction

It is a great pleasure for me to introduce these volumes of papers that originated in the Fifth World Congress of Central and East European Studies, held in Warsaw in the week 6–11 August 1995, under the auspices of the International Council for Central and East European Studies and of the Institute of Philosophy and Sociology and the Institute of Political Studies of the Polish Academy of Sciences.

In the period since the previous world Congress, held in Harrogate, England, in July 1990, that part of the world that is the focus of Slavists' special attention had undergone the completion of changes that were already in train but the outcome of which was still uncertain. Moreover, given the inevitable time-lag between the conception of a major scholarly event and its occurrence, the major concerns at the beginning of the decade were not yet those of charting and analysing the transition from communist rule to some other form of political, economic and social entity and the impact of this on the societies and cultures of Russia, the Soviet Union and the countries loosely referred to as 'Eastern Europe': far less ambitious expectations were still the order of the day. Even though Poland had led the way in abandoning communist rule, shortly followed by all the other countries in 'Eastern Europe', it took some considerable imagination and conviction for the Executive Committee of the International Council to take the bold decision to hold the 1995 Congress in Eastern Europe, a decision that evoked a very positive response from our colleagues in Warsaw.

The different international climate immediately made itself felt, as scholars from the region were able to attend in large numbers a conference organised by a body that had been almost exclusively 'Western' in its previous experience. No longer were they specially invited guests (who on previous occasions had sometimes been denied exit visas to attend such Congresses), and it was a moving experience for me, as General Editor of the Congress proceedings, to receive letters and other communications by fax and e-mail from countries that in 1990 had no separate existence, or from provincial cities in the heart of post-Soviet Russia. Moreover, the opening of archives and the opportunities for new kinds of research, by scholars based in the countries concerned and by those entering from outside, meant that by 1995 there was much new information available, and scholars from the two 'sides' inevitably had much to say to one another.

The traditions in which the different groups had been trained meant that the styles of scholarship were not totally compatible, and there is a learning process in train that is likely to continue for some years. However, both the Congress itself and, more especially, the collaborative ventures such as this series of volumes containing selected papers, give opportunities for professional colleagues from around the world to make their own contributions to the new (and sometimes old) scholarly debates in ways that were hitherto impossible.

While not every paper that was presented or offered for publication was considered suitable for inclusion in the various thematic volumes, and individual editors sometimes had to make difficult choices and disappoint some authors, the endeavour as a whole must itself be seen as part of the global process of learning about the Slavic, Eurasian and Central and East European world: its peoples, its languages, its literature and cultural life, its history, politics, societies, economies, and its links with the rest of the world. Interest in the region is likely to grow, with new opportunities for contacts at various levels, and these volumes will, I am certain, serve both to educate and to inspire scholars and students anxious to understand.

It is very pleasant indeed to acknowledge once again the association of the Congress and the International Council with Macmillan, who will be publishing these volumes in the United Kingdom, and particularly the highly professional support and the keen personal interest of Tim Farmiloe for the whole project. If I may add a personal note, I should like to express my gratitude to John Morison and the Executive Committee of the International Council for charging me with the function of General Editor; to the editors of individual volumes, to whom fell the difficult tasks of assessment and selection followed by the tedium of editorial preparation; to my wife, Ethna, for her assistance in keeping track of several hundred typescripts, letters, faxes and e-mail messages; and to the many scholars who have patiently (and sometimes not so patiently — such are the pressures of modern academic life!) contributed to this complex international publishing venture. The collapse of communist rule has contributed sharply to globalisation, and the creation of this series of volumes has placed me at the hub of a world-wide enterprise, with editors on several continents and authors located in many countries of the world. It has provided me with a new kind of learning process for which I am humbly grateful.

Trinity College, Dublin   RONALD J. HILL

Notes on the Contributors

Dr Bob Arnot, Department of Economics, Glasgow Caledonian University, Scotland.

Paweł Bożyk, Warsaw, Poland; former Finance Minister of the Polish People's Republic.

Professor Paul G. Hare, Centre for Economic Reform and Transformation, Department of Economics, Heriot-Watt University, Edinburgh, Scotland.

Dr Herman W. Hoen, Faculty of Economics, University of Groningen, The Netherlands.

Professor Masaaki Kuboniwa, Institute of Economic Research, Hitotsubashi University, Japan.

Dr Vladimir Mau, Institute for the Economy in Transition, Moscow, Russia.

Professor Ken Morita, Hiroshima, Japan.

Vladimer Papava, P. Gugushvili Institute of Economics, The Georgian Academy of Sciences, Tbilisi, Georgia.

Dr Joseph L. Porket, Ruislip, Middlesex, England.

Professor Steven Rosefielde, Department of Economic, University of North Carolina, Chapel Hill, USA.

Professor Valdas Samonis, Centre for Russian and East European Studies, University of Toronto, Canada.

Hillel H. Ticktin, Institute of Russian and East European Studies, University of Glasgow, Scotland.

1 Overview

Paul G. Hare

Introduction

When thinking about the processes of transition that have been under way for several years now in the former communist world of Central and Eastern Europe and the former Soviet Union, there are several questions that it is interesting to ask:

- What is the nature of the system that collapsed, characterised by communism and central planning among other features?
- Why and how did the former system of political control and economic management collapse?
- How do post-communist states manage the dual processes of state-building and economic reforms, and are these processes fundamentally different for new states and old ones? As far as the economic transition is concerned, what strategies make most sense?
- Can anything useful yet be said about the *destination* of the transition economies, in either political or economic terms, or both? Related to this, can anything of a more normative nature be said, concerning where these countries *ought* to be heading?
- What have we learned from the recent experience of the economies in transition concerning the relative performance of alternative economic systems? (and, more broadly, of alternative socio-political systems?)

These are the questions that we examine in this opening chapter, referring where relevant to individual chapters of the book. Hence this chapter serves the twin purposes of: (a) introducing the issues which, in their different ways, the ensuing chapters deal with for particular countries and periods; and (b) introducing the chapters themselves to give readers an initial guide to the book.

1

In places I find it unavoidable to offer my own judgements on certain chapters. In doing so, however, I should stress here that those chapters included in this volume are all contributions whose ideas I find intellectually interesting and in most cases quite challenging. Hence my disagreements and arguments should not be taken to imply that I think certain chapters are inadequate, for if that were the case such chapters would not have been included at all. Rather, certain chapters are good examples of particular lines of argument which I regard as important contributions to debate, while also, at times, considering their arguments to be wrong. When this is my view, I shall say so, as the reader will shortly discover.

Communism and Central Planning

Transition to some form of market-type economy, accompanied by some form of more or less democratic polity, is proving more difficult and complex than many of the more naïve observers of Eastern Europe expected at the start of this decade. Among the reasons for this situation is our imperfect understanding of the *ancien régime* in the region. Actually, it is misleading even to start by referring to a single regime since, although all the CMEA countries were characterised by one-party, communist government, plus economic management by central planning, there was also substantial and at times increasing differentiation along several important dimensions:

- the historical background: previous experience of democratic government and/or market-type (capitalist) economic systems;
- the steps towards political reforms already taken up to the late 1980s, including loosening of Party control over various aspects of economic life;
- the extent and form of economic reforms already introduced by the mid-to-late 1980s, including toleration of private businesses, decentralisation or loosening of planning (or both), price reforms, banking system reform, fiscal reforms, and so forth;
- the degree of openness to the West (especially the EU) in terms of both trade relationships and foreign investment (for example, through joint ventures);

- The extent to which the given country was perceived by others or perceived itself as 'in crisis' or 'failing', economically, politically, or in both aspects.

Hence any notion of a core or typical communist or central planning *model* should also pay attention to the rather large differences along these lines when examining any individual country's experience.

The core model itself, however, can be characterised relatively sharply as a socio-economic system with predominantly state ownership of productive assets, government by a single party (the Communist Party), and an almost complete inter-penetration of political and economic control over the whole society. What the latter implies is that instead of the horizontal economic relationships of a market-type economy (between firms and their customers and suppliers, and so on) one finds a predominance of vertical relationships (such as between firms and their supervising ministries) (see Hare, 1990). In terms of their own self-definition, the countries operating this system variously referred to themselves as 'socialist', 'state socialist', or even 'communist', and claimed to draw their inspiration and guidance from the works of Marx and Engels, Lenin and Stalin (and the inheritors of the latter's traditions in Eastern Europe). However, such essentially ideological conceptions are not of great interest for present purposes, although one could no doubt debate endlessly about the rights and wrongs of particular formulations of the basic 'creed'. Since this is not intended to be an ideological essay, I shall resist the temptation to dwell on this issue.

For economic management purposes, the key operational feature of this system was central planning, with the five-year plans setting out the basic direction and structure of investment for the forthcoming period, and annual (and sometimes even shorter-term) plans providing plan targets for individual firms. Most foreign trade was conducted as a state monopoly, and within the socialist world it was usually conducted on the basis of government-to-government contracts agreed each year as part of the annual planning process. Pricing was mostly under state control, only very limited aspects of economic life functioned according to market principles or involved the private ownership of the means of production, and the financial institutions (mostly the banks) allocated credits in accordance with the prevailing plan. Economic criteria played a slowly increasing, but generally modest, role both in foreign trade (for example, little attention was paid to notions of comparative advantage) and in the selection of investment projects for inclusion in the plans. Although many details of what firms could do were laid down in the plans, households were freer in the sense that individuals were able to change jobs easily, and they were also free to use their income from work (and of other types of income there was practically nothing, apart from social welfare payments, including pensions) to purchase any available goods and services. In practice (though it is questionable how far this was a necessary or inherent feature of the system), plans were usually quite taut, involving (inefficiently) high levels of resource utilisation. The result was twofold: a labour market featuring both centrally-set wages and persistent excess demand for labour, thereby facilitating the labour turnover just referred to;[1] and markets for consumer goods that experienced widespread and persistent excess demand which, given centrally fixed prices, could only result in shortage (see Kornai, 1980).

Those countries which abandoned parts of central planning early, such as Hungary and Poland, typically relaxed or gave up the practice of breaking down the annual plans into detailed instructions for each state-owned enterprise. Also, some plan instructions slowly gave way to the wider use of more economic levers to influence production and consumption decisions, and in limited spheres of economic life private production was permitted. However, Party rule remained in place and the fundamentals of the old system were scarcely changed.

Why did the socialist system change at all, prior to its ultimate collapse at the end of the 1980s? As with all systems evolving dynamically, there were both internal and external factors. The former, the internal factors, concerned the shifting balance of interest groups within any given socialist society, the top levels of the ruling Party having to contend with strong sectoral and regional interests, enterprise managers seeking greater independence from the central planners,

---

1. In fact, many of the socialist countries experienced rates of labour turnover higher than those normal in most market-type (capitalist) economies, sometimes to the great consternation of the central planners. This was despite the fact that in the USSR, in particular, labour mobility was constrained by the internal passport system, and throughout the region the lack of a functioning housing market also inhibited mobility. Hence most labour turnover involved purely local job changes.

workers seeking better conditions with fewer controls, and the like. In the absence of markets, all conflicts over resources were necessarily mediated through the political process: hence the Party–state could be held responsible for outcomes that would not even be regarded as government concerns in market-type economies, and to avoid such wide-ranging responsibility one can well understand the temptation – far from always resisted – to deal with 'economic' conflicts by suppressing them. Many of the early rounds of economic reform in the socialist countries were attempts to make central planning somewhat more flexible, somewhat more decentralised, acknowledging inherent limitations over the government's ability to control events in every detail. Nevertheless, as we know, most reform attempts were at best partial failures and many were reversed or abandoned quite rapidly: Party leaders saw the loss of control associated with reforms as too dangerous, and also sought to 'correct' the shortcomings of reforms by imposing new central controls. Hence the appearance of a cyclical reform process with, in many countries, no very clear long-term tendency.

The latter, the external factors, are mostly concerned with the comparative performance of the socialist countries – relative to one another (in particular, to the Soviet Union), relative to the developed West, relative to near neighbours (thus, Austria was very significant for Hungary and Czechoslovakia, Germany for Poland, Scandinavia for the Baltic Republics). In terms of living standards, the region was clearly failing to catch up with the developed, capitalist world, even though officially measured growth rates (usually based on income measured in NMP terms, rather than the standard SNA concept of GDP[2]) were still apparently rather high in many countries until well into the 1980s. In this sense, most official figures from the period do not convey a strong impression of a system in deep crisis: but these figures were clearly significantly misleading. Aside from living standards, a further indicator of the lagging performance of the socialist countries was the region's participation in world trade, its share having declined steadily

2. NMP is net material product, a measure of national product or income used in the socialist bloc. It fails to count so called non-productive services as part of the national income. SNA refers to the system of national accounts recommended as standard by the United Nations, and used by most countries in the world. GDP is gross domestic product, the national product or income measure used in the SNA system.

since the early 1950s. Moreover, the nature of much socialist trade was indicative of economies at relatively low levels of development, being largely inter-industry (Ricardian) trade, rather than intra-industry trade. The latter, for instance, is more characteristic of advanced regions of the world competing through quality improvements and other innovations. In the more developed parts of the world, international trade depends less and less on inherited factor endowments, and increasingly upon technological advance. In this type of competitive interaction, too, the socialist world was largely outclassed.

The Collapse of the Old System

Here one can talk about the collapse of communist governments in particular countries, or focus on the general factors that brought about the disintegration of the communist system in the whole of Europe. In the present book, the chapters by Ticktin and Arnot are concerned specifically with these issues in relation to the former Soviet Union, and I therefore refer to them below.

On the general question, it is tempting, and probably far too simplistic, to suggest that communist systems collapsed because they were failing economically and were perceived (despite histories of mass repression) to be politically weak enough to be overthrown by popular pressure reflecting mass discontent. However, this sort of explanation is pretty vacuous, since *ex post facto* it is virtually certain to be a reasonable description of what happened, whereas it provides a very weak basis for convincing *ex ante* projection of political collapse and disintegration. This is because there are many societies and situations where the above conditions appear to be in place but regimes do not collapse (hence these conditions cannot be regarded as *sufficient* conditions for political transformation, though they may be *necessary*), and more importantly, the key terms 'economic failure' and 'political weakness' are not specified in any operationally useful manner.

For the USSR, Arnot (Chapter 10) nevertheless criticises Western economists for failing to predict the Soviet collapse and attributes that failure to the predominantly static character of neo-classical economic theory, rendering it unable to grasp the dynamics of the Soviet system. Ticktin (Chapter 8) also rejects formal models and hypotheses on the grounds of their static character. Having dismissed 'bourgeois economics', Arnot stresses the need for 'an integrative and historical approach that could lay bare its laws of motion', namely the laws of motion of the USSR. One can hardly dispute the desirability of such a dynamic conception of socio-economic processes in the former Soviet Union, which makes it rather regrettable that, for all its interest in other respects, Arnot's chapter provides not the smallest hint regarding the possible shape of this conception.

By implication, Arnot gives the impression that Western economists did such a poor job of predicting the Soviet collapse because they are mostly imbued with the so called neo-classical 'ideology'. I think this involves him in a serious methodological error. First, it was not my impression that Marxists (or anyone else for that matter) managed to predict the timing of the Soviet collapse any better than mainstream economists did; political scientists also fared no better, to my knowledge. Many social scientists, of all persuasions, believed that the Soviet-type system was stagnating and decaying, and that its economic performance was seriously lagging behind even slowly growing parts of the world such as Western Europe (as indicated above). Most (including the present author) probably believed that it would collapse eventually, without being able to say much of interest about the likely timing.

Second, the question of the dynamic analysis of a social system is many times more difficult than Arnot and Ticktin seem willing to concede. It is not the case that Marxists who use more dynamic terminology in their studies of socio-economic formations actually possess more effective analytical tools than those of us who remain committed to more conventional, neo-classical methods of economic analysis. Dramatic and assertive words do not make good theory; even less do they make for good forecasting of critical events in political and economic history (except through luck, which also has nothing to do with good theory). I would argue, instead, that neo-classical (and most other) theory is predominantly static not because its exponents are stupid or lazy (or politically incorrect!), but essentially because dynamic analysis is unbelievably difficult – and many people have tried to do it.

Because this point is so important, let me illustrate what I mean and then suggest an implication that is especially relevant for the present discussion. Consider the elementary theory of market equilibrium. Standard economics would run in terms of a supply and demand curve, finding the equilibrium price and quantity at their intersection (E). In the event of an increase in demand, we would then shift the demand curve to the right and 'predict' that the new equilibrium (E') will occur at the intersection between the original supply curve and the new demand curve. In many markets and in a surprisingly wide range of situations, this type of analysis yields remarkably good predictions of market outcomes. Nevertheless, it is irredeemably static, and it must be conceded that we have very little idea of the precise dynamic mechanisms that enable a market to shift from an initial point such as E to a new equilibrium such as E'.

Marxists, I believe, use different language, but face the same eventual difficulty. Their discussions often sound more dynamic as they refer to competitive processes, crisis conditions (where I might talk, more neutrally, about entry and exit from the market!) and the anarchy of the market. Indeed, the last of these is often attacked as a failing of the capitalist mode of production (to be superseded under socialism), whereas I would see it as a great strength, the market operating a vital social selection process through which economies achieve ever higher levels of output and productivity. That aside, the fact remains that no social scientists have yet discovered means of making really sound predictions about change in dynamic environments.

So what do we do? One possibility is simply to say that we cannot predict change, that we lack the models that would allow us to do so. The next – and in my view better – approach is to use a combination of empirical observation and static theory. Empirically, we observe that for most of the time, most socio-economic systems exhibit an appearance of stability: they may be changing, but the process is gradual and not usually marked by sharp discontinuities. We may not understand well why this is so, but we can see that it is. If, in addition, we conceive of socio-economic systems as being in some sort of equilibrium state (the details of which I would hesitate to specify, though they are inessential for the argument), then, if we observe little or no change in some period, the hypothesis that the socio-economic system being studied should remain unchanged at least for a little longer is surely not unreasonable. Hence the observation that Western economists failed to predict the collapse and disintegration of the Soviet Union in 1991 is neither surprising nor particularly reprehensible. Not only does it reflect the present state of our social theories (including the Marxist variants), but it has the great merit that predicting 'no change' can be wrong only once (and hence was right most of the time), whereas predicting 'imminent collapse' (as many Marxist groups did, year after year!) was nearly always wrong. Which is the better approach to social prediction?

Ticktin discusses five approaches to explaining the disintegration of the USSR, rejects them all, and then puts forward his own theory. The five approaches are termed the accidental, the economically necessary, non-market illegitimacy, élites' subjective desires (to maintain power and privilege in the economy), and the multifactorial. Most of these are, in any case, only partial explanations for what happened in the final stages of the USSR.

Ticktin is right, in my judgement, to attack the simple view that the USSR failed owing to its own inherent economic incompetence and must therefore move to the market system. I would argue that this simple view is wrong basically because I do not regard economic incompetence as a sufficient explanation for the failure of any system. Ticktin, though, objects to it on the grounds that it is 'ideological'; he insists that there is no implication that Russia must move to the market, since he is confident that we can devise a better economic system than the market. Later, he argues that there is a need for an alternative form of integration, neither planning nor the market, a system that might be called 'true socialism'. Since we are then told nothing about this putative system and how it might emerge, it is hard not to regard this assertion as at least as ideological as the line that he seeks to criticise.

One of the standard arguments about economic slowdown in the centrally planned economies relates to the transition from extensive to intensive growth. The former involves capital accumulation accompanied by massive transfers of manpower from agriculture to industry, while the latter refers to the period when reserves of labour are largely exhausted, implying that growth must rely far more heavily on the pace of technological improvement. Rapid investment might well be going on, and capital-labour ratios might be rising in both situations (though at different rates), but the nature of growth in the second (intensive) phase differs greatly from that in the first (extensive) phase.

Specifically, intensive growth is necessarily far more dependent on successful innovation and technological improvement than extensive growth, and hence places greater demands on the R&D system and its links with production and the ultimate 'customers' of new products and processes. Ticktin appears to reject this general line of argument, although his reasoning is neither clear nor, in so far as I could understand it, compelling.

Overall, therefore, Marxist approaches to explaining the downfall of communist systems offer some interesting lines of argument, but at the end they are no more convincing than more conventional arguments which, as we have seen, can say a good deal about the malfunctioning of a socio-economic system without being able to predict either its collapse or its likely future. Dismissing 'the market' as some sort of ideological construct neither helps to explain the end of communism nor takes us very far towards understanding what could (or should) follow it.

State-building and Economic Reforms

Rebuilding the state

Once communist regimes collapsed, and some of their states disintegrated, the process of transition could get under way. In some countries, economic aspects of the process had already commenced long before 1989, with particularly extensive market-oriented reforms being introduced in Hungary and somewhat less change in Poland. Nevertheless, in all countries the collapse of the old system signalled the need both to redefine and to reconstruct the state, a dimension of transition whose importance and urgency was greatly underestimated at the start of transition. Papava (Chapter 12), however, strikes the right note when he argues that the business of constructing the state must indeed be considered one of the key aspects of transition. This is partly because the remnants of the communist state are not well suited to running a market-type economy, partly because many of the countries that emerged from the ruins of communism had not previously been independent countries.

One of the more challenging aspects of the early post-communist period has been the disintegration of several of the original states in the region, and the collapse into civil and inter-ethnic strife of some of the successor states. The disintegration of the Soviet Union was especially dramatic, giving rise to 15 new states, but this was quickly followed by the declaration of independence by part of Moldova, warfare between Armenia and Azerbaijan, civil war in Georgia, and more recently the unsuccessful attempt by Chechnya to secure its independence from Russia. In Eastern Europe itself, Yugoslavia disintegrated in 1991, with warfare engulfing parts of Croatia and the whole of Bosnia until the Dayton Peace Accords came into force in late 1995. Despite a large NATO presence in Bosnia, it will be some time before we can feel confident about the durability of the 'peace'. Further north, Czechoslovakia split into two states, the Czech Republic and the Slovak Republic, with effect from the start of 1993; this at least was a peaceful dissolution. It would be surprising if these unsettling (and often, still unsettled) developments marked the end of a process of political change, since some of the forces that have been at work are still very much in play.

One of the first lessons concerning the transition, therefore, is that the nature of the state, including even its geographical extent and its ethnic complexion, is very much in question. This raises the issue of the state's role in the economy during the transition, which is partly a matter of assessing the influence of various interest groups over economic policy, partly a question of the competence or ability of the state in the new conditions, and lastly a problem of designing forms of intervention that positively promote transition itself, rather than blocking it. Even more so than in more settled and developed economies, there are few aspects of economic policy in transition economies that can be fruitfully and comprehensively discussed without making some reference to their political configuration.

Papava puts forward the hypothesis that state formation in so-called 'new states' such as Georgia is more complex and difficult than in the more established states, those that were already separate entities and that possessed the institutional structures of a modern state. This is an intuitively appealing notion and he explains why it makes sense in the Georgian case. Nevertheless, I am now convinced, as a result of recent research on Central Europe, the Baltic States, Ukraine and Moldova, that it is not correct. The reason is not so much that there is anything wrong with the Georgian story, rather it has to do with processes of state formation in the established states. Far from finding transition relatively easier to manage because the state was already 'in place' and functioning tolerably well, these countries, too, have had to undergo an extensive and difficult process of rebuilding the state structures to suit the new conditions. There is very little indication that they have had a notably easier time than the new states.

Porket (Chapter 4) examines the role of the state in different types of economic formation, noting its changing role in Western, market-type economies, and the variety of socialist models. In the immediate post-communist world there was a serious institutional vacuum in the countries concerned, in a situation where there was no remotely adequate theory of the transition to the market, including on the role of the state in promoting that process. Moreover, there is not just one type of market economy, since one can easily distinguish at least three: *laissez-faire*; the free market (but operating within a well-defined environment of rules and laws); and an interventionist model. While political democracy and the market economy might both be viewed as desiderata, they are not independent and can sometimes come into conflict. Although successful economies almost always possess both, democracy in the early stages of building a market economy can impede the process of marketisation, and even with democracy there is significant variation in the detailed structure of the state institutions. For the transition economies, in particular, there is a great deal of tension over the proper role of the state in either actively promoting the development of, or simply accommodating to, the demands of the market economy. Within that, and despite its apparent demise in the East, socialist notions are still alive in Western thinking about the state, especially in regard to its function in the areas of redistribution and social policy. These issues, too, have so far proved controversial and problematic in the East.

In Chapter 5, Samonis links the discussion of the state with that of transition *per se* by outlining some steps towards a normative theory of the transition process. He insists that the state must be actively involved in building the market economy, and proposes three stages or aspects: building the fundamentals, de-Sovietisation, and developing the welfare state. Through a series of simple lessons and hypotheses, he argues (*inter alia*) for public sector incomes policy, active supply-side policies, and privatisation using unconventional approaches (while emphasising effective corporate governance). Welfare institutions and pension funds need to be created, and the labour market should be liberalised both by reducing trade union power and by facilitating labour mobility through such measures as housing market reforms and the development of an effective housing market. On trade, there are two aspects to consider: on the one hand, transition should be securely anchored in a wider process of East–West integration; on the other, industrial adaptation should be fostered through temporary, market-type forms of trade protection such as tariffs, this protection being gradually lifted as new directions of comparative advantage are established. Given this general approach, it is no surprise that Samonis argues for technical assistance to support institution-building and facilitate trade, rather than more general forms of financial aid, as the best form of Western help to the transition economies.

The standard transition package

At the start of transition a relatively simple, standard 'recipe' was advanced (see Portes, 1991). This included the following elements: (1) macroeconomic stabilisation; (2) price and trade liberalisation; (3) privatisation and enterprise restructuring; and (4) institutional reforms. There is a certain logic that appears to bind these elements together, and even their relative timing and speed of implementation were initially supposed to be more or less pre-determined. For a wide range of papers on these aspects of the transition process, see Hare and Davis (1997).

Price and trade liberalisation, for instance, were needed in order to eliminate the mass of domestic price distortions and to bring relative prices of tradables into line with relative world market prices in order to facilitate more efficient trade. However, given the prevalence of shortage conditions in the last years of communism it was expected (generally correctly) that this liberalisation would give rise to an initial burst of inflation, which might also be accompanied by worsening trade and budget deficits. Hence, in order to limit and contain these potentially serious problems, macroeconomic stabilisation would also be required, involving strict monetary management and control over credit emissions, often combined with the use of an exchange rate peg as a nominal anchor (as in Poland under the Balcerowicz plan of 1990). Needless to say, all this was much more difficult for the region's new states, since they had to start by establishing a central bank and issuing their own currency, often in very unfavourable conditions. Nevertheless, the presumption was that stabilisation and liberalisation would both be very rapid, with other aspects of the transition requiring more time and coming later.

Under communism, of course, the economies of Eastern Europe and the former Soviet Union were largely dominated by state-owned enterprises (SOEs), plus collective farms in agriculture, but it was understood that the creation of a strong private sector was crucial for bringing about and sustaining a successful transition to a market economy. The almost universal presumption, in 1990, was that the way to do this was via the large-scale, and preferably rapid, privatisation of SOEs. Consequently, there was extensive debate about how to privatise (by sale to a new owner, through auctions, through free distribution to the population, and so forth), how rapidly to privatise, how and to what extent to involve foreign investors in the process, whether firms should undergo restructuring before or after privatisation, how to deal with bad debts and excess employment, and many related matters. These are undeniably important questions, but they now appear rather less important than they did.

This is the case for several reasons. First, although evidence started to accumulate in various countries concerning changes in enterprise behaviour as they adapted to harder budget constraints and a more competitive market environment, these changes could be observed in both privatised and state-owned firms. Hence privatisation *per se* could not explain the observed changes, an observation not unfamiliar in Western countries (such as in connection with the UK's privatisation programme) but unexpected in the East. This has led to a great deal of re-thinking about just what does induce firms to adjust and restructure. Among other things, problems of corporate governance naturally arise here (see World Bank, 1995; EBRD, 1995).

In Russia in particular, a substantial proportion of firms has been privatised, mostly through the issue of vouchers to the population, and other forms of free, or nearly free, distribution of assets, prior to the achievement of stabilisation. This reverses what was otherwise considered the 'normal' transition sequence in which privatisation would mostly follow on from stabilisation and liberalisation. Moreover, the privatisation issues listed above were hardly dealt with at all in the Russian privatisation. So, on the one hand, it is clearly feasible to accomplish privatisation without tackling many supposedly key issues, while on the other hand it is then unclear just how far enterprise behaviour actually changes, and what other elements must be in place to bring about real change.

Second, in most countries, privatisation proceeded more slowly than expected or intended, yet the private sector still grew very rapidly. Much of this growth can be attributed to the unexpectedly rapid growth of the *new* private sector. Among other things this raises many questions about the proper way of supporting and fostering small and medium enterprises (SMEs) and the associated entrepreneurship and innovation.

The last item in the traditional transition package, institutional reforms, actually covers a long list of topics: reforms of commercial law to do with property rights, contracts and their protection, forms of business entity, accounting law, competition policy, and so on; tax reform at national and provincial or regional levels; banking, financial market reforms and credit policy; employment policy and labour market reforms; the social safety net; and others. All of these were acknowledged as important contributions to building the institutional infrastructure of a market-type economy, but many governments, their advisers, or both, failed to appreciate the urgency of such measures, with the result that some countries – especially in the Commonwealth of Independent States (CIS), embracing most of the former Soviet Union – have made only limited progress so far. Closely related to enterprise behaviour and privatisation, banking and financial market reforms in particular now seem far more vital than they did in 1990, since they provide mechanisms to replace the formerly planned allocation of investment with a market-determined process based on profitability; they also provide sources of funding and monitoring functions which are crucial in improving performance.

Especially for the CEE countries and the Baltic states (in EU parlance, these are the so called PHARE countries), one of the most central policy concerns for the remainder of this decade and into the next century has to do with these states' preparation for membership of and eventual accession to the European Union. Several EU Council of

Ministers meetings in recent years have issued declarations on this topic, not yet setting out a firm timetable but certainly offering the commitment to eventual membership for the Associated States, namely those which have already signed Association Agreements with the EU. By early 1996 this comprised 10 of the 11 PHARE countries (not Albania), and all were actively engaged in preparing themselves for entry by adapting various elements of their domestic policies to accord with EU norms and practices.

Experience in various countries

The above outline of the mostly economic aspects of transition processes leaves room for significant controversy over the precise means, policy tools and sequencing of reform steps. The most notable such controversy, addressed in several of the following chapters, is that between shock therapy and a more gradual approach to economic reforms. This issue is referred to, for instance, in the chapters by Bożyk (2), Hoen (3), Mau (9), Papava (12).

Bożyk, paying most attention to Poland, sees shock therapy as a drastic selection process to 'purge' uneconomic activities, while also eliminating demand inflation by suppressing aggregate demand. However, he points out that it cannot by itself eliminate cost inflation due to structural imbalances, and suggests that this might be a factor in the particularly severe output falls in the CIS countries, apparently implying an exceptionally high cost of shock therapy. My own view, though, is that at least some of the special problems experienced by the CIS countries are attributable not to shock therapy *per se*, but to its ineffective application (as Papava concedes for Georgia, Mau for Russia). Some of the institutional defects of the transition economies, including the absence of an adequate financial sector, inappropriate enterprise structure and badly functioning labour markets do, nevertheless, make it likely that shock therapy will work less well in transition economies than in already established market economies. For this reason Bożyk argues that it would be best to confine shock therapy to a short initial period when hyperinflation has to be dealt with, after which it should be followed by what he calls *evolutionary therapy*. The latter is not fully specified in the chapter, but it would acknowledge that reforms should mostly be gradual, with some sectors liberalised before others and with an active industrial policy in place to cope with the more difficult restructuring problems.

Hoen challenges the now traditional ways of thinking about shock therapy and gradualism by pointing out that they generally place too much emphasis upon stabilisation and liberalisation, paying insufficient attention to privatisation, restructuring and institution-building. Both *ex ante* and *ex post facto*, there are undeniably political constraints on the feasible reforms, but what is ultimately important is their impact on enterprise behaviour. From this perspective, the usual ways of thinking about reforms in the Czech Republic and Hungary need to be inverted. The former's liberal rhetoric and quick stabilisation has been accompanied by a corporatist approach to economic management with active labour market policies and surprisingly little restructuring at enterprise level. In contrast, Hungary had no need for a shock therapy approach to stabilisation, but nevertheless applied something like a shock therapy approach in building up its market institutions, thereby forcing rapid changes in enterprise behaviour. Hence, in Hoen's view, the Czech Republic should be characterised as gradualist, Hungary as the fast ('shock') reformer.

The political constraints on the course of reforms are discussed in a particularly interesting way by Mau, focusing on the largest and in some ways the most problematic of the transition economies, Russia. As other observers have noted, although Russia formally inherited the state institutions of the USSR, it was initially a very weak state, not helped by Yeltsin's early failure to reform the structures of state power. Reform debates and decisions had to take place in a very difficult environment with many contending interest groups operating with ill-defined 'rules of engagement'. These groups included the president himself, his government, the parliament (the State Duma), regional authorities, and a range of sectoral and local lobbies.

Payment problems between firms, rising fuel prices and threats of bankruptcy strengthened a producers' lobby or interest group. By 1992, this group formed a powerful pro-inflation bloc, preferring inflation to the perceived alternatives of large-scale open unemployment or bankruptcy. Only the unpleasant experience of near-hyperinflation induced them to accept measures that gradually brought about monetary stabilisation in Russia. Nevertheless, regional (and at times, even separatist) pressures remained strong, with Russian economic space being carved up in various ways to protect local production and deliveries. Only very gradually were inter-federal relations stabilised in Russia. There was constant struggle between those wanting to preserve or even extend their existing monopoly powers, and those seeking greater openness and competition. Surprisingly, despite the sharp fall in Russian output and incomes accompanying the reform process, people proved to be remarkably tolerant, with few strikes or other disturbances, especially in industry. At the political level, though, stabilisation remains fragile, dependent on continuing consistency of macro-economic policy in an environment still lacking clear 'rules of the game'.

Destinations and Economic Performance

In the end, for all its political ramifications, transition is really about economic performance. Given the immense sacrifices in the early years of the process, resulting from the initial post-communist recession (or slump, in many cases), one hopes that economic growth will not take too long to restart, and that before long the populations of the region will be able to enjoy much-improved living standards. This recovery and growth stage of transition is already well established in most of Central and Eastern Europe, although not yet in the CIS countries. Thinking about transition from the standpoint of growth and economic performance suggests a number of important and interesting questions:

- How deep is the post-communist slump and what are the factors that might facilitate or impede recovery and the renewal of growth?
- How can sustainable growth at reasonable rates be fostered in the region?
- Can anything yet be said about the ultimate destination, in terms of the evolving economic systems, of the post-communist countries?

The first question is partly empirical, partly conceptual. The empirical part of the puzzle is addressed by Kuboniwa (Chapter 6), who presents a very careful appraisal of the output decline in Russia. By using electricity balances as a basis for developing growth projections by branch, he finds a much smaller (though still severe) decline in industrial output than that shown in offical Russian statistics as reported by Goskomstat (1991-94: about 25 per cent compared with an official decline of 50 per cent); he also finds an adjusted GDP decline in the range 27-35 per cent, depending on the precise assumptions made. Thus there is no doubt that a serious decline has occurred, but its magnitude is much less than that usually reported.

Rosefielde (Chapter 11) takes a very pessimistic view of Russia's prospects, arguing that recovery from the recent sharp decline will be especially difficult owing to factors inherited from the communist era, notably anti-competitive institutions and highly inflexible and badly allocated capital equipment, much of which is simply useless in the new conditions. He considers it rather strange that CIA figures rated the Soviet Union so highly in the 1980s in economic terms, although it is hard to avoid the suspicion that there might have been a political element in such appraisals. Certainly, more recent calculations place Russia at a much lower economic level than used to be thought. Moreover, there is greater emphasis now upon the barriers – institutional, political, legal, and so forth – to the emergence of a real market economy.

This last observation raises questions, of course, about what we should mean by the adjective 'real' in this context. But I take it to mean a market economy in which the bulk of production is produced by private economic agents, and all the key markets (including the markets for labour, capital, finance, housing and foreign exchange that did not exist under central planning) exist and function tolerably well, supported either by a clear and enforced legal framework (including adequate regulation, where relevant) or by generally accepted custom and practice. Russia is clearly some way from this situation and its likely direction of evolution from the present position is not yet clear, for both domestic and wider, international reasons. Domestically, the political situation remains fluid, while externally Russia's relationships with CIS partners are also not yet settled. There are those in Russia who would like to revive some notion of the former Soviet empire, drawing CIS states into closer political and economic alliance with Russia. Significant moves in this direction would certainly exert an impact on Russia's domestic economic policies, most probably not favouring an open, liberal market economy. Alternatively, if Russia's CIS ties remain relatively loose and the country sustains a more open orientation emphasising trade and other economic links with the West, then the eventual prospects for building a more normal market-type economy are far better.

Going beyond market-oriented reforms to the business of generating and sustaining growth, Morita (Chapter 7) discusses Polish economic reforms in Japanese perspective. What was evidently crucial for Japanese recoevery and eventual economic success following the Second World War was the combination of high investment rates and extraordinarily efficient investment that was quickly achieved. There were high rates of saving, especially by private individuals (perhaps taking account of the lack of provision of social welfare by the state), and by unincorporated businesses. Nevertheless, the early post-war period in Japan was also marked by severe structural problems and imbalances. The Dodge stabilisation plan of 1949 was a form of shock therapy, and at the time it was accompanied by fierce debates between the advocates of shock and more gradual approaches to reform, as in Eastern Europe today. Land reform and measures to deconcentrate business helped to unlock some of the rigidities of the Japanese system, paving the way for decades of rapid growth. The Japanese experience suggests that there is an important role for a strong and pro-competitive industrial policy.

Comparing Poland with Japan, it appears that the Polish 'shock' was rather weaker than that applied earlier in Japan, and that the associated structural reforms have also been weaker. For Morita, this then casts doubt on the sustainability of Polish growth, even though Poland initially recovered sooner and more solidly from its post-socialist recession than any other country in the region. The key resides in saving and investment. By the mid-1990s, Poland was investing only about one-fifth of its GDP in new investment. While not a bad investment ratio compared with some of the more developed OECD countries (such as the US or the UK), it is well below Japanese rates and is not enough to generate significant expansion by Poland to EU output and income levels within a reasonable period of time. Hence, for those countries which have already implemented the basic 'transition package' of reforms, the next vital step must be to find ways of stimulating much higher rates of domestic savings (none of the countries in the region can sensibly rely on foreign investment for their future growth), and then to ensure that the resulting resources are invested productively. Given popular concerns over current living standards, and hence understandable resistance to further cuts in personal consumption, it is clear that this will be no easy task, anywhere in Central and Eastern Europe. Yet for long-term political stability, and for successful political and economic integration into Western Europe, it is vital.

References

EBRD (1995), *Transition Report 1995* (London: European Bank for Reconstruction and Development).

Hare, Paul G. (1990), *Central Planning* (Chur: Harwood Academic Publishers).

Hare, Paul G. and Junior Davis (eds) (1997), *Transition to the Market Economy*, 4 volumes (London: Routledge).

Kornai, János (1980), *The Economics of Shortage*, Vols A and B (Amsterdam: North Holland).

Portes, R. (1991), 'Introduction', *European Economy*, Special edition No. 2, pp.1–16 (Brussels: Commission of the European Communities).

World Bank (1995), *From Plan to Market*, World Development Report 1995 (Washington, DC: The World Bank).

Part I

Systemic Change

2 Gradualism versus Shock Therapy

Paweł Bożyk

Introduction

The strategy pursued in Central and Eastern Europe to move from centrally planned to free-market economies rests on frail theoretical foundations. Its starting-point is the shock therapy ('Big Bang') used to fight inflation in South America, Asia and Europe.[1] Certain successes on this front, especially in South America, persuaded the IMF that it was a cure also applicable to the countries of Central and Eastern Europe which were suffering similar travails as inflation soared in the course of transforming economies from central planning to free-market systems.

However, after a few years of experiment it was found that this was a risky measure which did more harm than good. For the causes of inflation in Central and Eastern Europe proved to be largely of a different kind than elsewhere, especially in underdeveloped countries with market economies.

Shock Elimination of Inefficient Activity

Economically, the shock method of combatting inflation boils down to the rapid and at the same time radical elimination of activity which is inefficient in terms of free-market criteria as determined in the conditions of an 'open' economy. These criteria were market-clearing prices of goods and services, positive real interest rates (that is, nominal rates set above the level of inflation), an exchange rate balancing supply and demand of foreign currencies, and so on.

---

1. See Paweł Bożyk, *Droga do nikąd? Polska i jej sasiedzi na rozdrożu* (Road to Nowhere? Poland and Its Neighbours at the Crossroads) (Warsaw: BGW, 1991).

In Central and Eastern Europe such shock therapy criteria were bound to mean nothing short of an economic revolution, for under the previous system the operating principles of the economy were completely different. Both production and consumption were to a large extent subsidised, so that the prices of an overwhelming majority of goods and services diverged significantly from equilibrium prices. Demand for these goods visibly exceeded supply, and in many areas there were shortages on the market.

Likewise, interest rates were below the inflation level, which meant that the state was subsidising investment. Moreover, the size of these subsidies differed according to subject and object, with the result that capital made available for expansion was cheaper for some activities than for others.

Also subsidised was employment. Officially, unemployment did not exist, but in a sizeable proportion of enterprises work-forces were considerably bigger than the actual manpower requirements. So what in effect occurred was 'hidden unemployment'. The subsidisation of employment also varied from sector to sector: in some industries wages were lower than the free-market value of labour; in other activities and occupations, by contrast, they were higher than the free-market value. This is because the prevailing trend in the centrally planned economy was towards the compression of wages around the average level of earnings in the economy as a whole.

Another area in which prices were differentiated was foreign exchange. The official exchange rate was set at a level in the region of the average across the economy. Thus, the official rate differed basically from the unofficial (or black-market) rate as determined by marginal magnitudes. Moreover, within the state sector, too, the exchange rate was administratively differentiated; foreign exchange was cheaper for some importing enterprises and more expensive for others.

The way to the application of shock therapy in practice was opened up with the liberalisation of all markets (goods and services, capital, labour, foreign exchange). The withdrawal of the state from the subsidisation of economic activity on these markets was bound to result in increases in the prices of goods and services, factors and foreign exchange.

On the goods and services market the products that had to be eliminated were in the first place those which were more expensive than imports. Unfortunately, in the countries of Central and Eastern Europe whose economies had for almost fifty years developed autonomously, goods which could not compete with world production constituted the bulk of output.

On the labour market, what had to be eliminated were jobs which in a free-market perspective were no longer required. The wages of the surviving employees were determined by the supply-and-demand relationship. The results were, on the one hand, unemployment, and on the other, wage growth.

On the technologies market, all production structures and methods found redundant from the point of view of free-market requirements were eliminated. But at the same time there was a rapid growth of demand for technologies that served to bring into balance the demand for goods and services produced by means of such technologies.

A basic reorientation was also triggered off by shock therapy on the foreign exchange market through the elimination of state intervention and the related system of distribution of foreign exchange at prices lower than the equilibrium level. All this was replaced by a single exchange rate fixed at (or near) the equilibrium level, which led to those segments of external trade which could not show a profit being forced out of business.

The premise underlying shock therapy was that this elimination or selection process would be very swiftly accomplished, leading to the emergence within a matter of months of a completely altered economy bearing no resemblance to the central planning system, and 'purged' of all uneconomic goods, services and factors. This would be the turning-point in the systemic transformation of Central and Eastern Europe, the beginning of, in market terms, 'healthy' economic development. By 'healthy' was meant production restricted to goods which could be sold at prices set at the level of equilibrium between supply and demand.

All these assumptions would have been valid if inflation in Central and Eastern Europe had been solely of a demand-pull nature. The trouble was that only a small percentage of the inflationary growth of prices came into that category. Within a few months, too, this part of inflation was duly eliminated; here the Big Bang proved effective. Liberalisation of the consumer goods and services market combined with the introduction of wage controls resulted in prices growing at a rate several times faster than wages, which led in turn to overall supply and demand coming into balance.

What proved impossible was the elimination in the longer run of cost-push inflation, the reason being that it is not something that will yield to shock therapy, for behind cost-push inflation lie wholly different causes. Chief among them are the lopsided structure of production, obsolete technologies, defective industrial engineering and management methods, and so on. Removal of these requires large inputs, including investment, and is inevitably a long-term undertaking.

The effects of what are now over five years of the application of shock therapy in the Central and Eastern European countries are not very encouraging: by 1995, none of them had yet climbed back to its 1989 level of economic development. The countries that were closest to doing so, as far as industrial production was concerned, were Poland, Hungary, the Czech Republic and Slovakia. Poland was expected to pass that mark first – in 1996/97 – but paying a bigger price than the rest of this group in the form of large employment, a still high rate of inflation, a substantial decline in living standards, and the appearance of immense social inequality. The other three countries should get there later – at the end of the decade – but at a lower cost in terms of inflation and unemployment (especially the Czech Republic and Slovakia), only a small drop in the standard of living, and much less social inequality than in Poland.

A second group, comprising Lithuania, Latvia, Estonia, Bulgaria and Romania, is formed by countries which will not attain their 1989 levels of industrial production until after 2000. These countries have barely begun the process of making up lost ground, and are only steadily reducing the rate of fall in basic economic indicators. The best-placed is Latvia which was the first to cope with the problems of ever worsening crisis. But in all the countries in this group the slump in production was very steep, and inflation and unemployment continue to be high.

The third group of countries, which consists of the former Soviet republics and Albania, is still at the stage of plummeting basic economic indicators, and at a rate that is accelerating, not slowing, from year to year. For the moment it is hard even to estimate when these countries will re-attain the 1989 economic development level since they have not even begun the process of making up lost ground and in the vast majority of them the fall in industrial production amounted to over 80 per cent and in national income to over 50 per cent.[2] Inflation is astronomically high: in some of these countries, consumer goods prices in the first five years of systemic transformation rose over 27,000-fold.

The proponents of shock therapy did not bargain for such a steep slump. They assumed that an essentially universal remedy would quickly produce good results in all countries subjected to shock treatment. Although they expected that the costs of shock therapy might initially be heavy, they considered that they would be short-lived and would in sum be smaller than if another method of transformation were followed.

Radical transformation embracing the whole economy was expected to bring the free-market economic mechanism into play already in the initial period and with effects typical of the economies of developed countries in the form of equilibrium, improved efficiency and technological advance. If this did not happen, then the reasons, according to the advocates of shock therapy, are to be sought in the inconsistent application of this method of systemic transformation, not in any defects in the therapy itself. It is, they maintain, a universal method, and, provided that it is consistently applied, will in all conditions produce the expected results.[3]

In my opinion, this reasoning is untenable and the causes of the massive economic breakdown in the countries of Central and Eastern Europe lay in the therapy in question being ill-suited to the needs of systemic transformation in this region.[4]

2. See World Economy Research Institute, *Poland: International Economic Report 1994/95* (Warsaw: Warsaw School of Economics, 1995), pp. 29–37; Paweł Bożyk, 'Kolejny rok zmian' (Another Year of Change), *Życie Gospodarcze*, 1995, No. 13, and 'Komu bliżej do kapitalizmu' (Who's Closer to Capitalism), *Przegląd Kulturalny*, 1995, No. 9 (12 May).
3. See Jeffrey Sachs and David Lipton, 'Poland's Economic Reform', *Foreign Affairs*, Summer 1990.
4. See Paweł Bożyk, *Któredy do Europy?* (Which Way to Europe?) (Warsaw: Graf-Punkt, 1994), pp. 41–3.

Factors Determining Choice of Methods of Systemic Transformation

The real sphere and its institutional environment in Central and Eastern Europe at the turn of the 1990s differed basically from the conditions in countries with market economies, whether developed or developing. So, although some of the symptoms of crisis to be found in market-economy nations and in Central and Eastern Europe were similar (inflation, external debt, balance of payments deficits, and so on), the causes were totally different.

Countries with market economies had the institutional arrangements typical of them, and regulations to match, in the real sphere. Although the effectiveness of these mechanisms varied from country to country, the logic behind them was the same. In Central and Eastern Europe, on the other hand, the institutional arrangements in place at the time when the region embarked on systemic transformation were diametrically different from those of a market economy. Institutions characteristic of the latter were missing, laws and regulations differed, and there was no banking, financial, taxation, tariff or other system geared to free-market operation. Furthermore, the real sphere had been shaped according to a completely different stereotype. The ownership structure was inappropriate; the predominant form was not private but state ownership, which is resistant to free-market rules.

Also inappropriate was the structure of enterprises. Instead of thousands of small and medium-sized firms, Central and Eastern Europe was dominated by large enterprises employing many thousands of workers.[5] Practically speaking, that eliminated these enterprises as free-market players since they are incapable of responding flexibly in the short term to changing supply and demand: they are not equipped to deal with daily movements in prices, floating exchange rates and other such parameters of free-market competition. The majority of these enterprises cannot, for technological or other reasons, be broken up into smaller ones. Nor can they be privatised within a period of a few years because of a shortage of the capital required to undertake the necessary restructuring and modernisation.

At the same time, there was a lopsided structure of production. Instead of competing firms, the pattern in Central and Eastern Europe

---

5. J. Sachs, D. Lipton, 'Poland's Economic Reform', op. cit.

was tilted towards monopolies which dominated individual industries. To this day almost two-thirds of the production of all goods still comes from monopolists which not only control the volume of supply and prices, but also interfere in the sphere of consumption.

The structure of output was also distorted, the emphasis during the years of central planning having been put on heavy industry, metallurgy, mining, engineering, and the like at the expense of consumer industries and, especially, services. This structure determined long-term economic development objectives (levered primarily by investment growth), which was glaringly at variance with criteria in a free-market economy where priority is given to short-term goals, and consumption in particular. From the point of view of free-market criteria there were no buyers for much of this output, so its volume was cut back, which made it unprofitable. At present it burdens national budgets with subsidies and awaits either modernisation or liquidation.

A major barrier to the introduction of free markets proved to be lack of mobility of production factors, and not only labour but also capital and technology. The presence of labour surpluses in one region and shortages in another does not by any means indicate that the labour market can adjust to equilibrium. The main obstacle is a scarcity of housing and very high rents which often exceed employment incomes. The immobility of capital is due to a low rate of accumulation (and investment) in national income, high costs of investment, and so on. The greatest degree of flexibility in this field is displayed by technology, although its low standard in Central and Eastern Europe gives rise to a need for imports from outside the region. But here there is the barrier of these countries' large external debt.

If we add a shortage of management staff with the qualifications and ability to run business enterprises, banks and other financial institutions in a free-market environment, the situation is further complicated. Instead of entrepreneurship, socialism produced an army of administrators of state-owned assets trained to execute the orders passed down the bureaucratic chain of command. A large proportion of them are not equipped to manage small, wholly market-oriented firms on their own; they are incapable of taking the risks involved in decisions where uncertainty has to be weighed against potentially high profits. Developing the large numbers of specialists needed in this field requires considerable outlays and time, and in addition depends not only on building up the necessary network of training facilities but also on many years of practical experience.

Similarly, many years of laborious action will be needed to change the mentality, habits and mores of state sector employees whom 'real socialism' had accustomed to 'gain without pain'. The overwhelming majority of them were corrupted by a lack of strict discipline at work and the various forms of work-dodging that went with it (phoney sick leaves, down periods due to bad organisation, overmanning and the accompanying feather-bedding). Another plague in Central and Eastern Europe are the recurrent strikes and other job actions in support of demands for pay increases, improvements in working conditions and fringe benefits.

Finally, it will also take time to develop a financial sector (especially banking and fiscal), foreign trade infrastructure and so forth that meet free-market requirements. Their underdevelopment and shortages of modern technology, suitably qualified staff and experience lead under shock therapy conditions to pathological developments in the functioning of the free market, including the growth of a 'grey sector', tax evasion, corruption, and the like.

These are further encouraged by an inconsistent legal system modernised piecemeal, uncoordinated, and often under the influence of the arrangements of the central planning period. The result is frequent violations of the principle of the operation of free markets under the rule of law.

All these factors, which I call a *decalogue of limitations on the application of shock therapy in Central and Eastern Europe*, argue for the choice of a different solution in the form of evolutionary therapy.

The Evolutionary Therapy Scenario[6]

There is a debate in progress in the literature about whether evolutionary therapy (gradualism) can be treated as an alternative to shock therapy or is solely and exclusively one of the forms of the Big Bang.[7]

6. See Paweł Bożyk, 'An Evolutionary Mode of Transformation of External Relations', Paper presented at Sixteenth World Congress of IPSA, Berlin, August 21-15, 1994.
7. See *Economic Transformation in Central Europe. A Progress Report*, edited by

According to D.M. Nuti and Richard Portes, the differences between gradualism and shock therapy are small since, on the one hand, the possibilities of implementing gradual changes are limited, on the other, there are areas of the economy in which Big Bang-style therapy is not feasible.[8]

In the opinion of these two authors there are no good reasons for shrinking from shock methods of freeing prices, introducing a single exchange rate, decentralising and liberalising external trade, privatising state-owned enterprises, eliminating production subsidies from government budgets, and so on. Furthermore, they argue, in many cases shock therapy is essential since otherwise there would be a danger of the transformation process being dragged back as a result of dilution of the new rules of operation of the economy. For instance, temporary maintenance of subsidies might result in a lack of interest in improving productivity and discontinuance of the restructuring of production.

On the other hand, gradualism is essential in construction of the new institutional system, which is of its nature a longer-term process. In short, this point of view is an attempt to strike a balance between these two modes of transformation.[9]

My approach to the problem is different. Basically, Nuti and Portes agree with the idea that shock tactics are the only way of fighting inflation that serves the purposes of systemic transformation in Central and Eastern Europe. For them gradualism is nothing other than a gentler version of shock therapy.

To my mind, this idea is wrong, since gradualism is a far more universally employable method than shock therapy. The latter can and should be used only in a hyperinflation situation, assuming of course that the causes are of a demand-pull nature. The time-frame must, however, be short and the degree of radicalism a function of the rate of inflation. The period of application of shock therapy has to be brief because of the immense social costs that it exacts. If these costs grow

Richard Portes, CEPR and Commission of the European Communities, 1993, pp. 12–14.

8. Ibid., p. 12.
9. The cited authors consider that only in the former East Germany was shock therapy applied in pure form. Nevertheless, despite massive financial assistance from Bonn, the costs were high. What we have had in the rest of Central and Eastern Europe, according to Nuti and Portes, is a mixture of shock therapy and gradualism.

over a longer period of time there is the danger in a democratic system of the complete evaporation of popular support for the reformers.

The amount of radicalism in fighting inflation should depend on the amount of popular support for changes of this kind and needs to be treated on a purely case-by-case basis. If it is widespread (as it was in Poland in the first months of transformation in 1990) the radicalism of the fight against inflation can be greater. In cases where there is a reluctance on the part of the public to accept the high costs involved (as in Hungary and the Czech Republic) the radicalism of the therapy should definitely be much less.

The fact that shock therapy works as a means of bringing demand-pull inflation under control cannot be taken to mean that it will work equally well as a mean of systemic transformation. These are two wholly different spheres of application. In the second case shock therapy cannot be even so much as considered without the prospect of external subsidisation of the reforms. Failing that, the inevitable result will be social conflict.

Consequently, in Central and Eastern Europe, lacking as it does significant sources of external subsidisation, the one and only course that can be followed is gradualism. Furthermore, it should embrace not only the institutional sphere but, in the first place, the real sphere. Moreover, the latter is more difficult to transform than the former; it takes longer and is more costly. As far as this is concerned I am in basic disagreement with Nuti and Portes.

After all, systemic transformation in the real sphere is a matter not only of changes in supply and demand relations on the goods and services market but above all of changes in the economic structure, broadly defined, including the structure of production and investment. The means employed for this purpose by shock therapy is a shake-up of market price relationships, which is not a very efficient way of doing things. Better results are likely to be produced by means of industrial policy, which by definition belongs among the instruments of evolutionary therapy.

Nor does the shock therapy scheme allow for the abolition of subsidies for production which is unviable from the point of view of short-term market criteria. The development of a number of industries is governed a priori (also in advanced market economies) by long-term criteria which often differ from the short-term market criteria. They must, therefore, be supported out of the government budget: otherwise the costs of closing them will be greater than the costs of subsidies. Sometimes certain kinds of production cannot be scrapped in the first place and so have to be supported by the state over a longer period. Hence elimination of subsidies must take an evolutionary form since it is inherently a function of changes in economic strategy and policy and has to be harmonised with action in many other areas of systemic transformation.

Likewise, the liberalisation of external economic relations, foreign trade included, should not be effected by shock treatment methods since it involves substantial costs. It, too, should be harmonised with policies concerning structural change in the economy, industrial policy in particular.

Lastly, the privatisation of state-owned enterprises should of its nature also be an evolutionary process. Some of the efficient firms in this sector should not be privatised at all; commercialisation and adaptation to free-market rules are enough. Privatisation of some of the large enterprises has to be spread out in time in view of the shortage of capital. But what can be privatised quickly are small and medium-sized enterprises, especially in the trade sector.

On the other hand, in the institutional sphere there are far greater possibilities and needs for shock changes, although the process of laying the groundwork is necessarily a long and laborious one. This is especially true of the legal system. Here, gradualism would lead to considerable inconsistencies in the law, generate pathological disorders and impede the whole transformation process.

Shock treatment is also likely to be a better way than gradualism for tackling reform of the banking system, although in this case, too, its success depends on solid preparation of the ground. But gradualism would create the danger that advantage might be taken of inconsistent regulations for wrongful (possibly even strictly illegal) purposes. This applies also to the transformation of the fiscal, tariff and other systems.

The general conclusion to be drawn from the above considerations can be formulated as follows. There are no rational grounds for supposing that the real sphere of the economy is better suited to effective transformation under shock therapy conditions than the institutional sphere. In my opinion, the opposite assertion comes closer to the truth.

At the heart of the evolutionary transformation scenario lies a desire to minimise the costs which consist of, on the one hand, the costs of changes in systemic infrastructure and, on the other, the costs of replacing one mechanism with another. Systemic infrastructure comprises the real sphere, and the economic mechanism the institutional sphere.

The basic premise of the evolutionary scenario is that there should be no contradictions between the changes going on in these two spheres. In particular, harmony must be observed in transformations of the elements of the economic mechanism (prices, exchange rate, interest rates, money-creation rules, and so on). Thus, we rule out a situation in which we introduce an economic mechanism in an out-and-out free-market version but forgo privatisation of the economy. But also ruled out is the direct opposite: rapid and radical privatisation of the economy while leaving in place a mechanism in which some prices are government-controlled, exchange rates are not allowed to find their level, interest rates are lower than inflation rates, and in foreign trade a sizeable proportion of transactions is excluded from liberalisation.

Our assumption in formulating the evolutionary transformation scenario is that the chief restrictions on the pace of reform lie in the real sphere, above all in the restructuring of production. This has to be the touchstone of the pace of reform in the institutional sphere, although some running ahead in certain areas is perfectly admissible.

Acceptance of these principles rules out the possibility of transforming the whole economy in a short period of time. But it does not rule out rapid transformation of that part of the real sphere which lends itself to complete liberalisation in the short term.[10]

Complete liberalisation can be undertaken already in the initial period of markets for goods whose supply and demand is in balance, which can compete with imported products and which, simulaneously, also fulfil the conditions of the free-market systemic infrastructure: that is, production is not monopolised and competition in the market is not limited. In other words, there is a large number not only of buyers but also of sellers, and their positions are adequately balanced.

In this sector a completely free-market mechanism can, under the evolutionary transformation scenario, be put in place at once, which in the transition from a centrally planned economy would require the state

10. Paweł Bożyk, 'Ewolucyjny wariant transformacji powiazan zewnetrznych' (The Evolutionary Variant of Transformation of External Relations), *Ekonomista*, 1993, No. 3. pp. 283–300.

to relinquish its price and wage controls, abolish supports for production (consumption), introduce in this sector a realistic exchange rate, free access to currencies bought at equilibrium prices, and so on. There would also be free access to internal markets for foreign exporters. The liberalised sector would also be able to borrow at a single positive (real) interest rate and taxes would be payable according to the binding tax system. Nor would there be any limitation of foreign direct investment in this sector.

The introduction of free-market economy rules could go ahead without an 'inflationary shock' and a drastic fall in living standards. Liberalisation would start with the private sector, small-scale state and co-operative enterprises, private farming and several other sectors which were already, under the centrally-planned economy, operating within parameters of a more or less free-market nature.

The sector left unliberalised at the start of the process would be the rest of the economy which would initially be subject to the rules of a government-regulated market – but by means of indirect controls in all but exceptional cases (such as energy sources). Firms in the non-liberalised sector could also employ the parameters of the liberalised sector (for example, purchase foreign currencies at a lower exchange rate, borrow at positive interest rates, and so on). However, these parameters would a priori be disadvantageous to them.

The basic indirect forms of government intervention in the non-liberalised sector would be the following: production and export subsidies; customs duties and other charges on imports; non-tariff restrictions; preferential investment and production credits; sales of foreign currencies at prices above the market rate, and so forth. All these instruments would be a means of protecting parts of the economy against foreign competition in the initial stages of reform.

The presence of a separate non-liberalised sector means *ex ante* that some economic entities are unable to compete on the general terms of the liberalised sector, while their early failure and bankruptcy could cause far greater social and economic losses than the costs to the state of propping them up until they become competitive. How large this support should be and how long it should be maintained are matters for government discretion. In this scheme the government is a rationally functioning institution with the ability to make accurate evaluations of the economic situation and efficiently coordinate market mechanisms and eliminate pathological phenomena. Of course, such a conception of government functions is completely opposed to the approach of the 'shock therapists' who maintain that the state is incapable of performing these tasks properly.

The non-liberalised sector as described here should be seen as a stepping-stone to a free market system. The transition should be furthered by: privatisation; de-monopolisation through the development of a competitive production structure; enhancement of competitive power through technological modernisation; economies of scale; better organisation and management; the creation of such market institutions as stock exchanges, commercial banking systems and efficient fiscal and tariff agencies; the commercialisation and privatisation of management in state-owned enterprises, and so on.

A key advantage of a liberalised economy – the *terminus ad quem* – is the transparency of its ground-rules which are the same for all. Therein lies the attraction and fairness of the free market. But we must also remember that it is fair only if and when there is the proper systemic infrastructure to guarantee equal chances to all the players. If this is lacking, pathological social phenomena arise which nullify the benefits of the system. The whole point of a separate non-liberalised sector is to protect the economy from their appearance.

Concluding Remarks

The evolutionary (or, as it might also be called, sectoral) approach to systemic transformation proposed in this chapter differs fundamentally from shock therapy. The latter has been applied in Central and Eastern Europe chiefly for political reasons, 'on the wing', as it were, and without regard for the social and economic costs. It was not preceded by the necessary theoretical spadework and in particular by discussion among specialists.

The result has been profound economic crisis in this part of Europe. Today, several years into the transformation, it is not yet too late to replace shock therapy with gradualism, especially in the Central and Eastern European countries classified in this chapter in the third group: in those countries it is certain that shock therapy will not produce the expected results, at any rate in any foreseeable future.

3 'Shock versus Gradualism'

The Inappropriateness of the Labels Applied to the Strategies in Central Europe

Herman W. Hoen

Introduction

Economists face severe difficulties when suggesting strategies for the transition from a centrally planned to a market economy in Eastern Europe. To quote Van Brabant (1993, pp. 81–2), 'they know next to nothing about undoing the planning environment and coming to grips with the wide-ranging legacies of the earlier communist dominance in societal affairs'. After the collapse of the communist systems, many economists initially defined the desired economic order negatively and mistook the creation of a market economy for the destruction of mandatory planning (see Wagener, 1992, p. 365). Within this conception, system reversibility is implicitly acknowledged; that is, a market economy is expected to emerge instantaneously – or at least very quickly – by pressing the switch. At present, economists increasingly recognise that the transition from a centrally planned to a market economy entails the implementation and the evolution of new institutions (see, for example, Schmieding, 1993). Some of these institutions can be implemented rather quickly, but others will be the unintended result of long-term historical development. This perception stresses the irreversibility and path-dependency of system development.

The controversy over the desired nature of the transition, often referred to as the 'shock-versus-gradualism' debate (see Balcerowicz,

1993; Slay, 1994), seems to reflect the lack of well-accepted conceptual economic models, but it nevertheless set the stage for discussing the transition strategies in Central and Eastern Europe. This chapter highlights the transition policies applied in Poland, Hungary, former Czechoslovakia and its successor states (the Czech Republic and Slovakia). The bulk of the relevant literature classifies the Polish transition as a clear example of a shock therapy, at least in the initial stages (see Berg and Sachs, 1992; Bruno, 1992; Calvo and Coricelli, 1990), whereas the Hungarian policy is mostly perceived as a gradual case (Hare and Révész, 1992; Székely and Newbery, 1993). As far as the Czechoslovak economy is concerned, labels vary from a shock therapy – although starting somewhat later than in Poland – to a monetarist-inspired, liberal, non-government-intervention approach (Jeffries, 1993, pp. 378ff.). It is obvious, though, that after the split of Czechoslovakia, policies in the Czech Republic and Slovakia diverged (OECD, 1994).

This chapter challenges the appropriateness of these tags. Taking the key elements of the transition into account, they reveal a bias towards stabilisation and liberalisation of the economy and tend to neglect other key elements of the transition, such as (micro-economic) restructuring of production through privatisation and institution-building. It will be argued that, if the latter are taken into account, there are firm reasons to qualify the Hungarian transition as a shock treatment, whereas the Czech Republic presents a fine example of gradualism.

The outline of this chapter is as follows. Section 2 focuses on the 'shock-versus-gradualism' debate and addresses the issue of the extent to which this polemic is able to contribute to the design and evaluation of transformation policy. The notion of a pointless debate is not fully subscribed to, but it will be argued that the debate makes sense only in so far as one is willing to distinguish among the key elements of the transition, and, accordingly, to indicate the elements concerned. Before studying the transition policies conducted in the Central European countries, Section 3 briefly presents a survey of their economic performances. The background of a common contraction in economic activity during the first years of transition leads to the hypothesis that the frequently attached labels over-emphasise differences in the strategies applied, and, at the same time, neglect policy similarities. Therefore, the subsequent sections separately compare the reform policies in terms of stabilisation (Section 4), liberalisation (Section 5), privatisation and consequential restructuring (Section 6), and institution building (Section 7). The last section summarises the main conclusions.

Sense and Nonsense of the 'Shock-versus-Gradualism' Debate

The 'shock-versus-gradualism' debate concentrates on different opinions with respect to the speed and sequencing of reforms. Each of the measures to be adopted in the process of transition is associated with adjustment costs, so the issue is whether all the measures should be implemented at the same time and at maximum speed, or whether the total welfare costs can be minimised by sequencing the implementation of the necessary reforms. The dispute gave rise to much incomprehension, since the labels 'shock' and 'gradual' are tangible only when the type of reform is indicated. The agenda for the transition consists of an enormous list of required reforms (see Falk and Funke, 1993; Laski et al., 1993), but it can be divided into the following four main categories: stabilisation, liberalisation, privatisation, and a number of institutional reforms that are to provide a framework for the good functioning of markets (see Van Brabant, 1993, p. 77).

Within this continuing debate, advocates of shock treatment focus most strongly on stabilisation and liberalisation. Regarding stabilisation, they stress the necessity of a restrictive monetary and fiscal policy in order to combat budget deficits and external disequilibria (see Berg and Sachs, 1992; Lipton and Sachs, 1990). But the core element of a shock treatment is the rapid elimination of domestic price control by the state. In fact, price liberalisation is essential for macro-economic stabilisation, as well as for micro-economic restructuring. A general increase in the price level has to eliminate the monetary overhang, while changing relative prices should improve allocative efficiency. As soon as the aggregate price level is stabilised, relative price adjustments provide the incentives to bring about a more efficient allocation of resources. Producers will economise on the utilisation of inputs, while consumers are expected to experience welfare gains, because they will no longer be forced to substitute initially unwanted for eventually unavailable commodities. However, in a shock-therapist's perception, liberalisation involves not only the freeing of prices, but also the exposure of domestic enterprises to international competition. This involves the introduction of an internally convertible currency for current account transactions. The shock approach ultimately rests upon the conviction of general equilibrium, and it is rational behaviour on the part of market participants that is of crucial importance for the achievement of such an equilibrium. Independently of any past experience, they will optimise utilities by following price information. Within the shock approach inspired by neo-classical theory, the nature of transition is a matter of instantaneous adjustment of rational agents without a past (see Hoen, 1995).

Whereas proponents of shock treatment primarily focus on conditions under which there exists market equilibrium, adherents of gradualism tend to be preoccupied with scrutinising what happens if these conditions are not being fulfilled (see, for example, Van Ees and Garretsen, 1994; Murrell, 1992). Almost obviously, they stress that liberalisation of prices and foreign trade should be spread over a longer period of time. In the discussion so far, the arguments have particularly focused on the notion that rapid and complete price liberalisation, in combination with a restrictive monetary and fiscal policy, thwarts the importance of certain components of liquidity in the short run (see Kregel et al., 1992; Schmieding, 1993). These solutions are deemed to lead to non-welfare-maximising developments, since prices (interest rates) will not reflect the marginal profitability of investments, but will rather be subject to problems of project selection and moral hazard (see, for example, Stiglitz, 1992). Besides, an immediate and definite exposure to international competition may lead to the termination of production which in the longer run could have been profitable. But most importantly, they oppose *laissez-faire* solutions because well-functioning markets need special institutions. Part of these institutions also have to guarantee that privatisation will indeed enforce production restructuring. Hence, advocates of a gradual approach to a large degree focus on a different aspect of the transition. Their claim is that without proper institutional guidelines with respect to property rights, freedom of contract, liability and competition rules, shock treatment will induce a gratuitous decline in economic activity. Furthermore, they point to the fictitious aspects of the concept of a free market. Most specifically, this criticism relates to the fact that advocates of a shock approach try to implement a kind of capitalism which has not existed for a long time. In a more general sense, it focuses on the necessity of state intervention during the period that markets still do not function properly. As will be shown below, this last point in particular leads to misleading characterisations.

Does this imply that those in favour of shock treatment have no valuable contribution to make with respect to privatisation and institution-building? Since neo-classically-inspired shock therapists assume well-functioning markets – the only institution explicitly taken into account – it has indeed very little to add in this respect (see Murrell, 1991). However, recently, various economists have tried to include institutions within the neo-classical concept, and refer to their framework as neo-institutional, thereby excluding those institutionalists who criticise the rational-choice model (see Eggertsson, 1990, pp. 22ff.). Since these economists focus on the right to use productive resources, it can be deduced that the implementation of a well-defined system of decentralised property rights is the most important task in this field. The sooner this can be accomplished, the better. It has to be emphasised, however, that speed is the only relevant criterion for the way in which property rights should be transferred from the state to private persons. The most appropriate mechanism for rapid privatisation follows straightforwardly from the Coase theorem, which states that, under zero transaction costs, no matter what the distribution of property rights looks like initially, it will always end up disposed in the most efficient way.

Even though the logic of shock treatment or gradualism can to a certain extent be deduced from economic theory, the ultimate choice is highly dependent on political restrictions. The decision to conduct a shock approach, or not, is a *political* decision. This highly complicates matters and fuels further incomprehension. Shock treatment is generally perceived to add to the credibility of the transition strategy in a society which, owing to its experiences of earlier communist reforms, may be rather sceptical; but at the same time, it can be considered a strategy which anticipates a possible reversal once negative consequences are revealed (Roland, 1994). Therefore, in the perception of shock therapists, successor governments have to be saddled with insuperable costs in case they want to revoke decisions *ex post facto*. Political authorities would be most susceptible to this kind of 'scorched-earth policy' in a revolutionary atmosphere immediately after the collapse of the communist system. A gradual approach is a response to the perceived political feasibility. It focuses on the possibility and the necessity of compromise. Political barriers have to be lifted beforehand, and therefore the policy should reduce expected costs related to a reversal and persuade sceptics to support the reforms for the time being. It seems an obvious strategy in the case when the political scene is dominated by uncertainties about the welfare gains of transition, for instance when past communist reforms resulted in a relatively prosperous inheritance.

To what extent does the derivation of strategies from pure economics differ from that in which the choice of either 'shock' or 'gradualism' is due to the nature of political constraints? As far as the differences are concerned, it has to be appreciated that a transition policy based upon the nature of political restrictions under all possible circumstances assumes system reversibility, with a gradual approach seeking to reduce the costs of return, whereas a shock treatment aims to maximise them. In this respect, these different aproaches further nourish confusion. But there are also similarities, especially related to the ability to implement all the necessary reforms. As stated above, when discussing stabilisation and liberalisation, fast implementation in principle seems feasible. But it is not just for political reasons, but also because of technical constraints, that privatisation and institution-building cannot be prepared in a short period of time, let alone be implemented. Therefore, it has to be concluded that governments applying shock treatment will not only be seeking to raise the costs of reversibility – that is, the pure neo-classical case of the creation of a market as the destruction of mandatory planning – but for reasons of political survival will also have to consider the feasibility of reforms in the longer run. Hence, the whole 'shock-versus-gradualism' debate may reduce to a semantic discussion, unless one is willing to distinguish the key elements of the transition to a market economy. As will be shown in the remainder of this chapter, this has not been the case so far and has therefore resulted in inappropriate labels.

The Economic Performance in Central Europe: Was the Crisis Really Necessary?

The Central European countries applied different policies during the first years of transition. Their divergent courses were partly due to different ideas that the policy makers had when starting with the transition – whether or not supported by Western advisers – and partly the result of differences in their scope for policy manoeuvre. Before further exploring the nature of the strategies applied in these countries, this section briefly outlines their economic performance in the first half of the 1990s and, on the basis of these factual developments, will present hypotheses on the differences in reform policies.

As can be seen from Table 3.1, all four Central European countries severely suffered in terms of falls in Gross Domestic Product (GDP). Poland was the first country that suffered from a heavy decline in production, but also appeared to be the first country that experienced positive GDP growth. With a time-lag of approximately one year, Czechoslovakia and Hungary were the next to suffer from the transition crisis. In Table 3.1, economic performances of Slovakia and the Czech Republic have been calculated in retrospect, but it goes without saying that during the last two years of the federation both the Czechs and the Slovaks were heavily hit by the recession. Whereas the Czech Republic halted the fall in economic activity in 1993 and realised a moderate positive growth for 1994, Slovakia still experienced a negative growth performance in 1993, although at a decreasing rate, but achieved a remarkable growth performance in 1994 (see Bank Austria AG, 1994, for an excellent analysis of Slovakia). Hungary is believed to have followed a more gradual path of transition, but the decline in economic activity was no less than in the other countries. Other calculations also reveal that during the first five years following the collapse of communism, all the countries under consideration were confronted with a cumulative contraction of GDP within a range of 18 to 22 per cent (see Zloch-Christy, 1994, p. 124).

With economic activity declining over successive years, unemployment started to rise to a 1995 level of approximately 15 per cent in all the Central European countries, whereas the budget deficits crept above the critical IMF-approved level of 5 per cent of GDP – the Czech Republic taking a different stand in these respects. The initial price shock, as a result of price liberalisation was certainly larger than expected, but what is more noteworthy is that in none of the countries were the stabilisation programmes successful enough to bring inflation rates down to single-digit levels on a yearly basis, Poland in this regard remaining a notorious negatively performing outlier.

Table 3.1   Development of important economic indicators:
The Czech Republic, Hungary, Poland, and Slovakia,
1990–94

Czech Republic	1990	1991	1992	1993	1994
GDP change (%)	−0.5	−15.1	−7.1	0.0	2.1
Inflation (%)	15.3	20.4	11.7	20.8	12.5
Budget deficit (% GDP)*	−0.9	1.1	4.0	4.3	−0.1
Unemployment (% active population)	0.8	4.1	2.6	3.5	3.1

Hungary	1990	1991	1992	1993	1994
GDP change (%)	−3.7	−12.0	−5.0	−1.0	5.2
Inflation (%)	28.9	33.8	21.8	23.0	17.9
Budget deficit (% GDP)	0.1	4.3	7.3	5.7	7.6
Unemployment (% active population)	1.7	6.6	12.0	12.6	10.5

Poland	1990	1991	1992	1993	1994
GDP change (%)	−11.6	−7.6	1.0	2.5	5.5
Inflation (%)	586.0	70.3	43.0	35.3	32.2
Budget deficit (% GDP)	−2.7	3.8	8.0	4.9	3.0
Unemployment (% active population)	6.3	11.8	13.6	15.3	16.8

Slovakia	1990	1991	1992	1993	1994
GDP (change in %)	−2.5	−15.8	−6.0	−4.7	4.4
Inflation (%)	15.6	25.1	10.1	27.5	14.5
Budget deficit (% GDP)*	−0.9	1.1	4.0	6.8	5.7
Unemployment (% active population)	1.5	11.8	10.4	14.1	14.5

* Figures for 1990, 1991, and 1992 apply to Czechoslovakia.

Source: PlanEcon Report, various issues.

The outcomes seem to fit into the general framework of J-curves (see Brada and King, 1992), which assumes the inevitability of a transition crisis and suggests that a drop in economic activity is unavoidable before there is an improvement in economic performance. In fact, adherents of a shock and of a gradual approach towards the transition both confirm the inevitability of such a contraction in economic activity. It applied to all the Central European countries under consideration and mainly stems from three factors. First, the transition towards a market economy implies a reallocation of means of production from loss-making to profitable industries and services. This shift will not proceed without friction and necessarily coincides with a short-term decline in output. Second, a price has to be paid for the attainment of macro-economic equilibrium. Third, contrary to a supply-constrained centrally planned system, a demand-constrained market economy has to remain flexible by not producing part of the potential output (Ellman, 1993). During the adjustment processes, production will decline, as apparently was the case in Czechoslovakia, Hungary, and Poland. Of course, the question remains whether or not the transition crises as they occurred in these countries were too severe, and, therefore, whether part of the pain could have been eased by applying other policies.

The tabulated economic indicators confirm the inevitability of the transition crisis, but they also suggest either that the frequently attached labels of shock versus gradual over-emphasised differences in the strategies applied, or that the common decline in output has to be explained by exogenous shocks. Although the latter view cannot be completely ruled out (see Brada and King, 1992), this chapter maintains that there are firm reasons to challenge the appropriateness of the frequently suggested labels. In order to underpin this line of thought, the next section tries to identify the 'shock' and 'gradual' elements in the policies applied in Central Europe by following the agenda of transition as listed in Section 2.

Stabilisation Strategies in Central Europe

With respect to stabilisation, the labels still correspond to those usually suggested, and therefore can be rather briefly illustrated. The shock approach towards stabilisation is most clearly embodied in the Polish reform programme, which was implemented by the Mazowiecki government in January 1990 (see Lipton and Sachs, 1990). A restrictive monetary policy, tight wage control, severe cuts in subsidies, in combination with the liberalisation of the vast majority of prices and external trade relations, were the main ingredients of this IMF-approved policy implemented by Finance Minister Balcerowicz. A huge decline in economic activity as a negative consequence of this shock treatment was expected to last for a rather short time, and, moreover, had to be evaluated as a necessary reduction of inefficient production.

In many ways, the Polish policy served as a point of reference for the transition in Central and Eastern Europe. However, it did not serve as an example for all of these countries. Hungary, in particular, followed a deviating path. The Antall government, which came into power in May 1990, speeded up the reforms initiated by the Hungarian communists in the 1970s and 1980s, instead of disposing of this legacy as soon as possible. With respect to stabilisation, certain Keynesian-inspired elements supporting a more gradual approach are clearly visible. Most importantly, the government tried to maintain the purchasing power of the population in order to avoid a dramatic decline in aggregate demand. For example, contrary to the Polish macroeconomic stabilisation scheme, there were no serious attempts to tax away wage increases completely to the extent that these exceeded inflation. The liberal wage policy led to a situation in which Hungarian employees were among the best paid in Central and Eastern Europe (see Köllő, 1993). In comparison with the surrounding countries in transition, falls in real wages were rather moderate.

The fact that stabilisation policy in Hungary reveals some gradual strands does not necessarily imply that the Hungarian authorities were solely inspired by the arguments put forward by adherents of a gradual approach towards the transition. In fact, it may very well have been the case that policy contingency was less than in Poland, because of the relatively smooth political changes – to some extent initiated from within the socialist party – meant that the former communists could not solely be blamed for the decline in output necessary for the creation of the market economy. In contrast to this, the post-communist leaders in Poland could initially argue that the negative social impact of the shock therapy was just the result of the communist legacy. Hence, policy responsibility at the start of the transition was more intricate in

Hungary. Even if they wanted to implement a shock therapy, they were unable to do so because of public resistance at the start of transition. Here, it seems that the nature of the political restrictions shaped the policy.

After the political turmoil in 1989, stabilisation policy in Czechoslovakia to a large extent resembled that of Poland, but the implications were of a totally different nature (see Levcik et al., 1994). The Czechoslovak government implemented a monetary and fiscal policy that was restrictive in nature, but since macro-economic disequilibria in terms of the size of monetary overhang and hard-currency debts were rather modest, the Polish phenomenon of inflationary outbursts did not emerge. Of course, after the splitting of the federation in 1993, the policies of the Czech Republic and Slovakia diverged. Furthermore, the Czechoslovak government directly intervened in labour markets, as will be shown in the next section.

Liberalisation Strategies in Central Europe

As stated above, liberalisation is closely related to stabilisation. It was perceived as an important item in all the Central European countries, and, with the notable exception of labour markets, more or less the same deviations can be observed between Poland and Czechoslovakia, on the one hand, and Hungary, on the other. Poland and Czechoslovakia opted for a quick liberalisation of nearly 90 per cent of all prices within a period of approximately half a year (Berg and Sachs, 1992; Levcik et al., 1994). The only difference between the two countries was that Poland started price liberalisation in January 1990, whereas Czechoslovak prices were liberalised from the start of 1991. The emphasis on full liberalisation of prices, which implies a focus on allocative efficiency, reveals pure neo-classical strands. Furthermore, the efforts to implement a market economy almost overnight witnessed a strong belief in the possibility of pragmatically constructing a market economy. Owing to the rational behaviour of agents, the legacy of the past was not believed to thwart the purposes of the transition strategy in a serious way.

Although 90 per cent of prices in Hungary were liberalised by the end of 1991, the process took longer. During the period of reforms in the 1970s and 1980s, there were several attempts to free prices; most of them failed, but still genuine liberalisation was introduced as early as 1989 – before the system collapsed (see Csaba, 1992). The same holds for the liberalisation of foreign markets. In Hungary, import liberalisation as an important step towards currency convertibility was introduced before the political turnover and started from January 1989. It entailed the liberalisation of 80 per cent of all imports within a period of three years. After the communists were forced to resign, the time schedule was shortened, but compared with Czechoslovakia and Poland, both of which introduced internal convertibility more or less overnight and relied upon the idea that devaluation of the currency was the only mechanism to protect domestic industries, import liberalisation remained gradual. It implied that not all industrial sectors were exposed to world market conditions at once, whereas in Czechoslovakia and in Poland, foreign trade was liberalised almost overnight (see Ábel and Bonin, 1993; Hanel, 1992). It has to be added, though, that the observed differences should not be exaggerated. All the Central European countries under consideration effected genuine liberalisation of imports within an astonishingly short period of time, and even though the Hungarian currency was *de jure* not fully convertible, *de facto* it was from approximately half a year after the first post-communist government took office in May 1990.

Our remarks on austerity programmes already suggested that the liberalisation of labour markets contradicted common perceptions of the nature of the transition in the countries under consideration. Thanks to the legacy of the reforms in the 1980s, the Hungarian labour market was the most liberal and the authorities were not in a position to regain effective wage control. At the other extreme, the Czechoslovak authorities to a large extent directly intervened in this respect and at first continued to use decree powers of central planning in order to implement a tough wages policy by administrative means. Since 1991, wage restraints have been negotiated in the context of a tripartite council consisting of representatives of the government, the employers and the employees, after which the government has the power to set the negotiated results by decree. Therefore, the Czech Republic is unique not in the achievement of restricting wages, but in the fact that wage restrictions are accepted without major upheavals. Despite the liberal rhetoric of the former Prime Minister Václav Klaus of the Czech

Republic, corporatist labour relations seem to enhance the population's willingness to accept the cost of transition. Moreover, as part of the implicit 'social contract' the Czech authorities apply a very active labour market policy. In order to balance the demand and supply of labour in an as yet poorly-functioning market, the government mandates district labour offices to create socially useful jobs and introduces extensive retraining programmes for the unemployed (see Raiser, 1994). This active labour-market policy fits very well into the approach which connects gradualism with the nature of political constraints. In the Czech Republic, the government in office in the mid-1990s still seemed to enjoy the support of a large part of the population, whereas higher unemployment rates may have contributed to the major political shifts that led to the return of socialist governments in Poland and Hungary. But whatever the underlying motives may have been, the fact of the matter is that the Czech liberalisation of labour markets certainly did not entail a shock-like approach.

Privatisation and Restructuring in Central Europe

Privatisation dominates the agenda of transition in the formerly centrally planned economies. This also holds true for the Central European countries. Whereas price liberalisation in combination with a restrictive monetary and fiscal policy are supposed to support macro-economic stability, the importance of privatisation lies in micro-economic restructuring. Privatisation ultimately is bound to improve enterprise efficiency, since the budget constraints of private enterprises are harder than those of state enterprises. Large-scale transfers of property rights from the state to the public, however, have far-reaching consequences for the division of capital and income. So there may be a broad consensus with respect to the importance of privatisation, but because of massive welfare effects it remains to be seen how to transfer state property. Should privatisation precede restructuring, or should the two take place simultaneously? And, if there are firm reasons to sequence privatisation, what criteria should guide the decisions? The transfer of property rights in the Central European countries perfectly illustrates the different views in this respect.

Whereas Poland set the stage for stabilisation, Czechoslovakia did so for privatisation with the introduction of its so-called 'voucher scheme'. Voucher schemes can be considered as the most decentralised way of privatisation. By distributing vouchers to the population almost free of charge, and subsequently organising several auctions at which these vouchers can be exchanged for enterprise shares, the Czechoslovak authorities tried to create a capital market at once and provoke entrepreneurial behaviour. The danger of an extreme dispersion of ownership rights, which would lead to ineffective control over management, more or less disappeared as a result of the unexpectedly vigorous, spontaneous development of investment funds, which fulfil an intermediation function. There is no active role left for state interference as far as restructuring is concerned. Privatisation became an instrument for restructuring, and not the other way round.

Poland to some extent followed the Czechoslovak example after initial failures of so-called 'spontaneous privatisation', which basically implied that the former managers received ownership rights at reduced prices. But with respect to the implementation of voucher schemes, the Polish authorities did not completely rely upon the Czechoslovak *laissez-faire* approach. In order to avoid too much dispersion of enterprise shares, they deliberately created holding companies, each of which consisted of a number of state-owned enterprises operating in a common sector. These holding companies serve as financial intermediaries between the population and the state. The population cannot exchange vouchers for enterprise shares, but are allowed only to change them for shares of the holding company. This might be called an 'interventionist' voucher scheme which is designed to let privatisation and restructuring proceed simultaneously. It has to be added, though, that because of the subsequent vacillations of political power, Polish privatisation was been seriously delayed (see Nunnenkamp, 1994). So far, the liquidation of state-owned enterprises – not necessarily implying bankruptcy – has been predominant in the Polish privatisation, that is, the direct sale of state assets without transforming the enterprise into a partnership issuing shares.

With the exception of the restitution of land – and in regard to the restitution of other expropriated assets – the Antall government in Hungary did not make use of vouchers, although time and again the option of voucher schemes was discussed in parliament. The Hungarian authorities decided to sell state property after spontaneous privatisation had led to an enormous distrust of the population towards the reforms in general. A specially established state property agency was required to select enterprises for privatisation (see Mihályi, 1993). By setting this up, the state actively interfered, since it implicitly made decisions about which sectors were believed to be vital and should not be left solely to the market. On top of that, the Hungarian parliament decided in summer 1992 to create an additional state organ, the State Assets Management Company, that was to be responsible for the management and supervision of those firms which were expected to remain wholly or partly in state hands in the longer term. Although the establishment of this state body was meant to support the state property agency by more clearly distinguishing privatisation from the operational management of state enterprises, two functions which until then had been combined within the State Property Agency, it also set a definite boundary to the scope of privatisation in Hungary. (It has subsequently been superseded, as SAMCo and the SPA have now been merged, and many of the companies expected to remain in state hands are now being privatised.)

Although it is extremely risky to generalise on privatisation experiences, it can nevertheless be asserted that arguments related to a more gradual sequencing influenced decision-making more in Hungary than happened in Czechoslovakia and Poland. Hungarian privatisation seems to accompany some kind of industrial policy, which has to be interpreted as guiding the market. Furthermore, the fact that the Hungarian policy refrained from the idea that privatisation should in principle include all companies amplifies this line of thought. Czechoslovak and Polish privatisation experiences were somewhat different. The voucher privatisation in Czechoslovakia was introduced in order to privatise the whole industrial sector at maximum speed. It can even be maintained that giving away state property to the population at large, without taking welfare considerations into account, is rather close to the Coase theorem, which posits that no matter how the property rights are initially divided among the population, they will eventually always be distributed in the most efficient way. In other words, transaction costs associated with the redistribution of ownership rights, once privatisation was completed, are assumed to be zero. In this respect, the Czechoslovak experience presents a neo-classical-inspired shock approach. But there are certainly gradual elements as well. These are to be found in the subsequent restructuring. The enormous dispersion of property rights among the population places great confidence in individual entrepreneurship as the driving force that has to accomplish economic change. Furthermore, the distribution of property rights implies that the state is not inclined to restructure state properties. This is envisaged as the essential task of the new private owners. Restructuring is assumed to be a waste of time and money as far as the state is concerned. On top of that, the Czechoslovak authorities refrained from intervention aimed at the prevention of dispersed ownership rights. The emergence of investment funds was a process of spontaneous evolution. The Polish option is extremely hard to categorise, but seems to a large extent to resemble the Czechoslovak case, except that the deliberate creation of privatisation intermediaries, rather than *laissez-faire* voucher privatisation, may be interpreted as a deliberate attempt to preserve interest in certain pivotal sectors. However, as privatisation schemes were delayed in this country, it is difficult to identify the main theme in the process.

The ultimate proof of successful privatisation is in the changed economic behaviour of privatised firms. Privatisation in itself may be rather quick, but at the same time will not improve enterprise efficiency, since the enforcement of market-conforming behaviour needs more than privatisation alone. Hence, the speed of privatisation as a criterion for distinguishing shock treatment or gradualism is a meaningless exercise, unless limiting conditions in the institutional sphere of market building are also taken into account. It is shown in the next section that an assessment of these conditional matters will turn our initial perceptions upside-down.

Building Market Institutions in Central Europe

Institution-building is intended to provide a framework for the proper functioning of markets and most specifically refers to those reform attempts that will have an impact on incentive structures and basically try to achieve a hardening of the budget constraints, that is, to ensure that enterprises can no longer *ex post facto* adjust the budget to the costs (see Raiser and Nunnenkamp, 1993). It is difficult to sum up all the relevant measures, but one might suggest that most of the reform attempts which try to enforce financial discipline upon enterprises are closely linked to the implementation of a new financial system.

As financial markets were completely absent in the formerly centrally planned economies, or at the most functioning in a embryonic phase, investment capital needed for restructuring the economy is mainly to be supplied by banks. However, the banking sector is seriously constrained in supplying credits. The state banks inherited bad portfolios, because, under central planning, credits resulted from *ex post facto* adjustment to changes in the real sphere of the economy (see Dittus, 1994). Therefore, once a market economy was required to replace this passive financial system, the banks started with the burden of several decades of poorly performing loans, and hence were not in a favourable position to generate new investment capital.

Surveying the creation of investment capital, one can observe delays that are common to all Central European countries. Although Hungary implemented a two-tier banking system as early as 1987, the implementation of an efficient mechanism of capital allocation did not emerge. Since the enforcement of financial discipline was ineffective, the large state-owned enterprises received the bulk of the credits, whereas tight credit controls squeezed investment opportunities for new private enterprises (see Estrin, Hare and Surányi, 1992). But after being in power for about a year and a half, in December 1991 the Antall government introduced a whole package of institutional measures which, among other goals, sought to put an end to any further lending to uncreditworthy state-owned enterprises (see Dittus, 1994). A pivotal part of this institutional package was the enforcement of a bankruptcy law. Furthermore, in order to tackle the problems due to the inherited stock of bad loans, the banks were forced to make special provisions to build up their reserves. Also, an enormous number of state-owned as well as private enterprises were judged bankrupt. This policy certainly does not fit into the perception of a gradual strategy of transition, since it was a pure shock treatment (see Bakos, 1994).

Notwithstanding a commonly accepted shock approach, the Czechoslovak authorities to a large extent directly intervened and complemented their tight monitoring of banks with financial support for distressed enterprises (see Dittus, 1994; Levcik et al., 1994; Raiser, 1994). To a far greater extent than in Hungary, banks were able to write off non-performing loans, whereas new provisions were more relaxed. In addition, the Czechoslovak government founded a special 'Consolidation Bank' in an attempt to reduce the financial burden on enterprises in the process of privatisation. Czechoslovak policy was explicitly aimed at preventing the above-mentioned credit crunch, since the spread on interest rates (that is, the difference between borrowing and lending rates) could remain within reasonable margins. This had a positive impact on lending possibilities for private investment projects. In the meantime, however, the Consolidation Bank evolved from one of the largest creditors into an important institution in the field of restructuring large enterprises. This actually hampered the process of restructuring. Besides, a bankruptcy act did not come into effect before April 1993, and by the middle of the decade only a few liquidations had occurred. Moreover, the bankruptcy act explicitly disallows the closing of state-owned enterprises during the process of privatisation (Orenstein, 1994, p. 7)). For political reasons, the Czech government has tolerated the survival of a large number of loss-making enterprises, while it is also not in the interests of the large commercial banks to initiate bankruptcy procedures (see Levcik, 1994). The Polish policy is less easy to interpret. A main characteristic seems to be slowness, since arrangements with respect to poorly performing debts became effective only in March 1993. But it is doubtful whether this can be perceived as gradual; it can rather be viewed as muddling through as a result of continuous political disputes.

In sum, with respect to creating market institutions, the labelling of Hungary as gradualist in comparison with the Czech and Polish shock treatment is completely misleading. Taking the reforms aimed at hardening budget constraints into consideration, it rather seems the other way round. In the absence of well-functioning markets, the Czech authorities in particular were very willing to intervene.

Conclusions

This chapter focuses upon the strategies applied in the Central European countries. On the basis of the dichotomous framework of a rapid versus a gradual transition, Polish and Czechoslovak policies are mostly labelled as 'shock', whereas the Hungarian transition is perceived as a case of gradual sequencing. In order to put things in perspective, this chapter firstly has reconsidered the theoretical under-pinnings of this dichotomous framework, and subsequently pinpointed the reasons for incomprehension, thereby challenging the appropriate-ness of the frequently suggested labels.

It can be concluded that the 'shock versus gradualism' dispute blurs stabilisation, liberalisation, privatisation and institution-building, which constitute the key elements of transition. In addition, the suggested labels of a neo-classical shock approach in Poland and Czechoslovakia contrasted with a strategy of a gradual sequencing in Hungary only make sense with respect to stabilisation and liberalisation. Considering privatisation and institutional reform, the attached labels are even completely misleading, especially in the case of Czechoslovakia. Despite the fact that speed drove privatisation, it can be asserted that there are important elements of a gradual approach to be found in the Czechoslovak experiment. These are to be found in the limiting conditions of building market institutions. In this respect, the Czecho-slovak authorities intervened broadly. In order to prevent a credit crunch, they applied a policy of tight monitoring of banks supported by substantial capital injections, whereas in the labour market there were direct wage controls in the context of corporatist labour relations. On the other hand, Hungary seems to be the only country with a bank-ruptcy law which is indeed effective, and, therefore, the Antall govern-ment appeared to a certain extent to be a wolf in sheep's clothing.

References

Ábel, István and John P. Bonin (1993), 'State Desertion and Converti-bility: the Case of Hungary', in István Székely and David M.G. Newbery (eds.), *Hungary: An Economy in Transition* (Cambridge: Cambridge University Press), pp. 329–41.

Balcerowicz, Leszek (1993), 'Common Fallacies in the Debate on the Economic Transition in Central and Eastern Europe', Working Paper 11 (London: European Bank for Reconstruction and Development).

Bakos, Gábor (1994), 'Hungarian Transition after Three Years', unpublished paper prepared for the 35th Annual Convention of the International Studies Association, Washington D.C.

Bank Austria AG (1994), *The Slovak Republic After One Year of Independence* (Vienna: Bohmann Druck & Verlag).

Berg, Andrew and Jeffrey Sachs (1992), 'Structural Adjustment and International Trade in Eastern Europe: The Case of Poland', *Economic Policy*, No. 14, pp. 117–55.

Brabant, Jozef M. van (1993), 'Lessons from the Wholesale Transformations in the East', *Comparative Economic Studies*, Vol. 35, No. 4, pp. 73–102.

Brada, Joseph and Arthur King (1992), 'Is there a J-curve for the Economic Transition from Socialism to Capitalism', *Economics of Planning*, Vol. 25, No. 1, pp. 37–53.

Bruno, Michael (1992), 'Stabilisation and Reform in Eastern Europe: A Preliminary Evaluation', *IMF Staff Papers*, Vol. 39, No. 4, pp. 319–47.

Calvo, Guillermo A. and Fabrizio Coricelli (1992), 'Stabilizing a Previously Centrally Planned Economy: Poland 1990', *Economic Policy*, No. 14, pp. 176–226.

Csaba, László (1992), 'From Reforming to Transforming the Economic System in Hungary: A Survey', *Comparative Economic Studies*, Vol. 34, No. 3–4, pp. 96–106.

Dittus, Peter (1994), 'Corporate Governance in Central Europe: The Role of Banks' (Basel, Bank for International Settlements), mimeo.

Ees, Hans van and Harry Garretsen (1994), 'The Theoretical Foundations of the Reforms in Eastern Europe: Big Bang versus Gradualism and the Limitations of Neo-Classical Theory', *Economic Systems*, Vol. 18, No. 1, pp. 1–13.

Eggertsson, Thráin (1990), *Economic Behaviour and Institutions* (Cambridge: Cambridge University Press).

Ellman, Michael (1993), *General Aspects of Transition*, in Piet Hein Admiraal (ed.), *Economic Transition in Eastern Europe* (Oxford, Basil Blackwell), pp. 3–22.

Estrin, Saul, Paul Hare and Marta Surányi (1992), 'Banking in Transition: Development and Current Problems in Hungary', *Soviet Studies*, Vol. 44, No. 5, pp. 785–808.

Falk, Martin and Norbert Funke (1993), 'Zur Sequenz von Reformschritten: Erste Erfahrungen aus dem Transformationprozeß in Mittel- und Osteuropa', *Die Weltwirtschaft*, No. 2, pp. 196–206.

Hanel, Petr (1992), 'Trade Liberalisation in Czechoslovakia, Hungary, and Poland Through 1991: A Survey', *Comparative Economic Studies*, Vol. 34, No. 3-4, pp. 34-53.

Hare, Paul and Tamás Revész (1992), 'Hungary's Transition to the Market: The Case Against a Big Bang', *Economic Policy*, Vol. 14, pp. 227-64.

Hoen, Herman W. (1995), 'Theoretically Underpinning the Transition in Eastern Europe: An Austrian View', *Economic Systems*, Vol. 19, No. 1, pp. 59-77.

Jeffries, Ian (1993), *Socialist Economies and the Transition to the Market: A Guide* (London and New York: Routledge).

Köllő, János (1993), 'The Transformation of Shop Floor Bargaining in Hungarian Industry', in István Székely and David M.G. Newbery (eds), *Hungary: An Economy in Transition* (Cambridge: Cambridge University Press), pp. 275-95.

Kregel, Jan, Egon Matzner and Gernot Grabler (eds) (1992), *The Market Shock: An Agenda for the Economic and Social Reconstruction of Central and Eastern Europe* (Vienna: Austrian Academy of Sciences).

Laski, Brus, Dragoslav Avramovic, János Fath, Michael Landesman and Dariusz Rosati (1993), 'Transition for the Command to the Market System: What Went Wrong and What to Do Now?' (mimeo) (Vienna: Wiener Institut für Internationale Wirtschaftsvergleiche).

Levcik, Friedrich, Milo Pick, Ota Turek and Josef Pöschl (1994), 'The Czech Economy: Internal and External Developments since 1989 and Future Options', Forschungsbericht No. 203 (Vienna: Wiener Institut für Internationale Wirtschaftsvergleiche).

Lipton, David and Jeffrey Sachs (1990), 'Creating a Market Economy in Eastern Europe: The Case of Poland', Brookings Papers on Economic Activity (Washington, DC: The Brookings Institution), No. 1, pp. 75-147.

Mihályi, Péter (1993), 'Hungary: A Unique Approach to Privatisation – Past, Present and Future', in István Székely and David M.G. Newbery (eds), *Hungary: An Economy in Transition* (Cambridge: Cambridge University Press), pp. 84-117.

Murrell, Peter (1991), 'Can Neoclassical Economics Underpin the Economic Reform of the Centrally Planned Economies?', *Journal of Economic Perspectives*, Vol. 5, No. 4, pp. 59-76.

—— (1992), 'Evolutionary and Radical Approaches to Economic Reform', *Economics of Planning*, Vol. 25, No. 1, pp. 79–95.

Nunnenkamp, Peter (1994), 'Governing the Economic Transition of Hungary, Poland and Former Czechoslovakia', paper presented at the 7th World Congress of Social Economics, Verona, 3–7 August 1994.

OECD (1994), *The Czech and Slovak Republics* (Paris: OECD Economic Surveys).

Orenstein, Mitchell (1994), 'The Political Success of Neo-Liberalism in the Czech Republic', Working Paper Series, No. 68 (Prague: Center for Economic Research and Graduate Education – Economics Institute of the Academy of Sciences of the Czech Republic).

PlanEcon Report, various issues.

Raiser, Martin (1994), 'Ein tschechisches Wunder? Zur Rolle politik-induzierter Anreizstrukturen im Transformationsprozeß', *Kiel Discussion Paper*, No. 233 (Kiel).

—— and Peter Nunnenkamp (1993), 'Output Decline and Recovery in Central Europe: The Role of Incentives Before, During and After Privatisation', *Kiel Working Paper*, No. 601 (Kiel).

Roland, Gérard (1994), 'The Role of Political Constraints in Transition Strategies', Discussion Paper, No. 943 (London: Centre for Economic Policy Research).

Székely, István and David M.G. Newbery (eds.) (1993), *Hungary: An Economy in Transition* (Cambridge: Cambridge University Press).

Schmieding, Holger (1993), 'From Plan to Market: On the Nature of the Transformation Crisis', *Weltwirtschaftliches Archiv*, Vol. 129, No. 3, pp. 216–53.

Slay, Ben (1994), 'Rapid versus Gradual Economic Transition', *Radio Free Europe/Radio Liberty Research Report*, Vol. 3, No. 31, pp. 31–42.

Stiglitz, Joseph E. (1992), 'The Design of Financial Systems for the Newly Emerging Democracies of Eastern Europe', in Christopher Clague and Gordon C. Rausser (eds), *The Emergence of Market Economies in Eastern Europe* (Cambridge, MA: Basil Blackwell), pp. 161–85.

Wagener, Hans-Jürgen (1992), 'Debate on the Transition of Post-Communist Economies to a Market Economy: The Legacy of the

Past and the Uncertainty of the Future', *Acta Oeconomica*, Vol. 44, No. 3/4, pp. 363-70.

Zloch-Christy, Iliana (1994), *Eastern Europe in a Time of Change: Economic and Political Dimensions* (Westport, CT, and London, Praeger).

4 The Visible versus the Invisible Hand
A Tension Inherent in Post-Communist Economies

J. L. Porket

The collapse of communism in Eastern Europe and the Soviet Union has fatally discredited the idea of totalist authoritarianism (conceived as authoritarian politics and political control over the economy and society) and boosted the idea of liberal democracy (conceived as democratic politics and free-market economics). Francis Fukuyama went even further, arguing that liberal democracy may constitute the end-point of mankind's ideological evolution and the final form of human government, and as such constitute the end of history.[1]

Yet so far, free-market economics has triumphed neither in Western societies nor in post-communist ones. Both continue to experience a multi-dimensional tension between economic individualism and economic collectivism. The tension revolves round the role of the state in the economy. The importance of this lies in the fact that the role the state plays in the economy has an impact not only on efficiency and welfare, but also on individual liberty and the nature of the political system.[2]

Expressed differently, the tension between economic individualism and economic collectivism is a tension between the invisible hand and the visible hand, between limited government and big government. It

1. Francis Fukuyama, *The End of History and the Last Man* (London: Penguin Books, 1992).
2. J.L. Porket, 'Tensions in Post-Communist Economies', paper presented at the conference on International Privatisation: Strategies and Practices, University of St. Andrews, Scotland, 12–14 September 1991, and J.L. Porket, *Unemployment in Capitalist, Communist and Post-Communist Economies* (Basingstoke: Macmillan, 1995, pp. 186–8.

implies that in both Western and post-communist societies socialism is far from dead, although it has changed its spots: after a period when it was in retreat and disarray, it started to reinvent itself, to rethink its policies.[3]

The Historical Background

The tension between economic individualism and economic collectivism dates from the rise of nation-states and the emergence of national economies towards the end of the fifteenth century. During the sixteenth and seventeenth centuries and most of the eighteenth century, the state in Western Europe pursued mercantilist policies, that is, it extensively regulated both foreign trade and domestic economic activity. These policies had a dual purpose: one was to build up economic power to strengthen the state; the other was to use the power of the state to promote economic growth, enrich the nation (conceived as a great commercial company), and further self-sufficiency.[4]

Besides encouraging evasion, mercantilist policies frequently had harmful consequences. Moreover, as early as the second half of the seventeenth century they began to be challenged by the advocates of economic freedom and competition. Finally, the principle of state regulation of economic activity gave way to the *laissez-faire* principle, to the doctrine of economic liberalism.

Economic liberalism reached its apex between the last quarter of the eighteenth century and the last quarter of the nineteenth century. It reduced – but did not eliminate altogether – the role of the state in the economy. Hence, it did not amount to unrestrained *laissez-faire*, to 'anarchy plus a constable', as satirised by Thomas Carlyle. At the same time, on the Continent the role of state in the economy (including industrialisation) continued to be greater than in Britain.

Nevertheless, already in the last quarter of the nineteenth century economic liberalism came under pressure. Protectionism was on the increase.[5] A trend towards monopolistically inclined corporations

---

3. J.L. Porket, 'Socialism on the Retreat, but not Dead', *Slavonic and East European Review*, Vol. 71, No. 1 (January 1993), pp. 133–6.
4. On mercantilism see Rondo Cameron, *A Concise Economic History of the World*, 2nd edn (Oxford: Oxford University Press, 1993), Chapter 6.
5. The reaction against free trade was discussed by T.G. Williams, *The History of*

appeared. The foundations of the modern welfare state were laid. Socialist movements emerged,[6] often bitterly disagreeing over the form of the envisaged socialist society and the means and timing for achieving it.

Between 1914 and 1945, economic liberalism was weakened by the First World War, the Great Depression, the rise of totalitarian regimes, and the Second World War.[7] These events usually resulted in greater government intervention in the operation of the market. However, in some cases they resulted in the substitution of state coordination for market coordination (for example, in imperial Germany during the First World War, in Nazi Germany in the mid-1930s, and in Britain during the Second World War), and in one case (the Soviet Union in the early 1930s) in the substitution of command socialism for market capitalism.

After the end of the Second World War, the retreat of economic liberalism intensified. In the West, socialist tendencies were strong. It was widely believed that sustained economic growth, full employment and the provision of welfare were among the proper ends and responsibilities of government. Nationalisation of the means of production came into fashion, as did Keynesian economics, indicative planning, micro-economic regulation, and corporatism. Simultaneously, the welfare state expanded considerably.

Under the force of circumstances, though, reaction set in about the mid-1970s. Keynesian economics began to fall into disrepute, and neoclassical economics began to gain ground, to become most influential during the 1980s. The market, the private sector and welfare pluralism were rediscovered. In order to roll back the frontiers of the state, free the market, and increase efficiency, privatisation and deregulation were put on to the agenda.

Outside the West, the political and economic system established in the Soviet Union not only survived the Second World War, but was imposed on Eastern Europe.[8] As a result, in Eastern Europe state

---

Commerce (London: Sir Isaac Pitman & Sons, 1926), Chapter XIV.

6. Cf. Albert S. Lindemann, *A History of European Socialism* (New Haven, CT: Yale University Press, 1983), Chapter 4.

7. According to Richard M. Ebeling, the First World War brought the Liberal Epoch to an end, while the Second World War only reinforced the Collectivist tendency: see his 'Liberalism and Collectivism in the Twentieth Century', *Political Studies*, special issue, Vol. XLI (1993), pp. 66–77.

8. An analysis of successful and failed communist take-overs since 1917 is to be

ownership of the means of production was substituted for private ownership, and state co-ordination was substituted for market co-ordination. Nevertheless, in both the Soviet Union and Eastern Europe the market mechanism was used to distribute the labour force among planned jobs and the planned supply of consumer goods and services among households; second economy activities, mostly (albeit not exclusively) illegal or semi-legal, abounded; and various economic reforms were attempted in the decades prior to the late 1980s, when communism suddenly collapsed.

Also the emerging countries of the Third World fell under the sway of socialism after the end of the Second World War. Indeed, many a developing country either followed the Soviet example and tried comprehensive and *dirigiste* planning, or practised indicative planning. Yet, by the end of the 1970s the attractiveness of the Soviet model of planned socialist development started to fade even in those Third World countries which in the preceding quarter of a century or so uncritically acclaimed it as a magic formula able to transform poverty and underdevelopment into a developed socialist economy.

Post-Communist Options

Since communism collapsed suddenly, a temporary systemic vacuum (a kind of no man's land) tended to appear in post-communist societies. This implied the emergence of elements of anarcho-capitalism, of a chaotic situation in which legal norms regulating private economic activity either do not exist at all or are widely ignored.[9] However, in at

found in Thomas T. Hammond (ed.), *The Anatomy of Communist Takeovers* (New Haven, CT: Yale University Press, 1975); see also Bogdan Szajkowski, *The Establishment of Marxist Regimes* (London: Butterworth, 1982).

9. Despite that, under anarcho-capitalism private economic activity can be regulated by gradually and spontaneously developing informal rules (conventions): see Paul H. Rubin, 'Private Mechanisms for the Creation of Efficient Institutions for Market Economies', in Lászlá Sőmőgyi (ed.), *The Political Economy of the Transition Process in Eastern Europe* (Aldershot: Edward Elgar, 1993), Chapter 9. Rubin's conclusion was that '[w]hile it is important to create efficient legal structures, business in new economies need not wait until these structures are established. The history of legal structures and examples from developed countries indicate that there are private mechanisms which can support trade without the assistance of the state.'

least two countries (namely, Poland and the Soviet Union) elements of anarcho-capitalism already manifested themselves before the collapse of communism.

The sudden collapse of communism meant, too, that although post-communist societies rejected totalist authoritarianism, originally their main goals were only loosely defined and the ways of achieving them had not been worked out. The avowed goals included the introduction of the rule of law and a democratic political system, the substitution of market capitalism for command socialism, and the formation of a civil society.

Market capitalism (a pluralistic and competitive economic system) was adopted as a goal because, in the prevailing view of that time, it separated the economy from political power, was the only economically viable alternative to command socialism (a non-pluralistic and non-competitive economic system), and had a vastly superior economic performance. Moreover, communism collapsed at a time when in the West the market was reasserting itself and privatisation was on the agenda.

However, while by 1989 there existed a considerable number of theories predicting the imminent downfall of capitalism and the inevitable rise of socialism, there was no theory dealing with (and, hence, providing guidance to) the transformation of command socialism into market capitalism. Although economists in both Western and post-communist societies broadly agreed that the core components of economic transformation were macro-economic stabilisation, liberalisation, privatisation, and institution-building,[10] they were far from unanimous when it came to the important question of the dynamics of its implementation – the issues of the transformation's speed, comprehensiveness, sequencing, and dependence on the state.

Concerning the last-mentioned issue, disagreement existed about the role of the state during economic transformation, about whether economic transformation should be planned and managed by the state, or left to the market. In connection with the former view, it was frequently emphasised that a strong state with a coherent transformation design was needed if the economy was to free itself from the strangling grip of the state. The models discussed included Anglo-American capitalism,

---

10. In addition, economists in both Western and post-communist societies generally agreed that economic transformation required an adequate social safety net.

the German social market economy, the Swedish welfare state, Latin American and East Asian economies, and even the Chinese economic reform.[11]

Actually, economic transformation should be seen as a process of interaction between government policies and market forces, taking place in a wider intra-societal (domestic) and extra-societal (international) environment. To a large extent, its outcome depends on the government's orientation, that is, on its commitment to market capitalism. At the same time it should be remembered that there are three variants of market capitalism, namely, the *laissez-faire* variant, the free-market variant, and the interventionist variant.

Under the *laissez-faire* variant, which assumes perfect competition while failing to consider externalities, the role of the state is confined to providing national defence, maintaining law and order, and stepping in when private initiative is lacking. This variant is frequently misunderstood and misrepresented: there is a tendency to view and depict it as being identical to anarcho-capitalism in the sense given above.

The free-market variant recognises that all markets need not be perfectly competitive and that externalities occur. Consequently, the role of the state widens in certain important respects, but remains of necessity limited. In addition to providing national defence, maintaining law and order, and stepping in when private initiative is lacking, the state is expected to foster competition and to deal with externalities.

While under both these variants the state is predominantly means-oriented in the sense of being concerned with process or procedure, under the interventionist variant it is more or less goal-oriented in the sense of being concerned with an end-state or final outcome. In order to achieve specific economic or social objectives other than allocative efficiency, such as stable economic growth, full employment, or a desired distribution of income, it intervenes in property rights, the operation of the free market, the outcome of economic activity, or a combination of these.

However, not only the market, but government intervention in the economy too can fail: that is, it need not attain its objectives and can produce unintended consequences. One of its unintended consequences

11. See, for example, John Gray, 'From Post-Communism to Civil Society: The Reemergence of History and the Decline of the Western Model', in Ellen Frankel Paul, Fred D. Miller, Jr., and Jeffrey Paul (eds), *Liberalism and the Economic Order* (Cambridge: Cambridge University Press, 1993), pp. 26–50.

is second-economy activities (tax evasion, benefit fraud, and so on). Their existence in capitalist market economies illustrates the point that in these economies there are limits to effective interventionist policies, to the extractive, allocative, distributive and regulative capabilities of government. In a word, market forces cannot forever be denied.

Of the three variants of market capitalism distinguished above, the free-market variant had relatively strong support immediately after the collapse of communism. Gradually, though, a shift towards the interventionist variant began to manifest itself. This follows both from the available sample surveys[12] and from the behaviour of sitting governments, opposition parties, pressure groups and voters.[13]

Moreover, the interventionist variant of market capitalism has been advocated for post-communist societies by quite a few Western scholars. To give just one example, in 1994 Ivan T. Berend criticised the model of economic transition chosen by Eastern and Central European political elites and contended that '[i]nstead of a religious-ideological free-market approach, a more pragmatic, organic transformation via a regulated mixed-market economy would better serve a relatively smooth and successful transformation and structural adjustment – one with a relatively large publicly owned sector, strong state direction and intervention in labor, investment and structural (industrial) policy, as well as a combination of liberalisation and, in certain fields, protection of the domestic market.'[14]

12. See Wolfgang Seifert, *East Germany and Eastern Europe Compared*, Studies in Public Policy No. 233 (Glasgow: Centre for the Study of Public Policy, University of Strathclyde, 1994), pp. 14–16, and Porket, *Unemployment in Capitalist, Communist and Post-Communist Economies*, Chapter 14.

13. *Inter alia*, ex-communists (albeit usually under a different name) returned to power in free parliamentary elections in a number of post-communist countries, including Romania, Bulgaria (1990 and again December 1994), Lithuania (1993), Poland (September 1993), Ukraine (March-April 1994), and Hungary (May 1994). On Poland between 1989 and 1993, see Voytek Zubek, 'The Reassertion of the Left in Post-communist Poland', *Europe–Asia Studies*, Vol. 46, No. 5 (1994), pp. 801–37.

14. Ivan T. Berend, 'Self-Regulating or Regulated Market Economy? On the Model of East-Central European Transformation', in Robert W. Campbell (ed.), *The Postcommunist Economic Transformation* (Boulder, CO: Westview, 1994), p. 62.

Economics and Politics

After the collapse of communism, the goals endorsed by post-communist societies included not only the introduction of market capitalism, but also the establishment of political democracy. This gave rise to an important (though often underestimated) question, namely, that of the relationship between the two elements.

The available evidence suggests that while market capitalism is not tied to democracy, modern democracy is dependent on market capitalism: historically, it has arisen exclusively within market capitalism, and has been unable to survive except when coupled with it. Hence, market capitalism is a necessary (albeit not sufficient) condition of modern democracy.[15] It follows that market capitalism is of greater importance for society than democracy, and that as long as market capitalism is not institutionalised in a society, the establishment of a stable democratic political system therein is at risk.

Yet, although modern democracy is dependent on market capitalism, simultaneously it creates conditions for the emergence of the critics and opponents of market capitalism, who reject both its *laissez-faire* variant and its free-market version and advocate either its interventionist form or socialism of one kind or another. This constitutes the paradox of democracy: in extreme cases, democracy can develop a self-destructive tendency by undermining market capitalism.

Consequently, in democratic political systems the electorate can elect a government committed to the pursuit of interventionist or socialist policies. However, even if the elected government pursues free-market policies, it can be pressed by the opposition, pressure groups, or both, for more regulation, more industrial policy, more trade policy, and more social policy. Expressed differently, modern democracy is vulnerable both to changes in the mood of the time and to sectional interests powerful enough to influence the elected government and to exploit majorities.

15. On the relationship between economic and political systems see, for example, Peter L. Berger, *The Capitalist Revolution* (Aldershot: Wildwood House, 1987), Chapters 4 and 8; J.L. Porket, *Work, Employment and Unemployment in the Soviet Union*, pp. 4–6; Gerhard Schwarz, 'Limitations to the Interdependence of Systems', in Kurt Dopfer and Karl-F. Raible (eds), *The Evolution of Economic Systems* (London: Macmillan, 1990), Chapter 3.

Not surprisingly, this paradox of democracy is noticeable in post-communist societies, too. In these societies, the political pluralisation triggered off by the collapse of communist rule on the one hand has paved the way for the transformation of command socialism into market capitalism, and on the other hand has made opposition and resistance to the extent and pace of transformation possible.

Opposition and resistance to the extent and pace of transformation have been fuelled partly by vested interests, partly by the strains of economic transformation. Since in representative democracy politicians have to compete for votes, the combination of vested interests and the strains of economic transformation has frequently resulted in the pursuit of populist policies, which have retarded both economic transformation and economic growth.

Although representative democracy does not automatically lead to prudent and effective government, nearly all the world's most prosperous countries have a democratic political system and a capitalist market economic system, while nearly all the world's least prosperous countries have neither feature.[16] This close correlation between political freedom and economic prosperity suggests that the long-term prospects for post-communist societies depend on their establishing and keeping both democratic politics and free-market economics.

However, certain conditions must be fulfilled if representative democracy is not to undermine market capitalism and, thus, itself. These are the rule of law, a limited government (that is, one with a limited scope of political power), a strong government (one that does not incessantly yield to any and every opposition and pressure group demand), the existence of a well-trained bureaucracy, and the exercise of political self-restraint by the electorate.[17]

Socialism's Changing Spots

By its nature, modern democracy makes possible both the advocacy of interventionism and socialism and the pursuit of interventionist and socialist policies. The electoral defeat of Sweden's Social Democrats in

16. See *The Economist*, 27 August 1994, pp. 17–19.
17. Of these five main conditions, the second, fourth and fifth were mentioned by Samuel Brittan, *Capitalism with a Human Face* (Aldershot: Edward Elgar, 1995), Chapter 5.

1976 and that of the British Labour Party in 1979, the ousting of the Social Democratic Party from the government of Germany in 1982, the collapse in France of the so-called Mitterrand experiment of 1981-82,[18] the privatisation and deregulation movements in the West, and the collapse of communism in 1989 may have created an impression of socialism's death-knell. In the early 1990s, though, it began to enjoy a revival.

Contemporary Western socialism may be divided into two main strands. One, market socialism, accepts that free markets are desirable but argues that the private firms which operate in them should be organised along socialist lines. Hence, it favours workers' co-operatives, employee share ownership plans (ESOPs), and worker participation in decision making as methods of redistributing power and wealth within firms.[19] The other strand, called here neo-socialism, accepts market capitalism, although with the proviso that both the market and private ownership of the means of production would be regulated by the state which, simultaneously, would pursue redistributive and welfarist policies.

Of these two strands of contemporary Western socialism, neo-socialism is more widespread. One of its features is its interventionist orientation. While it distances itself from traditional interventionism which replaces the market, it advocates 'new interventionism' which seeks to guide (use and shape) the market. According to Robert Wade, for instance, 'new interventionism' is characterised by the fact that it 'uses price and non-price methods to channel investment away from unproductive uses, expand technological capacity, strengthen links with foreign firms and give a directional thrust to selected industries'.[20]

Another feature of neo-socialism is its protectionist orientation.[21] Although it is not averse to tariffs on imports, import quotas and import

18. Serge Halimi, Jonathan Michie and Seumas Milne, 'The Mitterrand Experience', in Jonathan Michie and John Grieve Smith (eds), *Unemployment in Europe* (London: Academic Press, 1994), Chapter 6.

19. See, for example, David Miller, *Market, State, and Community* (Oxford: Clarendon Press, 1989); Julian Le Grand and Saul Estrin (eds), *Market Socialism* (Oxford: Clarendon Press, 1989); David Schweickart, *Against Capitalism* (Cambridge: Cambridge University Press, 1993); John E. Roemer, *A Future for Socialism* (London, Verso, 1994).

20. *The Economist*, 4 April 1992, p.91; see also Malcolm Sawyer, 'Industrial Strategy and Employment in Europe', in Michie and Smith (eds), op. cit., Chapter 11.

21. In John Gray's view, new protectionism is needed because unfettered global free

controls in order, for example, to offset international cost differences, promote infant industries, or safeguard jobs, it also calls for equalisation of labour costs in the countries of origin. On the surface, the call for 'fair labour practices' in exporting countries is compatible with free trade. In fact, if put into effect, it would stifle foreign competition by increasing labour costs in countries with lower labour costs.

The last (and central) feature of neo-socialism is its distributionist orientation. Believing ardently in equality,[22] it is a staunch exponent of income and wealth redistribution and of welfare statism. Its language is that of social justice,[23] fairness, solidarity, cooperation, partnership, collective responsibility, communitarianism, economic and social rights, entitlements, the poor–rich (disadvantaged–privileged, loser–winner) dichotomy, compassion, caring, positive discrimination, affirmative action[24] and the like.

In sum, command socialism is currently out of fashion in the West, and so are theories predicting the imminent downfall of capitalism and the inevitable rise of socialism, that is, theories based on the principle of socio-economic determinism and a linear definition of history. What is alive, though, is socialism in the sense of calls for a redistribution of power, wealth and income by means of activist government.

Socialism in this sense is driven by sentiments, desires, events and circumstances, takes various guises, lacks a theoretical framework and a clear vision, focuses on particular issues, and advocates or pursues policies that tend to be populist, paternalistic, unrealistic and damaging.

  trade makes people economically insecure and poses the threat of social and political upheavals: 'Into the Abyss?', *The Sunday Times*, 30 October 1994, p. 26.
22. According to Roy Hattersley, for instance, the ultimate objective of socialism is freedom, and the extension of liberty requires the creation of a more equal society within which power and wealth are more evenly distributed; in organising equality, the state must play a positive role: *Choose Freedom* (London: Michael Joseph, 1987), pp.21–3 and 144.
23. Social or distributive justice is the opposite of procedural justice. Its critics (among whom is F.A. Hayek) maintain, for instance, that in a free society no agreement exists about desirable distribution, that social justice is a demand by particular groups for a privileged position, that one source of the calls for it is pure envy, and that its pursuit would lead to a loss of personal freedom and the emergence of a totalitarian order: see Norman P. Barry, *An Introduction to Modern Political Theory*, 2nd edn (London: Macmillan, 1989), Chapter 6.
24. On affirmative action see Lynn Turgeon, *State and Discrimination* (Armonk, NY: M.E. Sharpe, 1989), and David Edmonds, 'Race against Positive Discrimination', *New Statesman and Society*, 15 April 1994, pp. 22–3.

At the same time, its standard-bearers (intellectuals, educators, opinion-makers, and left-wing politicians) frequently shy away from left-speak and from using the term 'socialism', and are to be found even among the self-proclaimed liberals.

To give an example of what contemporary socialism stands for, Stephen K. Sanderson's view deserves mention. After admitting that command socialism had weaknesses, he goes on by saying that 'I have gradually come to the conclusion that perhaps the best we can do, at least for the foreseeable future, is to extend to as much of the world as possible something like the Swedish model of social democracy. This means a capitalist system that has a large number of built-in protections in terms of minimum standards of income, health care, education, and other aspects of the modern welfare state, but at the same time a great deal of economic planning. A world state that would seek to combine the best elements of the plan and the market, while at the same time eliminating or neutralizing their worst elements, seems to me to be the most appropriate path to follow.'[25]

Besides being alive in Western societies, socialism is alive in post-communist societies, too. The available evidence suggests that, although only a minority continues to favour a socialist command economy, many people have retained nostalgia for the communist cradle-to-grave welfare state and desire a nanny state. It is not surprising, then, that – as already once mentioned above – over the years support for the interventionist variant of market capitalism has increased.

In this connection, the findings of four sample surveys given in Table 4.1 are of interest. The table shows that between October 1991 and November 1994 support for a free-market economy (defined as one largely free from state control) varied considerably from one post-communist society to another, being lowest in Armenia, Belarus, Georgia, Kazakhstan, Russia and Ukraine. It also shows that during this period the support fell in practically all post-communist societies. On the other hand, it does not show the preferences of the opponents of the free-market economy and of those respondents who did not answer.

The falling support for a free-market economy seems to be a response to the impact of the progress of transformation with its costs and benefits on the satisfaction of people's needs and wants. Expressed

25. Stephen K. Sanderson, *Social Transformations: A General Theory of Historical Development* (Oxford: Basil Blackwell, 1995), p. 374.

Table 4.1 Percentage of respondents who feel that the creation of a free-market economy, that is one largely free from state control, is right for their country's future

	October 1991	November 1992	November 1993	November 1994
Albania	67	72	71	67
Bulgaria	62	55	47	40
Czechoslovakia	61	–	–	–
Czech Republic	–	55	51	47
Estonia	59	49	52	48
Hungary	65	56	46	44
Latvia	57	36	41	38
Lithuania	75	63	57	46
Poland	56	56	53	49
Romania	35	65	52	71
Slovakia	–	51	40	42
Slovenia	–	61	41	47
Armenia	–	31	24	24
Belarus	–	32	26	26
Georgia	–	48	–	22
Kazakhstan	–	–	–	25
Russia	47	37	31	22
Ukraine	–	34	31	28

Sources: European Commission, *Central and Eastern Eurobarometer*, various issues.

differently, it reflects a gap perceived by people between their expectations and reality which continues to be in a state of flux and, consequently, breeds uncertainty. At the same time, many people probably do not realise that what they experience at present in the economic sphere is not free-market capitalism.

However, in post-communist societies socialism has not only domestic supporters: it is advocated for these societies by at least some Western scholars. According to Maurice Glasman, for instance, '[t]he dilemma facing all these countries is that there is no alternative to the market, but the market is no alternative. *Socialism* is no longer an ideology but a necessity in a market society. It takes many forms but always resists unregulated markets in labour, money and property.'[26]

The European Union

Since interventionism and socialism are not dead in Western societies, they are not dead in the European Union either.[27] Being part of the international environment of post-communist societies, the European Union has an impact on these societies by, *inter alia*, fluctuations in the level of its economic activity, its economic policies and practices, its legislation, and the thrust of its economic (as well as political and social) thought.

Although on 1 January 1993 the European Community officially became a single market, this has not eradicated interventionist, corporatist, welfarist, and protectionist strivings within it. Its critics contend that the single market is over-regulated, over-protected,[28] and over-centralised, as well as run by a bloated bureaucracy, subsidy-dependent, and fraud-ridden. They also point out that some member states have become past masters at going slow on the implementation of unwelcome policy directives.

The Maastricht treaty likewise has its critics. In their view, because its ruling ideas are common policy-making and harmonisation of taxes, labour laws, welfare provisions, and so on, it does virtually nothing to increase individual economic freedom, but much to centralise the exercise of political power.

Nevertheless, most East European post-communist societies are keen to become full members of the European Union, which early in May 1995 published its version of what the East European applicants need to do to qualify for membership. Yet, despite containing hundreds

26. Maurice Glasman, 'The Great Deformation: Polanyi, Poland and the Terrors of Planned Spontaneity', in Christopher G.A. Bryant and Edmund Mokrzycki (eds), *The New Great Transformation? Change and Continuity in East–Central Europe* (London: Routledge, 1994), p. 213.

27. Cf. George Ross, *Jacques Delors and European Integration* (Cambridge: Polity Press, 1995).

28. According to Martin Wolf, 'the EU combines liberalism within and mercantilism without. ... The EU is, in short, mercantilist': 'Cooperation or conflict? The European Union in a Liberal Global Economy', *International Affairs*, Vol. 71, No. 2 (April 1995), pp. 325–37.)

of pages of dense detail on the administrative and legal procedures by which the EU legislation must be adapted and implemented by applicants, this 'route map' left many questions unanswered, including, for example, that of the date by which entry negotiations could begin. (With selected countries, negotiations opened in March 1998 – Ed.)

While most East European post-communist governments are keen to become full members of the European Union, public opinion is divided. In 1994, Table 4.2 shows, in practically all post-communist societies only a minority of the population believed that the aims and activities of the European Union were generally positive. In the same year, as shown in Table 4.3, in the majority of these societies there was a not negligible minority believing that in the relationship between their own country and the European Union the latter would benefit most.

Table 4.2 Image of the European Union in post-communist societies, November 1994 (per cent)

	Positive	Neutral	Negative
Albania	72	15	3
Romania	51	25	6
Poland	42	23	7
Bulgaria	37	23	6
Slovakia	37	37	7
Slovenia	37	42	7
Latvia	35	39	7
Lithuania	34	41	4
Czech Republic	34	40	6
Hungary	32	28	8
Estonia	29	38	5
Armenia	46	27	8
Kazakhstan	41	38	2
Belarus	32	32	7
Ukraine	30	25	2
Russia	26	35	6
Georgia	25	35	13

Source: European Commission, *Central and Eastern Eurobarometer*, No. 5 (March 1995), Annex, Figure 13.

Table 4.3   Beneficiaries of the relationship between post-communist
societies and the European Union, as perceived by post-
communist societies, November 1994 (per cent)

	Our country benefits most	Both benefit equally	The EU benefits most
Albania	61	23	5
Lithuania	37	38	9
Latvia	31	22	19
Estonia	26	29	20
Bulgaria	21	37	13
Hungary	20	40	14
Romania	20	48	19
Czech Republic	16	41	25
Slovenia	16	46	26
Slovakia	15	39	25
Poland	14	35	24
Georgia	23	33	16
Armenia	21	35	20
Ukraine	19	41	8
Belarus	17	23	20
Kazakhstan	11	41	25
Russia	8	26	36

Source: European Commission, *Central and Eastern Eurobarometer*, No. 5
(March 1995), Annex, Figure 14.

However, in the European Union, too, public opinion is divided over
a number of issues. According to a poll carried out in May 1994, for
instance, although 50 per cent of the respondents favoured the enlarge-
ment of the European Union to the Czech Republic, Hungary, Poland
and Slovakia, 30 per cent opposed it. At the same, while 51 per cent
regarded the European Union as effective, 42 per cent saw it as not
effective. And whereas 50 per cent were in favour of a more integrated
Europe as envisaged under the Maastricht treaty, 40 per cent preferred
a looser arrangement among independent nation-states.[29]

29. *Financial Times*, 1 June 1994, p. 4.

Conclusion

Both Western and post-communist societies, it has been argued, continue to experience a multi-dimensional tension between economic individualism (the invisible hand) and economic collectivism (the visible hand), which revolves around the role of the state in the economy.[30] Under the former, the state is means-orientated in the sense of being concerned with process or procedure. Under the latter it is goal-orientated in the sense of being concerned with an end-state or final outcome.

Naturally, in practice neither exists in its pure form. The role that the state plays in the economy depends on the established variant of economic individualism or economic collectivism. The main variants of economic individualism are *laissez-faire* capitalism, free-market capitalism, and interventionist capitalism, while the main variants of economic collectivism are neo-socialism, market socialism, command capitalism, and command socialism. If anarcho-capitalism is disregarded, *laissez-faire* capitalism is the extreme variant of economic individualism and command socialism is the extreme variant of economic collectivism. Interventionist capitalism and neo-socialism at least partly overlap.

The factors affecting the role the state plays in the economy include, *inter alia*, the orientation of the sitting government, opposition parties, pressure groups, and the electorate, and also the mood of the time. In democratic political systems they can support either free-market policies (and, hence, a low-tax, low-expenditure and low-regulation government) or interventionist–socialist policies (and, hence, a high-tax, high expenditure, and high-regulation government).

One of the reasons in democratic political systems for underlying support for interventionist or socialist policies is belief in welfare statism.[31] Yet, because the welfare state is financed through taxation

30. The five main interrelated dimensions of the tension concern the coordinating mechanism, the ownership of the means of production, the criteria applied to economic activity, the perceived sources of the individual's welfare, and the distribution of income and wealth.

31. In OECD countries, expenditure on public social programmes (including education, health care, transfer payments, and welfare services, but excluding housing) accounted on average for 13 per cent of GDP in 1960, for 25 per cent in 1980, and for about 27 per cent in both 1985 and 1990: see Edwin Bell, 'Social Policy and

and gives priority to consumption and redistribution over production (wealth creation), it is detrimental to economic growth and expansion. It also blunts the work ethic, gives rise to a dependency culture and, in its operation, is subject to the Say's Law, asserting that supply creates its own demand.

Consequently, political democracy can stand in the way of economic development. This occurs if, in the pursuit of interventionist or socialist policies, it overlooks the fact that the pervasive economic phenomenon of scarcity means that the basic economic problem is the allocation of scarce means (resources) among competing ends for the achievement of maximum results; that government co-ordination is less effective than market co-ordination; that not only markets, but governments also fail; that government failure is likely to be more damaging in economic terms than market failure; and that excessive government intervention in the economy undercuts economic freedom and encourages non-observance of legal and administrative norms.

However, political democracy can undermine not only market capitalism, but also the fabric of society and itself, because it offers opportunity for the emergence of values, attitudes and patterns of behaviour incompatible with social stability and democratic freedoms. These values, attitudes and patterns of behaviour include disregard for standards of morality, a rights-without-responsibility culture, dogmatic and intolerant single-issue fanaticism, and the dissolution of the family.

Economic Reality', *The OECD Observer*, No. 183 (August/September 1993), pp. 14–15.)

5 Road Maps to Markets
Issues in the Theory of the Post-Communist Transformation

Valdas Samonis[1]

Introduction

The fall of communism in Eastern Europe and parts of Asia is the most important development since the Second World War. Poland and Hungary were the first countries to start dismantling the communist legacy in the autumn of 1989, followed by many other countries including the newly independent ones after the dissolution of the Soviet Union, Yugoslavia and Czechoslovakia. They all face the post-communist transformation, including its crucial economic part. This long and truly historic process can be depicted as the transition from a centrally planned economy and communism to a market economy and democracy (see Chart 5.1). The post-communist transformation is a process of far-reaching political and economic consequences for the East, the West, and the entire global village, to use the term coined up by the great Canadian thinker Marshall McLuhan.

Chart 5.1   The post-communist economic transformation: a general scheme of the process

CENTRALLY PLANNED ECONOMY	MARKET ECONOMY
Macro-economic stabilisation	Social systems
Systemic change	
COMMUNISM	DEMOCRACY

1. Support for this research has been provided by the Social Sciences and Humanities Research Council of Canada and the Dean of Graduate Studies, University of Toronto. The usual disclaimer applies.

This chapter aims at developing key road maps and identifying main trends in the post-communist economic transformation as the crucial part of the overall process of change in the post-communist countries. The general objective is to promote an understanding of the process in the West as well as in the East by arriving at some approximation to a normative theory. Within this general objective, a number of specific ones will be pursued as represented by major lessons and hypotheses as advanced below (see Chart 5.2).

Chart 5.2: The post-communist economic transformation: a conceptual framework for advancement and testing of lessons–hypotheses

Create domestic markets		Join the global village	
Liberalise	Institutionalise	Liberalise	Institutionalise
LH1	LH3	LH7	LH9
LH2	LH4	LH8	LH10
LH6	LH5		

State–Market: The Crucial Dimension of the Post-Communist Change

The post-communist economic transformation, which has been going on in Eastern Europe since 1989, is a very complex process of historic magnitude and significance. Systemic change is at the heart of this transformation. An abject failure of the communist system makes it obvious that the new system will have to be built almost from scratch. There is a pretty widespread understanding that this new system – or rather its main features – will have to be imported from the West, first of all Western Europe, which thinking is neatly summarised by the slogan 'return to Europe' (Gomulka, 1991; Samonis, 1992b). A market economy (ME) of the West European type seems to be the goal of the great majority of East European reformers. The crucial dimension of systemic change seems to be the state–market dichotomy. Can the post-communist countries simply import the definition of the state's role from Western Europe – or North America, for that matter?

Western market economies have been developing gradually and more or less naturally over the past two centuries. Still, the role of the state in market economies and economic development in general seems to be a subject of a hot debate in the last two decades of the twentieth century (Hanusch, 1988; Krueger, 1990; World Bank, 1991; Colclough and Manor, 1992; *et al.*). Given the deadening legacy of communism as outlined below, it is unlikely that ME will be born as a result of spontaneous generation – *generatio spontanea*, as the process is known in biology. Even if it happened in such a way, it is unlikely that the transformation costs could be minimised in this way. This calls for an appropriately designed role of the state in building the fundamentals of a market economy, something along the lines of the Schumpeterian 'ordnungspolitische' (systemic) function. Markets cannot operate in a vacuum – they require a legal and regulatory framework that only governments can provide (Jackson, 1988; Stolper, 1984; World Bank, 1991).

Centrally planned economies have been constructed on the basis of the notion of the omnipotent state. The underlying conception was that the state knew best and could perform best in managing the national economy, relegating the role of the market to the absolute fringes. The eventual, miserable failure of this type of economy prompted some reformers of the post-communist economies (PCEs) to advocate the other extreme: the notion of an impotent state which is an echo of Adam Smith's 'night watchman' role or Friedrich von Hayek's views (Kornai, 1990; Hayek, 1944). However, the elimination or minimisation of the state's economic role is not likely to minimise the cost (including time) of transforming PCEs into MEs. This role will have to be optimised rather than minimised. Hence this chapter proposes a macro-analytical framework for the optimisation of the state's role during the post-communist transformation process. For this purpose, the process is divided into three stages as depicted in Chart 5.3: (a) building the fundamentals of a market economy (FME); (b) de-sovietisation (DS); and (c) welfare state (WS).

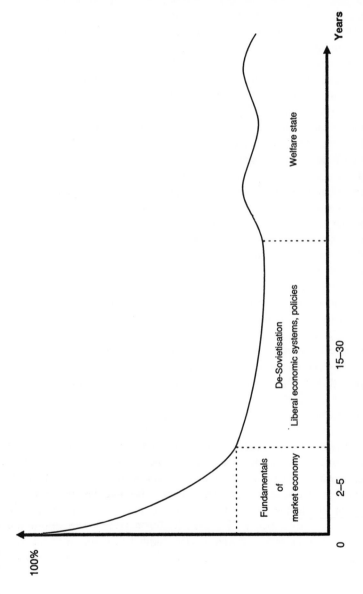

Chart 5.3   The state's role in the economic transformation: a conceptual framework

Building the Fundamentals of a Market Economy

The first stage is naturally about building the fundamentals of a market economy (FME), practically from scratch in most countries. By the end of 1993, all the post-communist countries were either at this stage of transformation or still had to enter it. In the optimistic scenario, building the FME may take some 2–5 years and will usually be associated with a decline of some 10–50 per cent in measured GNP per capita (see Chart 5.4). True, this decline may be overstated owing to inability to capture fully the private sector growth but will still be large, if the leading countries' transformation experience is any guide (Gomulka, 1991; Samonis and Hunyadi, 1993).

This can be explained largely by the fact that a PCE production structure is still effectively based on the principle of monopoly. Often some 50 per cent or more of the goods and services produced by the East European economies in any given sector come from a single enterprise or even a single plant. According to the theory of monopolistic behaviour, such enterprises do not act as takers of exogenously-determined production parameters (for example, prices): they try to influence them. If confronted with price liberalisation, for example, they act in basically two ways. Following the path of least resistance, they either pass price increases (as a cost-push inflation) forward to buyers of their output or, failing that, they limit their output or its growth to increase the monopoly rent. Such a production structure is only negatively responsive, meaning that it causes inflation or recession or both ('slumpflation') when reacting to liberalisation stimuli. This is especially true if the change is of the 'big bang' type (Gomulka, 1991).

Liberalisation and Institutionalisation: The Twin Challenges

At the most general level, the post-communist economic transformation is often regarded as the process of freeing up the economy internally and externally, that is liberalisation. The intellectual roots of liberalisation are grounded in the venerable Adam Smith tradition which extends to such luminaries as Ludwik von Mises and Friedrich von Hayek (1944). It is continued by Ronald McKinnon (1991) of Stanford and János Kornai (1990) of Harvard, who entitled their recent books *The Order of Economic Liberalisation* and *The Road to a Free Economy*,

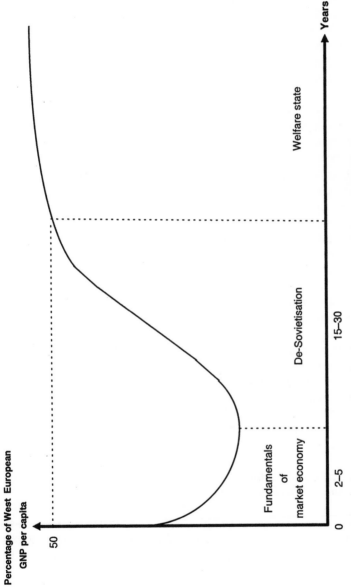

Chart 5.4 Modelling the supply response: the J-curve of economic transformation in the East

respectively. Other contemporary analysts adopt a similar perspective. This is not surprising given the focus of the liberal intellectual tradition on price theory as well as the most visible and discussed manifestations of the post-communist economic transformation (for example, price increases following the initial liberalisation). Liberalisation would constitute the entire process of transformation if the costs of making a transaction (concluding a contract, for example) in real-life market economies were zero, as the standard assumptions of the liberal tradition would imply. However, as demonstrated by the Nobel Prize winners Ronald Coase (1992) and Douglass C. North (1993), and also by Harold Demsetz (1988) and others, transaction costs in real life are usually greater than zero. Relevant information has to be collected, contracts have to be prepared, negotiations conducted, and so on. This calls for building an adequate institutional structure designed to govern economic exchange processes in a market economy so that transaction costs can be minimised. Without the necessary institutions, no market economy is possible. In the case of the post-communist transformation, there are additional arguments. This process is fragile and can quickly go wrong in several ways. It therefore has to be anchored in a stable institutional framework to secure irreversibility and steady progress. On top of that, institution-building (often from scratch) is a very important part of state-building in the newly independent countries. Hence, the post-communist economic transformation needs to have two aspects complementing each other: liberalisation and institutionalisation.

The state must play the crucial role in building the fundamentals of a market economy (FME). It should pursue a sort of affirmative action policy with regard to fledgling market economy relationships by building appropriate institutions. My proposal is that the state's role at this stage should be based on the infant market argument for state activism, somewhat parallel to the infant industry argument found in the development literature (Krueger, 1990).

Building the Fundamentals of a Market Economy in Post-Communist Countries: Main Lessons and Hypotheses

Given what was said above, this chapter's research strategy was based on the conceptual framework for the formulation and testing of lessons and hypotheses as portrayed in Chart 5.2, with the dual designation LH reflecting the dual nature of the propositions discussed; in some cases, hypotheses are well on the way to becoming simply lessons after four years of transformation experience and discussion.

Owing to the comprehensive and long-term nature of the post-communist economic transformation, it is only natural to ask where it should begin. In general terms, this question has been answered above by suggesting that it should begin with building the fundamentals of a market economy (FME). However, this does not take us very far. A debate on the appropriate sequencing of elements of this process was started in the world literature around 1990 but the issue is still far from being resolved. It seems, however, that there is at least some agreement that macro-economic stabilisation should be regarded as the first element (see Chart 5.1). It consists of the initial internal and external liberalisation (mainly in the markets for goods and services) and disinflation through appropriate fiscal (budget deficit reduction) and income (wage taxation) policies accompanied by monetary transformation (currency convertibility). The initial liberalisation means the removal of subsidies and controls on prices and foreign trade. Given that such a step releases most of the tensions built up during decades of repressed inflation, it naturally leads to a substantial but, it is hoped, once-off jump in the price level of practically all goods and services (corrective inflation). Disinflation is an effort to keep corrective inflation from becoming permanent. It requires bringing down and keeping the budget deficit within the manageable limits of some 5–10 per cent of GNP, which constitutes the first stabilising anchor. Some of these issues are similar to those faced by many overregulated, destabilised developing countries undertaking liberalisation efforts under the supervision of the International Monetary Fund (IMF). A pretty substantial, IMF-generated literature exists, also drawing on other sources, and this can be studied for workable solutions (see, for example, McKinnon, 1991).

Other issues are rather specific to the conditions existing in the post-communist economies. The question of currency convertibility and related foreign trade issues is the most important one. For a couple of decades, there was an implicit or explicit understanding in the world's 'reform literature' on communist economies that currency convertibility should be viewed as the last stage of reforms, a sort of crowning achievement. However, programmes for the post-communist transformation, especially the Balcerowicz Plan in Poland, emphasised the need to make the first step towards convertibility from the outset (Balcerowicz, 1992; Grosfeld, 1990). My hypothesis is that disinflation in the post-communist conditions requires firmly linking a domestic currency to a suitable convertible and stable Western currency or a basket of them through the institutional arrangement known as internal or current account convertibility. It should initially be based on a peg and subsequently replaced by a crawling peg or other less rigid arrangements aimed at managing the real (as opposed to nominal) exchange rate to optimise the process of East–West economic integration. Furthermore, as demonstrated by János Kornai (1990), there are irreducible differences in the hardness of budget constraints faced by public and private sector enterprises. Since the public enterprises are still dominant in a post-communist economy and their budget constraints are soft, an incomes policy is needed in the public sector to prevent or limit the inflationary wage-price spiral. So, in addition to the budget deficit reduction, two additional anchors are needed to liberalise and stabilise a post-communist economy. My first lesson–hypothesis therefore is:

LH1:   *Besides the usual instruments known from the practice of reform in overregulated developing countries, internal convertibility and a public sector incomes policy are two important anchors liberalising and stabilising a post-communist economy.*

A very large state sector and a very high degree of monopolisation are two defining features of the communist legacy. In all the post-communist economies, there is a dominant hard core of monopolistic state enterprises. According to the theory of monopolistic behaviour, they do not act as takers of the exogenously-determined economic parameters (such as prices). If confronted with price liberalisation and stringent macro-economic policies, they act in basically two ways. Following the path of least resistance, rather than cutting costs they either pass on price increases as a cost-push inflation to buyers of their output or, failing that, they reduce output or its growth to reap the monopoly rent. Such a production structure is only negatively responsive, meaning that it causes a slump in output or inflation or both ('slumpflation') when reacting to liberalisation stimuli. Still effectively based on the principle of state monopoly, post-communist production structures are therefore causing this double problem throughout the area. This further complicates the task of macro-economic stabilisation. Action on the demand side is a necessary but not a sufficient condition for achieving a liberalised and stable post-communist economy. Simultaneous action designed to stimulate the positive supply response is called for. Such a response is impossible without an early and credible commitment to liberalisation of factor markets. In particular, early privatisation of state enterprises should provide the main avenue for liberalising the market for capital. Privatisation should be accompanied by demonopolisation, which is best done by opening the economy to external competition but, if necessary (for instance, in large countries), should be helped by an administrative break-up of diversified conglomerates. The anti-monopoly agency should be instituted for this purpose. My second lesson–hypothesis can thus be formulated as follows:

LH2: *Sustained macro-stability on the goods and services markets cannot be achieved by acting on the demand side alone; simultaneous action (privatisation and demonopolisation) designed to liberalise the capital market and thereby stimulate a positive supply response is needed.*

Some of these issues have been researched relatively well. This stems in part from their place in the perceived sequence of stages but probably more from the transferability of experience gained in developing countries, as mentioned above.

The second element of FME, which should proceed more or less simultaneously with the macro-economic stabilisation, involves structural, that is systemic, change (see Chart 5.1). There is a growing consensus that a radical reconfiguration of property rights forms the core of systemic change. Privatisation should therefore be viewed as the backbone of transition from plan to market. There is a substantial body of world literature on Western (especially British) privatisation and various privatisation attempts in developing countries. This classical privatisation experience is, however, of a rather limited cross-border transferability in general and of especially low applicability to the conditions of the post-communist economies. Two main reasons for this are outlined below.

Administratively determined relative prices in the post-communist economies not only differ fundamentally from those in Western market economies but bear no relationship to scarcities either. Consequently, there is no rational basis for share valuation which is the defining feature of the classical privatisation. Furthermore, not only are there no investment banks, stock exchanges or other elements of the necessary structure of financial institutions; even basic accounting systems are geared towards measuring physical output rather than earnings, as is the case in market economies. On top of that, whatever trends in individual enterprise performance can be discerned, they are likely to be discontinued or substantially modified in the process of profound transformation. All this makes the valuation problem impossible to solve in practice. The second major problem stems from the very low purchasing power of the population. It usually represents less than 10 per cent of the book value of assets to be privatised. Owing mainly to the valuation and purchasing power problems, the classical privatisation methods are non-solutions as far as the post-communist privatisation is concerned. As has already been proved by the experience of countries at the forefront of the post-communist transformation (Poland and Hungary), more research needs to be done on the optimal ways of privatising the post-communist economies (Samonis and Hunyadi, 1992). At the most general level, there are two approaches to solving the privatisation problems: the classical one and the unconventional one, that is free distribution of shares to citizens (a sort of enfranchisement). If the efficiency (in terms of speed or cost, say) of transformation is the chief criterion, the choice between these two basic approaches (or any combination) will have to be predicated upon the assessment of the institutional features prevailing in any given post-communist economy (Samonis, 1994). The third lesson–hypothesis follows:

LH3: *Because of systemic and developmental differences, privatisation of the post-communist economies cannot proceed solely or even mainly on the basis of classical solutions described in the world literature; unconventional solutions (enfranchisement) and appropriate institution-building are called for.*

Reconfiguration of property rights to liberalise the market for capital is not an end in itself, though. It should be viewed as a means towards achieving better enterprise performance through a substantially improved institutional structure bringing about appropriate incentives and governance. The creation of effective enterprise governance should be viewed as the overriding consideration in the privatisation process and in systemic change in general. The broadest possible distribution of shares among the population, while desirable, might run against the barrier of low investment knowledge and governance problems. What is needed therefore is a network of private rather than state investment banks or similar institutions which would act as centres of investment knowledge and as controlling shareholders with regard to the newly privatised enterprises. Since this kind of knowledge and supervision expertise is practically non-existent in the post-communist economies, the investment banks suggested above should be created as joint ventures or other types of strategic alliances with Western financial institutions. The banks would gradually develop other functions, becoming universal banks familiar from the German and European experience. The East's fledgling stock exchanges have received wide coverage in the business press and some scholarly writings. While certainly helpful, they would play only a secondary role in my strategy of transformation, at least until a substantial spread of investment knowledge among the population can be achieved (Samonis, 1992a). Hence my lesson–hypothesis number four:

LH4:   *The creation of effective enterprise governance is the overriding criterion in the privatisation process; privatisation should proceed in tandem with the creation of predominantly private investment banks or similar institutions capitalised with Western expertise.*

As a solution complementing the above suggested structure of the post-communist financial institutions, pension funds should be established.

This brings us to the third element of FME, namely the creation of social systems (see Chart 5.1). Social issues form an inseparable part of the problems to be dealt with during the transformation. This calls for the liberalisation of the market for the second factor, namely labour. Theoretical considerations and the accumulated experience point to a very high probability of a substantial fall in the level of economic activity during the process. First, there is a slump, and then, it is hoped, a rebound in the gross national product, a development resembling the J-curve as portrayed in Chart 5.4. The first years of transformation saw some 10 per cent average annual slump in output throughout Eastern Europe. It seems inevitable that the overall economic situation (especially unemployment) will get worse before it gets better. The slump in the transforming countries was made deeper than necessary, however, judging by the experience up to 1993. It happened in that way because market co-ordination did not work properly after the initial liberalisation because of inadequate institutions. With regard to social issues, pension funds, unemployment insurance and welfare systems separated from each other and in part from the state budget will have to be designed and built from scratch, since these institutions were non-existent under communism when enterprises were acting as social institutions. In particular, the post-communist countries will have to substantially reduce welfare payments which are generally significantly above what these countries can afford. The system of 'workfare' (public works) will have to be introduced. Some initial research has been done on some of these issues (for example, Milanovic, 1993), but the results are far from adequate and call for more research. My fifth lesson–hypothesis follows:

LH5:   *The creation of separate pension, unemployment insurance and welfare systems, alongside other social institutions, is an inseparable part of the transformation; welfare payments will have to be reduced and based on the concept of workfare.*

Other important measures to liberalise the labour market will have to be undertaken as well. For example, the virtual absence of properly functioning housing markets in Eastern Europe causes low labour mobility since everybody tends to look for work only within commuting distance of his or her residence. Even more importantly, labour supply monopolisation (unionisation) is in direct contradiction to the need to liberalise this factor of production. Ways of decreasing the power and militancy of trade unions and changing their role will have to be found, if the supply response is to be boosted. Hence my sixth lesson–hypothesis:

LH6: *Supply response will depend on measures aimed at liberalising the labour market through the reduction of its monopolisation (unionisation) and the increase in labour mobility made possible by the development of housing markets.*

The process of joining the global village, that is integration into the world economy, is proceeding simultaneously with the creation of domestic markets. For analytical purposes and technical reasons, it is useful to treat these two transformations separately. There has been much controversy in the literature over the optimal way of opening the post-communist economies. Poland, for instance, did away with practically all the foreign trade restrictions at the outset of the process (Balcerowicz, 1992). Alternative solutions, such as that of Ronald McKinnon (1991), advocate a more gradual trade liberalisation. What is probably very important to do at the outset is the transformation of non-market-type protection into market-type protection. This should be done by way of the elimination of quantitative restrictions and introducing equivalent tariffs which will subsequently be subjected to a gradual reduction process. My seventh lesson–hypothesis follows:

LH7: *The external transformation should start with the translation of non-market-type protection into market-type protection, followed by gradual tariff reductions.*

To join the global village, the post-communist countries will need to develop ideas on what it is that they can bring to the world economy. Are they to rely exclusively on their skilled and cheap labour? Should national firms forget their historical and cultural roots and converge on the world-wide standards and norms of behaviour as soon as possible? In other words, what should their competitive advantage be based on once they liberalise their external economic relations? Michael E. Porter (1990) of Harvard came up with a comprehensive proposal on structuring a nation's competitive advantage on the basis of its unique historical and cultural traits. The proposal offers a way of harnessing national sentiments, previously suppressed by communism and now coming into the open so strongly. Instead of being a rather destructive force, they can work for the benefit of the post-communist economic development (Samonis, 1993a). Hence my lesson–hypothesis number eight:

LH8:   *The post-communist economies can best join the global village by developing their competitive advantage on the basis of unique traits of their historical and cultural development.*

Clearly, the West has an enormous stake in the post-communist economic transformation. It should therefore be ready to help in its own enlightened self-interest. Pouring money into the still largely untransformed economies is not the way to go, even if this money were easily available, which it is not. What is urgently called for is expertise and technical assistance in the creation of domestic markets and institutions and also a facilitating role in opening up Western markets to Eastern exports. This relates first of all to the so-called sensitive areas such as agriculture, textiles and steel. By opening its markets, the West, especially the European Union, can help the transforming countries much more than by sending financial aid. Hence my next lesson–hypothesis:

LH9:   *The West's proper role in the external transformation of the post-communist countries should be that of a source of expertise and technical assistance and a facilitator of market entry, but not of a provider of substantial financial aid.*

Many heated discussions have been conducted in the East as well as in the West regarding the optimal direction of integrational processes in the transforming economies. Two principal views have emerged. One advocates a regional – that is, East–East – integration, the other stresses the importance of early East–West integration. Given that the post-communist transformation is a long and very difficult process which can go wrong in several ways, it is important to secure whatever progress is made by anchoring it in a stable institutional framework which only the West can provide. The tenth and last lesson–hypothesis follows:

LH10:   *The post-communist economic transformation should be anchored in the institutional East–West integration to ensure the steady progress and the irreversible character of the process.*

Implications for Political Systems

Governments in the post-communist Eastern Europe operate under immense public pressure brought about by the Western demonstration effect. Now that these societies have more or less returned to Europe in a narrow political sense (they have adopted liberal democracy), the prevailing public opinion is that they should be able to catch up quickly with the West economically (Democracy, 1992). After two years of the post-communist transformation, President Lech Wałęsa maintained that, while the Polish people appreciated their political freedom, they had so far gained nothing from economic freedom. If this thinking continues and becomes something of a yardstick to evaluate government performance, the myopia of the political process known from the developing countries' experience could set in. Former communist parties returned to power in Lithuania, Poland and elsewhere. This increased the risk of 'hijacking' the change in directions which do not lead to a competitive market economy (Samonis, 1993b). It is then hard to see how these countries can accept the necessity of some short-term pain for a much bigger long-term gain and maintain an adequate level of political stability as well as a strong administrative capacity so badly needed to transform their economies (Krueger, 1990, pp. 199–200; World Bank, 1991, pp. 9–11).

This has definite implications for the type of government likely to maximise the efficiency of the first stage (FME) of the post-communist transformation. Within the realm of democratic solutions, presidential systems offer the best chance here, followed at some distance by majoritarian parliamentary systems. The proportional representation type of parliamentary systems would rank here as the least desirable choice.

De-Sovietisation

In the proposed framework, de-sovietisation comes after the stage of building the fundamentals of the market economy (see Chart 5.4). At the present time, the picture can be outlined in only a very rough manner. The de-sovietisation stage will concentrate on and strengthen the wealth-creating processes that have been started with the fall of communism. The central theme of this stage will be the transformation of Zinoviev's *homo sovieticus* into *homo oeconomicus* or somebody along the lines of the Schumpeterian entrepreneur (Schumpeter, 1960).

As part of an implicit social contract with the communist state, *homo sovieticus* renounced his freedom and human rights in exchange for the Orwellian 'care' by the Big Brother. The state is ultimately responsible for every facet of such a man's life. He does not have to be innovative or accept risk; he does not have to work hard. The state will continue to 'give' him whatever he needs for survival. He knows that no matter how creative, risk-friendly and hard-working he is, he will not be richer or more free than those who do not expend any effort beyond a minimum except when cheating on the state or fellow citizens, which behaviour is responsible for the zero-sum nature of communist economies. 'We pretend to work and they pretend to pay us' neatly summarises such behaviour. The society consisting of such people operates at the minimal level of possibilities (such as living standards), wasting human and natural resources at a rate unheard of in any free society.

Homo oeconomicus recognises that he is the ultimate shaper of his well-being. In the sphere of economic activity, he is the opposite of *homo sovieticus*. The only way this change can be brought about is by deliberately adopting liberal economic systems and policies for an extended period of time. These policies will be characterised by the minimal role of the state, especially in the area of social welfare. The proper role of the state will be limited to complementing the market by investing in infrastructure, both physical (such as roads or the environment) and human (such as education and health-care), as well as maintaining law and order and a stable macro-economy (low inflation, above all). Here, specific lessons can be distilled from Adam Smith's 'night watchman' proposal, from the neo-liberal school of economic thinking, and from the past forty years of economic development experience summarised in the World Bank's *World Development Report* (1991).

During the de-sovietisation stage, post-communist societies will have to re-learn the lesson that there is no such thing as a free lunch (Friedman, 1975). Such characteristics as hard work, self-reliance, innovativeness and adaptability will have to be promoted. The Schumpeterian entrepreneur will be the role model to follow (Schumpeter,

1960). Although compressed in time and with the usual late-comer advantages, the post-communist countries will have to repeat here the first half of the Western – including Scandinavian – development history. This stage will, it is hoped, result in a strong upward turn of a J-curve depicting the supply (output) response (see Chart 5.4). Per capita GNP will have to be raised from the present one-tenth or so of the West European level to something like one-half. Unfortunately, even in the optimistic scenario it could take a long time, probably a whole generation or more in some cases. Besides presidential systems, majoritarian parliamentary systems would probably be included in the category of the best solutions from the transformation efficiency point of view. This is because the central feature of this stage – rapid economic development – will more and more clearly serve the interests of the majority.

Welfare State

Only after the two first stages of the transformation have been more or less carried out will there be a realistic possibility of proceeding to a welfare state formula with its prominent redistributive function. To put it simply, production must come first, then distribution, for you cannot distribute what you have not got (Stolper, 1984). At this stage, the role of the state will start undergoing cyclical fluctuations, as observed in the second half of Western development history. Only then will it be possible to flirt with the now seriously compromised post-Second World War Swedish or other such models, should they still be of interest to more than a marginal proportion of the society. Politically, all the three basic systems (including proportional representation) may be equally acceptable at this stage since the transformation will be more or less complete and competing criteria will probably gain sharply in importance.

In Place of Conclusions

What are the main trends in the post-communist transformation? On the basis of theory and the first few years of experience, can road maps be constructed to guide the post-communist countries? What is the appropriate role of the state in this process? Given the legacy of communism, it is rather clear that no extreme solutions (omnipotent or impotent state, for example) are likely to minimise the cost of transforming post-communist economies into market economies. Instead, the state's role and other dimensions of the process will have to be optimised in response to the changing needs and priorities in the course of the transformation. This chapter has attempted to suggest some solutions applicable to the first stage of the transformation when new institutions have to be built. Taking a broad Schumpeterian social science perspective, the chapter has also proposed a macro-analytical framework which may be useful in the search for solutions to problems arising in the subsequent stages of the transformation. However, much more research is needed before the above lessons–hypotheses can simply be called lessons and one can answer all the above questions.

References

Balcerowicz, L. (1992), *800 dni: szok kontrolowany* (800 Days: A Controlled Shock) (Warsaw: Polska Oficyna Wydawnicza 'BGW').

Coase, R. H. (1992), 'The Institutional Structure of Production', *The American Economic Review*, September.

Colclough, Ch. and Manor, J. (ed.) (1992), *States and Markets: Neo-Liberalism and the Development-Policy Debate* (Oxford: Oxford University Press).

Democracy (1992), 'Democracy a Disappointment for Citizens of Eastern Europe', *The Globe and Mail* (Toronto), 29 January.

Demsetz, H. (1988), *Ownership, Control, and the Firm* (Oxford: Basil Blackwell).

Friedman, M. (1975), *There's No Such Thing as a Free Lunch* (LaSalle, IL: Open Court).

Gomulka, S. (1991). 'The Causes of Recession Following Stabilisation', *Comparative Economic Studies*, No. 2.

Grosfeld, I. (1990), 'Reform Economics and Western Economic Theory: Unexploited Opportunities', *Economics of Planning*, No. 1.

Hanusch, H. (ed.) (1988), *Evolutionary Economics: Applications of Schumpeter's Ideas* (Cambridge: Cambridge University Press).

Hayek, F. (1944), *The Road to Serfdom* (Chicago: University of Chicago Press).

Jackson, P. (1988), 'The Role of Government in Changing Industrial Societies: A Schumpeter Perspective', in H. Hanusch (ed.), *Evolutionary Economics: Applications of Schumpeter's Ideas* (Cambridge: Cambridge University Press).

Kornai, J. (1990), *The Road to a Free Economy* (New York: W.W. Norton).

Krueger, A. (1990), *Perspectives on Trade and Development* (New York: Harvester Wheatsheaf).

McKinnon, R. (1991), *The Order of Economic Liberalization: Financial Control in the Transition to a Market Economy* (Baltimore, MD: Johns Hopkins University Press).

Milanovic, B. (1993). 'Social Costs of the Transition to Capitalism: Poland 1990–91', World Bank Working Paper Series, No. 1165.

North, D. C. (1993), *Institutions, Institutional Change and Economic Performance* (New York: Cambridge University Press).

Porter, M. E. (1990), *The Competitive Advantage of Nations* (New York: Free Press).

Samonis, V. (1992a), 'Privatisation: The Backbone of the Post-Communist Economic Transformation', *Current Politics and Economics of Russia*, No. 2.

—— (1992b), 'Poland's Big Bang: Some Lessons After Three Years', *Geonomics*, September/October.

—— (1993a), 'The Shifting Competitive Advantage of Former Communist Countries: A Comparative Perspective', paper for the International Conference on US Competitiveness in the Global Marketplace, Washington, DC, 7–9 October 1993.

—— (1993b), *'Hijacking' Change in the Post-communist World? Lessons from Lithuania* (Toronto: University of Toronto).

—— (1994), 'Privatizing the Post-communist Economies: Towards the Political Economy of Enfranchisement', in T. Wiles (ed.), *In Transition: Society, Politics, and Economies in East Central Europe* (Bloomington: Indiana University Press).

—— and Cs. Hunyadi (1993), *Big Bang and Acceleration: Models for the Post-Communist Economic Transformation* (New York: Nova Science Publishers).

Schumpeter, J. (1960), *Teoria rozwoju gospodarczego* (The Theory of

Economic Development) (Warsaw: Państwowe Wydawnictwo Naukowe).

Stolper, W. (1984), 'The Relevance of Schumpeter's Ideas for Economic Policy', *Kieler Vortraege, Neue Folge*, 106.

World Bank (1991), *World Development Report 1991* (Washington, DC: The World Bank).

6 Russian Output Drop in Early Transition and its Macro- and Micro-economic Implications

Masaaki Kuboniwa

Introduction

One of the 'stylised' facts for the former Soviet-type economies in the early transition period is that there was a sharp fall in output coupled with a high inflation rate, which was an unexpected result for the suppliers of the reform package, namely the IMF and the World Bank. The drop in output officially measured in the early stages of the transition process was caused by the collapse of the traditional command and statistical system (see Winiecki, 1995). In the Soviet era, as was pointed out by many economists, including Seliunin and Khanin (1987) and Treml (1988), the official statistics of industrial production and national income suffered a general and continuous upward bias. This upward bias was mainly brought about by the traditional command system associated with its intrinsic incentive system, namely the distribution of bonuses, input requirements and output targets according to the extent of fulfilment of production plans. In this situation Soviet firms sent to the planning and statistical authorities reports which over-estimated output performance (a phemonenon known as *pripiska*). This type of paper output (write-ins) must have already disappeared by the early transition period.

Furthermore, under the shortage economy, state enterprises with soft budget constraints always needed larger volumes of inputs and capital goods than would have been needed in a developed market economy, which resulted in much higher input inventories in Soviet-type economies than in capitalist market economies (Kornai, 1980; Shmelev and Popov, 1989). This kind of inventory activity was also experienced by households. In the process of transformation, both the command system and its associated incentive system disappeared; thus, output on paper and excess input needs (over-sized 'slacks') also disappeared, and these in turn reduced industrial outputs. In the economic transition process, accompanied by a political transition, military expenditures also were remarkably reduced. This must have contributed to the marked decline in industrial output in the early transition period, especially in those countries with heavy concentrations of military production, such as Russia..

The steep drop in output was experienced by all of the former Soviet-type economies in the early transition period. However, it should be noted that Russia experienced one of the most serious falls in output officially registered. According to Goskomstat RF (State Statistical Committee of the Russian Federation), industrial output shows a decline of about 50 per cent for the period 1991–94 and GDP prior to the revision in October 1995 showed a decline of the same order. If this is true, then the transition has given rise to a crisis of production more terrifying than that which gripped the United States during the Great Depression of the 1930s. However, even assuming that production levels did indeed fall drastically in the first phase of the transition, we might suspect that the statistics greatly exaggerate the extent of that fall when we take into account the process of capital accumulation through 'insider' privatisation and tax evasion, vast capital flight, and conditions of living and employment. In short, there is reason to believe that the official statistics exhibit a strong downward bias.

Another well-known stylised fact is that the service economy has developed rapidly, but investigating industrial statistics is a more important priority since Russia's ability to compete in international markets is closely linked to its vast raw material resources and industrial base. This is apparent upon examination of influential commercial banks and enterprise groups which have achieved rapid growth in recent years. These business networks are frequently centred upon distribution firms handling oil, steel and non-ferrous metals. In other words, it can be stated that the continung rapid development of services and 'dollarisation' in the Russian economy can only be based on a continuing level of industrial production significantly higher than that reported in the official statistics.

We do not propose to offer support for either side of the superficial debates about 'shock therapy versus gradualism' or 'optimism versus pessimism', but rather to further our understanding of the macro- and micro-economic conditions of Russia in transition and of the obstacles to its structural transformation. This chapter investigates the major shift in the official output statistics from the upward bias in the Soviet era to the marked downward bias in the early transition period, resulting from the tax evasion, unregistered activities of firms and high inflation. The chapter provides preliminary observations on estimates of growth rates of Russian GDP and industrial output. These observations also provide a better understanding of the importance of macro-economic stabilisation policy for structural reforms because, among the disequilibria of a national economy, inflation reflects a socio-economic crisis regarding monetary instruments for the market, and the preservation of wealth and high inflation throws the behaviour of economic agents into confusion.

Inherent Problems in Industrial Output Statistics

Changes in the industrial production indexes compiled by Goskomstat are shown in Table 6.1. Every sector on the table experienced large drops in production from 1991 onwards. With the exception of light industry, which appears to be on the verge of extinction, the rate of decrease tended to level off only in 1995 although industrial performance for the first eight months of 1996 again showed an overall declining tendency.

Goskomstat made several revisions to the methodology of measuring growth rates of industrial outputs in the early transition period.

First, faced with the inappropriate deflators being employed in converting outputs in current prices to those in constant prices, they gave up using the traditional industrial production index based on

Table 6.1   Changes in Russian industrial output by sector, 1991–96

	Official data[a]						Official data[b]			
	1991	1992	1993	1994	1995	1996[c]	1993	1994	1995	1996[c]
	(Physical percentage change over previous period)									
Electricity	0.3	–4.7	–5.3	–8.8	–3	–0.4	–4.7	–9	–3	–
Electricity in kWh	–1.3	–5.6	–5.1	–8.4	–1.6	–0.6	–	–	–	–
Fuels	–6.0	–7.0	–15.0	–11.0	–2	–3	–11.6	–10	–2	–
Ferrous metallurgy	–7.4	–16.4	–16.6	–17.4	9	–4	–16.6	–17	9	–
Non-ferrous metallurgy	–8.7	–25.4	–18.1	–9.1	2	–4	–14.1	–9	2	–
Chemical industry	–6.8	–21.7	–21.8	–28.2	8	–13	–21.5	–25	8	–
Machine building and metal-working	–10.0	–14.9	–15.8	–38.1	–10	–14	–15.6	–31	–10	–
Wood and paper	–9.0	–14.6	–18.7	–31.2	–7	–20	–18.7	–30	–4	–
Construction materials	–2.4	–20.4	–17.6	–28.9	–8	–25	–16.0	–27	–5	–
Light industry	–9.0	–30.0	–23.4	–47.3	–31	–2.6	–23.0	–46	–29	–
Food industry	–9.5	–16.4	–9.2	–21.9	–9	–6	–9.0	–17	–8	–
Industry, total	*–8.0*	*–18.0*	*–16.2*	*–22.8*	*–5*	*–8*	*–14.1*	*–20.9*	*–3.3*	*–5*
	(Physical index; cumulative change: 1990 = 100)									
Electricity	100.3	96	91	83	80	–	91	83	80	–
Electricity in kWh	98.7	93.2	88.4	80.9	79.7	–	–	–	–	–
Fuels	94	87	74	66	65	–	77	69	68	–
Ferrous metallurgy	93	77	65	53	58	–	65	53	58	–
Non-ferrous metallurgy	91	68	56	51	52	–	59	53	54	–
Chemical industry	93	73	57	41	44	–	58	44	47	–
Machine building and metal-working	90	77	64	40	36	–	65	45	40	–
Wood and paper	91	78	63	43	40	–	63	44	42	–
Construction materials	98	78	64	46	42	–	65	47	45	–
Light industry	91	64	49	26	18	–	49	26	19	–
Food industry	91	76	69	54	49	–	69	57	52	–
Industry, total	*92*	*75*	*63*	*49*	*46*	–	*65*	*51*	*50*	–

Notes: [a] covers only large and medium-sized enterprises; [b] covers large, medium and small enterprises and joint ventures; [c] January–August only.
Electricity index in a broad sense (*elektronergetika*) is derived by aggregating electricity index in a narrow sense in terms of kWh (*elektroenergiya*) and steam index in terms of calories (*teploenergiya*).

Sources: Goskomstat RF, *Statistical Yearbook 1994*, *Statistical Yearbook 1995* and various issues of Monthy Report, and data directly provided by Goskomstat RF and CIS Statistical Committee.

enterprises' output reports and industrial output computed at comparable prices. Instead, they began to employ the physical industrial output index as the official figure, starting with the report of industrial output for 1991 (*Russian Statistical Yearbook for 1991*, published in 1992). The reason was that comparable price base statistics obtained from data on enterprises' performance reports were underestimating the decline in industrial production. In 1991, according to comparable price statistics, industrial production did not decline by more than 1.7 per cent, while production of machine-building and metalworking (MBMW) did not fall but rather grew by 3.9 per cent. However, Goskomstat felt that this outcome could not be observed in the actual products in physical terms.

According to a manual directed by the department of industrial production of Goskomstat, this new index is based on a GVA (gross value added)-weighted sample index method in order to reflect the dynamics of volume of major products in physical units.[1] For this index a standard set of representative industrial products is selected. The number of such products for the 1992 index was 372. Then sectoral production indexes (about 120) are computed on the basis of the production volume of representative products in kind for the current and previous year weighted by the previous year's prices. Production indexes of aggregated industrial sectors (about 15) or of industry in total are calculated as the volume of sectoral production indexes weighted by the proportions of GVA for the previous year. These indexes are adjusted to cover both civilian and military industrial production.

Second, starting with reports for 1993, Goskomstat began to revise measured industrial output aggregates to account for the growing share of activity of small enterprises and joint ventures in the industrial sphere. Until 1992, industrial output was estimated solely on the basis of reports from large and medium-sized traditional enterprises, which on average experienced sharper drops and contributed a downward bias to measured industrial output during the early transition. Time series (a) in Table 6.1 is based on this traditional method while time series (b), displaying the revised industrial output growth in the table, covers not only the output of large and medium-sized enterprises but that of

---

1. Goskomstat, *O raschete indeksa fizicheskogo ob"ema promyshlennoi produktsii* (Moscow: 1993).

smaller firms as well. In early 1995, the new method was made official
while time series (b) is available only for the period since 1992. Under
time series (b), annual industrial production was revised upwards by
approximately 2 per cent for 1993–95. A cumulative drop in series (b)
for 1991–95 is computed by chaining series (a) for 1991–92 with series
(b) for 1993–95. The cumulative drop in output of series (a) for 1991–
95 (1991–94) is 46 per cent (49 per cent), while that of series (b) is 50
per cent (51 per cent). Time series (b), based on industrial production
statistics in terms of current prices for 1994, indicates that industrial
production reached a level 12.7 per cent above that indicated in the old
time series (a). Broken down by sector, the differences for steel, non-
ferrous metals, chemicals and fuels (oil, gas and coal) were all under 10
per cent, while those for electricity, MBMW, wood and paper, construction materials, light industry and the food industry were all above 10
per cent.

These official revisions are still insufficient, since Goskomstat has
not yet dealt with problems related to under-reporting. Facing the collapse of the traditional incentive system and high inflation, firms began
to change their reporting strategies. Specifically, they began to send
reports underestimating output and income to Goskomstat and the tax
offices. We can easily imagine that this resulted in a marked downward
bias of industrial production. This implies that the industrial output in
Russia did not fall by as much as is shown by the official statistics,
even if there was indeed a remarkable drop.

Let us illustrate the downward bias of industrial output by looking at
the inconsistencies between the official figures for the output of the
electricity sector and other industrial outputs. Table 6.1 indicates that
the electricity industry suffered a very slight decrease in production
compared with other industrial sectors and to industry as a whole. This
is quite strange considering that for several decades, as shown in Figure
6.1, electricity grew at a rate which closely paralleled that of industry as
a whole.

There is no difficulty in aggregating electricity outputs because,
unlike the output of other industrial sectors, the output of different
electricity enterprises generated by whatever technology cannot be
distinguished. Furthermore, since electricity is supplied by naturally
monopolistic enterprises and through power transmission lines, the
electricity industry is quite different from industries such as oil, steel

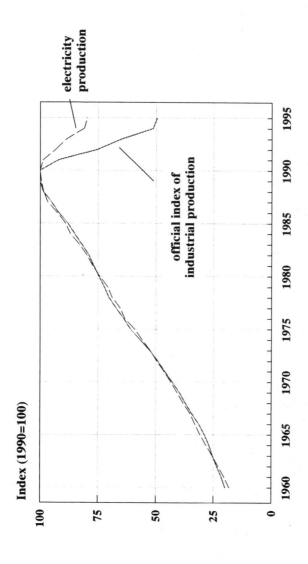

Index (1990=100)

electricity production

official index of industrial production

Figure 6.1 Official indexes of electricity production and industrial production in Russia (1990 = 100), 1960–1995

107

and non-ferrous metals, and manufacturing, all of which suffer sub-stantial theft and illegal diversions. In addition, since the hoarding of electricity is impossible, accumulation and inventories of electricity cannot occur. From the standpoint of national accounts statistics, another distinctive feature of electricity is that the margins for trans-portation and distribution are zero. These various factors imply that statistics for the production of electricity are considerably more reliable than those for the production of other industries. Because there is no inventory, the production statistics of electricity in value terms do not suffer any instability due to holding gains under high inflation. And, in the case of a vast country like Russia, the absence of transportation and distribution margins is especially helpful for statistical compilation. Finally, since there are no investment goods, the sharp fall in invest-ment which occurred during the early transition period had no effect on production statistics for electricity. Thus, it can be stated that the official figures for output and consumption of electricity are fairly reliable because they are hardly affected by aggregation, transportation margins, investment, inventory changes and sales through 'second' channels. For these reasons, in order to investigate statistics for all industrial production, it is reasonable to use the production and con-sumption of electricity as a starting-point, or 'control total'.

In estimating industrial output growth figures, we need the infor-mation on sectoral real growth rates of output shown in Table 6.2. The indicators used in deriving this table are as follows: industrial pro-duction volume index for industry, official agricultural output volume index for agriculture, index for construction and assembling works for construction, weighted volume index for transportation, official volume index of retail sales for trade and residual employment data for other non-material service sectors as a whole. Fixing the growth rates of sectors in Table 6.2 other than industry, we shall examine the possible variations of the growth rate of industrial output as a whole.

Estimating Industrial Output Growth by Electricity Balances

The balance of demand and supply for electricity can be defined in general as the following equation (all variables are in physical terms):

Table 6.2   Changes in Russian gross domestic output by sector,
1990–95 (annual percentage change in terms of volume
indexes or comparable prices)

	1990	1991	1992	1993	1994	1995
Industry	-0.1	-8.0	-18.0	-14.1	-20.9	-3.3
Agriculture	-3.6	-4.5	-9.0	-4.0	-12.0	-8.0
Construction	-8.0	-15.0	-37.0	-12.0	-7.0	-7.0
Transport	0.7	-6.8	-12.9	-9.6	-13.1	-3.8
Trade	11.7	-3.2	-3.5	1.9	0.1	-7.2
Other services	2.0	-0.9	-1.7	-2.1	-0.2	0.0

Notes: Figures for industry are given in Table 6.1; those for agriculture are based on the official output data in 1983 constant prices; figures for construction are derived from official construction and assembly work index provided by the CIS Statistical Committee; trade figures rely on the official retail trade sales index. The case of 'other services' is derived from the official employment data.

Source: Goskomstat RF, CIS Statistical Committee and author's estimates.

$$X_e(t) = D^{(1)}(t) + [(D^{(2)}(t) + D^{(2)}(t) + \ldots + D^{(m)}(t)] \qquad (1)$$

where:

$X_e(t)$ = gross domestic production of electricity in year t;

$D^{(1)}(t)$ = intermediate demand for electricity by the entire industrial sector in year t;

$D^{(k)}(t)$ = intermediate or final demand for electricity by the k-th non-industrial production sector or the k-th final demand sector at year t ($k = 2, 3, \ldots, m$).

Note that net increases in stocks and fixed capital formation are zero by definition. The above definition is true in both value terms and physical (kWh) terms. In value terms, since transportation and distribution margins are zero, the difference between purchasers' prices and producers' prices is basically represented by indirect taxes on electricity.

The rate of growth in production of electricity, g_e can be written as follows:

$$g_e(t) = \Sigma_k \alpha^{(k)}(t-1)\, g^{(k)}(t), \tag{2}$$

where:

$\alpha^{(k)}(t) = D^{(k)}(t) / \Sigma_k D^{(k)}(t)\ [\Sigma_k \alpha^{(k)}(t)=1];$

$g_e(t) = [X_e(t) - X_e(t-1)]/X_e(t-1);$ and

$g^{(k)}(t) = [D^{(k)}(t) - D^{(k)}(t-1)]/D^{(k)}(t-1),\ k=1, 2, \ldots, m.$

Therefore, given weights of demand for electricity in the previous period $\alpha^{(k)}(k = 1, 2, \ldots, m)$, the growth rate in electricity production in the current period g_e, the growth rates of the non-industrial sector's intermediate demand and final demand sectors' final demand for electricity $g^{(k)}(k = 2, 3, \ldots, m)$, then the industrial sector's intermediate demand growth rate for electricity $g^{(1)}$ can be uniquely determined. Namely, the rate of growth in industrial production, $g^{(1)}(t)$ is given by the following equation:

$$g^{(1)}(t) = [g_e(t) - (\alpha^{(2)}(t-1)\, g^{(2)}(t) + \ldots + \alpha^{(m)}(t-1)\, g^{(m)}(t))]/\alpha^{(1)}(t-1) \tag{3}$$

Using input coefficients or final demand coefficients, the components of demand for electricity can be expressed in the following manner:

$$D^{(k)}(t) = a_{e,k}(t)X^{(k)}(t),\ k = 1, 2, \ldots, m.$$

where:

$a_{e,k}(t)$ = the amount of electricity necessary to produce one unit of each sectoral product at year t', or the share of electricity consumption in the total final demand (final consumption + (net) exports); and

$X^{(k)}(t)$ = the total domestic output in each sector at year t ($k = 1, 2$) or the total final demand (final consumption + (net) exports) ($k = 3$).

Using the above formula, each sectoral growth rate of output $\gamma(k)$ can be written as follows:

$$\gamma^{(k)}(t) = [a_{e,k}(t-1)/a_{e,k}(t)][g^{(k)}(t)+1] - 1 \tag{4}$$

This formula implies that the growth rate of industrial production has a proportional relationship to the rate of increase in demand for electricity by sector along with technological change as represented by the decreasing rate of input coefficient. If it is assumed that input coefficients are stable, so that: $a_{e,k}(t) = a_{e,k}(t-1)$ is established, then it follows from (4) that: $\gamma^{(k)}(t) = g^{(k)}(t)$. This shows that each sectoral growth rate of output can be approximated by its change in the rate of demand for electricity.

We assume, as a first approximation, that the input coefficient and consumption coefficient are stable, so we can use equation (2) to calculate a plausible growth rate for industrial production. To do so, we first need information on $\alpha^{(k)}(t)$, the proportionate elements of demand for electricity (in the terminology of input-output analysis, the distribution coefficients of electricity). This information is provided in the input-output (I-O) tables (in terms of monetary values) or in the balance sheet of electricity (in terms of real kWh).

The structure of demand for electricity through 1994, shown in Table 6.3, is calculated directly from the balance sheet of electricity in physical terms. The distinction between intermediate demand and final demand for the electricity balance in terms of kWh is not clear. In the case of the MPS accounting system, construction, communications and a portion of trade make up intermediate demand within the 'other branches' category. A portion of transportation, housing and public utilities, and a portion of communications, cultural activities and health make up final consumption expenditures. The elements of the electricity balance include imports of electricity (competitive import type), but as these are negligible we may consider Table 6.3 as showing the breakdown of demand for domestic electricity for each element.

In Table 6.3, the electricity distribution coefficient $\alpha^{(1)}$ of the industrial sector shows a declining trend, falling from 0.61 in 1989 to 0.51 in 1994. The distribution coefficient for the transportation sector shows the same declining trend. In contrast, the distribution for agriculture and 'other branches' increases year by year. Two points should be noted regarding changes in the structure of demand for electricity since 1992. First, examination of the category 'other branches' from 1991 to 1993 indicates that only the housing and public utilities subcategory, which constitutes a part of personal consumption expenditures, showed increases. There was almost no change in the distribution coefficient for the 'communication-culture-health-trade' as a nonmaterial services sub-sector. The rapid increases in the trade and finance sectors must have cancelled out the rapid declines in the other non-material service sectors such as education and sciences.

Masaaki Kuboniwa

Table 6.3   Demand for electricity by sector (kWh basis), 1989–94

	1989	1990	1991	1992	1993	1994
	(Sectoral share, per cent)					
Industry	60.6	57.8	56.7	55.0	53.6	51.0
Agriculture	8.1	8.9	9.7	10.2	10.9	11.2
Transport	9.8	9.6	9.1	8.6	8.0	7.8
Other branches *of which:*	20.9	32.9	23.5	24.6	25.6	27.8
Construction	–	1.7	1.6	1.6	1.6	1.5
Housing and public utilities	–	–	9.0	9.6	10.5	–
Communications, culture	–	–	5.2	5.3	5.3	–
Health care and trade technical loss	7.9	7.8	7.7	8.1	8.2	9.0
Exports	3.6	4.0	4.4	4.4	4.5	4.8
Imports	–3.1	–3.2	–3.3	–2.7	–2.6	–2.5
Gross domestic output of electricity	100.0	100.0	100.0	100.0	100.0	100.0
	(Annual growth rate of sectoral demand, per cent)					
Industry	–0.4	–4.1	–3.3	–8.4	–7.5	–12.8
Agriculture	3.2	10.0	7.3	–0.5	0.9	–5.9
Transport	3.2	–1.7	–6.8	–10.3	–11.5	–10.8
Other branches *of which:*	2.9	9.9	1.3	–1.2	–1.3	–0.5
Construction	–	–	–5.0	–5.6	–5.1	–5.1
Housing and public utilities	–	–	–	0.7	3.7	–
Communications, culture	–	–	–	–3.8	–5.1	–
Health care and trade technical loss	–	–0.9	–2.3	–0.7	–4.0	–4.0
Exports	7.7	10.7	8.8	–6.8	–1.4	–3.9
Imports	4.0	3.6	0.3	–21.1	–10.8	–10.1
Gross domestic output of electricity	1.0	0.5	–1.3	–5.6	–5.1	–8.4

Sources: Goskomstat RF, *Statistical Yearbook,* 1994, p. 318; 1990, p. 316; 1995, p. 325; *Promyshlennost' Rossii 1995*, p. 130; and data supplied by Goskomstat RF.

Second, it is true that the industrial sector's share of demand for electricity has been declining, but this decline is much less than the decline implied in the official statistics.

Table 6.3 is based on physical volume data. By contrast, Tables 6.4 and 6.5 are based on data in current prices. Table 6.4 shows demand for electricity by sector as calculated from the Russian I–O tables at current 'producer prices (or basic prices)' for 1989–92. The elements of intermediate transactions and final consumption in the I–O tables indicate only Russian domestic product (non-competitive import type), so imported electricity is excluded from the elements. In addition, the I–O tables are on an MPS basis, so it is important to note that intermediate demand for electricity from the non-material service sector (passenger transportation, housing and public utilities, administration and finance, and science) is calculated as the final consumption expenditures of the public consumption sector. The producers' prices indicated here correspond to 'industrial producers' wholesale prices' in the Soviet traditional terminology because they exclude indirect taxes (turnover taxes until 1990, sales taxes and turnover taxes in 1991, and value-added taxes from 1992). The statistics in terms of current values for industrial production are estimated in terms of these prices.

The distribution coefficients $\alpha^{(k)}$ at a nominal base for the years 1989 and 1990 are relatively stable, so $\alpha^{(1)} \cong 0.56$, $\alpha^{(2)} \cong 0.18$ (for the non-industrial material production sector) and $\alpha^{(3)} \cong 0.26$ (for the final demand sector). Industrial production began to decline rapidly in 1991 but $a^{(1)}$ showed an increase toward 0.59, while $\alpha^{(3)}$ as the result of a major decline in the individual consumption distribution coefficient $\alpha^{(3)}$ showed a decline to 0.24 ($\alpha^{(2)}$ was almost constant). This could be understood primarily as resulting from the 1991 price reforms (rises in the cost of electricity for enterprises). The steady rise in the distribution coefficient for the trade sector (including restaurants) for 1989–91 reflects the prosperity of the cooperative trade sector. The extent to which the marked rise in the distribution coefficient for the trade sector from 0.04 for 1991 to 0.19 for 1992 appeared in the development of non-material service activities has not been determined. In other words, those figures in Table 6.4 which show that the share of the trade sector shot up from 4.3 per cent in 1991 to 18.5 per cent in 1992 do not match Table 6.3 at all.

*Table 6.4   Structure of demand for electricity in Russia (MPS basis), 1989–92
(percentage of electricity production at current producers' prices)*

		1989	1990	1991	1992
1	Electricity	0.9	0.9	2.3	2.2
2	Oil and gas	6.7	6.2	6.5	13.5
3	Coal	1.1	1.1	1.0	1.4
4	Other fuels	0.0	0.0	0.0	0.0
5	Ferrous metallurgy	3.9	3.9	3.8	4.4
6	Non-ferrous metallurgy	5.2	5.4	6.1	6.0
7	Chemical industry	11.5	11.6	11.2	8.0
8	Machine-building and metal-working	13.6	13.2	12.1	6.5
9	Wood and paper	2.9	2.9	3.2	2.5
10	Constructionmaterials	4.2	4.0	4.1	2.7
11	Light industry	2.1	2.1	2.5	1.7
12	Food industry	2.4	2.3	2.7	2.7
13	Industry n.e.c.	2.0	2.2	3.0	1.5
	Industry, total	*56.8*	*55.9*	*58.6*	*53.1*
14	Construction	3.8	3.4	3.0	1.3
15	Agriculture	3.6	3.9	3.5	1.8
16	Transport and communication	6.7	7.0	6.3	6.8
17	Trade	3.0	3.3	4.3	18.5
18	Other branches	0.2	0.4	0.3	0.3
19	Intermediate demand, total	74.1	73.9	76.0	81.9
20	Household consumption	10.0	9.0	5.5	0.9
21	Public consumption	12.9	13.9	15.2	11.4
22	Consumption, total	22.9	23.0	20.7	12.4
23	Net investment	0.0	0.0	0.0	0.0
24	Increase in stocks	0.0	0.0	0.0	0.0
25	Renovation investment	0.0	0.0	0.0	0.0
26	Losses	0.0	0.0	0.0	0.0
27	Exports	3.0	3.1	3.3	5.7
28	Final demand, total	25.9	26.1	24.0	18.1
29	Gross domestic output (GDO)	100.0	100.0	100.0	100.0

Notes: Input–output tables employed in this table are of a non-competitive type; the figures for 1992 are obtained by converting SNA to MPS.

Sources: Computed by using Goskomstat RF, Russian MPS Input–Output Tables for 1989–91 at Producers' Prices (MPS) and Russian SNA Input–Output Table for 1992 at Producers' Prices.

Table 6.5 Structure of demand for electricity in Russia (MPS basis), 1985–91
(percentage of electricity production at current purchasers' prices)

		1985	1986	1987	1988	1989	1990	1991	1992
1	Electricity	0.9	0.9	1.0	0.9	0.9	0.9	2.4	2.2
2	Oil and gas	6.3	6.3	7.0	6.9	6.7	6.2	6.6	13.5
3	Coal	1.4	1.4	1.1	1.1	1.1	1.1	1.1	1.4
4	Other fuels	0.0	0.0	0.0	0.0	0.0	0.0	0.0	0.0
5	Ferrous metallurgy	4.3	4.2	3.9	4.0	3.9	3.9	3.9	4.4
6	Non-ferrous metallurgy	5.4	5.3	5.1	5.1	5.2	5.4	6.2	4.4
7	Chemical industry	12.3	11.9	11.8	11.8	11.5	11.6	11.5	8.1
8	Machine-building and metal-working	13.3	13.1	14.2	14.0	13.6	13.3	12.4	6.5
9	Wood and paper	3.2	3.3	2.9	2.9	2.9	2.9	3.3	2.5
10	Constructionmaterials	4.3	4.3	4.5	4.2	4.2	4.0	4.2	2.7
11	Light industry	2.2	2.2	2.1	2.0	2.1	2.1	2.6	2.7
12	Food industry	2.4	2.4	2.4	2.4	2.4	2.3	2.7	2.7
13	Industry n.e.c.	2.2	2.3	1.9	2.0	2.0	2.2	3.0	1.5
	Industry, total	*58.3*	*57.6*	*57.8*	*57.3*	*56.7*	*55.9*	*59.9*	*53.2*
14	Construction	3.9	4.2	3.3	3.6	3.7	3.3	3.1	1.3
15	Agriculture	3.1	3.4	3.3	3.4	3.4	3.7	3.6	1.8
16	Transport and communication	6.9	6.7	7.4	7.5	6.7	7.1	6.5	6.8
17	Trade	2.2	2.3	2.7	2.8	2.9	3.3	4.4	18.6
18	Other branches	0.1	0.1	0.1	0.1	0.2	0.4	0.3	0.3
19	Intermediate demand, total	74.5	74.4	74.5	74.6	73.7	73.7	77.8	82.1
20	Household consumption	12.7	12.9	11.5	11.3	11.3	10.1	5.7	1.2
21	Public consumption	12.9	12.9	13.4	13.7	14.4	15.5	15.7	11.6
22	Consumption, total	25.7	25.8	24.9	25.1	25.8	25.6	21.4	12.8
23	Net investment	0.0	0.0	0.0	0.0	0.0	0.0	0.0	0.0
24	Increase in stocks	0.0	0.0	0.0	0.0	0.0	0.0	0.0	0.0
25	Renovation investment	0.0	0.0	0.0	0.0	0.0	0.0	0.0	0.0
26	Losses	0.0	0.0	0.0	0.0	0.0	0.0	0.0	0.0
27	Exports	2.2	−0.2*	2.8	2.7	2.9	3.0	3.3	6.2
28	Imports	−2.3	–	−2.2	−2.4	−2.4	−2.3	−2.4	−1.0
29	Final demand, total	25.5	25.6	25.5	25.4	26.3	26.3	22.2	17.9
30	Gross domestic output	100.0	100.0	100.0	100.0	100.0	100.0	100.0	100.0

Note: * denotes net exports

Sources: Computed by using Goskomstat RF, Russian MPS Input-Output Tables for
1985–91 and SNA Input-Output Tables for 1992 at Purchasers' Prices.

Table 6.5 shows the sectoral structure of demand for electricity calculated from the I–O tables for 1985–92 at current purchasers' prices. The elements in the I–O table include imports as well as domestic products (competitive import type). However, since there is almost no importation of electricity, the facts evident in Table 6.4 can be seen in Table 6.5 as well.

Goskomstat has compiled experimental SNA-based I–O tables at current purchasers' prices for 1991–92, and at producers' prices for 1992. These tables serve as the basis for Table 6.6, which shows the structure of demand for electricity. Table 6.6 totals the demand for electricity by non-material service sectors (education, cultural activities, and health; housing and public utilities; administration and finance; and science), and its complete accord with demand for electricity by public consumption shown in Table 6.4 can be easily verified. The share of demand for electricity from 'public consumption' for 1992 is calculated to be 11.6 per cent, below its share for 1991. As Table 6.6 makes clear, the expansion in the demand share by administration and finance did not offset the rapid decline in demand from the education, culture and health and science sectors.

Table 6.6 Structure of demand for electricity in Russia by sector (SNA basis), 1991–92 (percentage of electricity production at current prices)

	1991	1992	1992
	at purchasers' prices		*at producers' prices*
	competitive import type		*non-competitive import type*
1 Electricity	2.4	2.2	2.2
2 Oil and gas	6.6	13.5	13.5
3 Coal	1.1	1.4	1.4
4 Other fuels	0.0	0.0	0.0
5 Ferrous metallurgy	3.9	4.4	4.4
6 Non-ferrous metallurgy	6.2	6.0	6.0
7 Chemical industry	11.5	8.1	8.0
8 Machine-building and metal-working	12.4	6.5	6.5
9 Wood and paper	3.3	2.5	2.5
10 Constructionmaterials	4.2	2.7	2.7
11 Light industry	2.6	1.7	1.7
12 Food industry	2.4	2.4	2.4

13	Industry n.e.c.	3.0	1.5	1.5
	Industry, total	*59.9*	*53.2*	*53.1*
14	Construction	3.1	1.3	1.3
15	Agriculture	3.6	1.8	1.8
16	Transport and communication (T & C)	8.5	8.0	7.9
16a	Productive T & C	6.5	6.8	6.8
16b	Non-productive T & C	2.0	1.2	1.2
17	Trade	4.4	18.6	18.5
18	Other material branches	0.3	0.3	0.3
	Material intermediate demand	*74.5*	*74.4*	*74.5*
19	Education, health, culture	4.2	1.7	1.6
20	Housing and public utilities	4.4	4.7	4.7
21	Administration and finance	2.3	3.5	3.5
22	Sciences	2.7	0.5	0.5
23	*Intermediate demand, total*	*93.5*	*93.6*	*93.3*
24	Household consumption	5.7	1.2	0.9
25	Public consumption	0.0	0.0	0.0
26	Fixed capital formation	0.0	0.0	0.0
27	Increase in stocks	0.0	0.0	0.0
28	Exports	3.3	6.2	5.7
29	Imports	–2.4	–1.0	–
29	Final demand, total	6.5	6.4	6.7
30	Gross domestic output	100.0	100.0	100.0

Sources: Computed by using Goskomstat RF, Russian Preliminary Input-Output Tables for 1991–92 (SNA) at Purchasers' Prices and for 1992 at Producers' (Basic) Prices.

According to Table 6.6, demand for electricity from industry fell from 60 per cent in 1991 to 53 per cent in 1992. Demand from the MBMW, construction materials and light industrial sectors fell precipitously, but because the share of the oil and gas sector at purchasers' prices almost doubled, the total decline in industry's share at purchasers' prices was slight. The share of demand for electricity by the entire industrial sector in 1992 conforms to the figures in Table 6.5.

The distribution coefficient of electricity for the household sector dropped sharply in 1992 as can be seen in Tables 6.4, 6.5 and 6.6. This can be understood from Table 6.7, which shows that the price of electricity utilised by the household sector increased no more than

Table 6.7 Changes in electricity prices (rubles per kWh)

| | 1991 | 1992 | | | | 1993 | | | | 1994 | | | | 1995 |
		Q1	Q2	Q3	Q4	Q1	Q2	Q3	Q4	Q1	Q2	Q3	Q4	Q1
Household	0.04	0.12	0.22	0.26	0.35	0.37	0.39	5.43	5.82	6.27	13.00	20.51	25.41	41.75
Enterprises (producers)	0.03		0.55	1.00	1.98	3.14	4.61	12.66	17.53	28.61	41.87	53.45	58.40	81.59
of which:														
Industry										37.10	52.15	66.44	70.81	99.94
Agriculture										23.08	35.17	43.82	45.49	65.80
Enterprises (consumers)									17.66	33.12	48.93	56.20	62.08	90.63

Source: Goskomstat RF.

tenfold, while the price of electricity used by enterprises increased more than sixty times. This price differential began to shrink rapidly in 1993, causing the household sector's share of demand for electricity in terms of current value to begin another sharp rise from 1993.

As seen in the above discussion, there are many problems in the data on coefficients of electricity distribution. However, they are valuable in improving our estimate of industrial growth.

Simulation A: Assuming the stability of the input coefficients and the consumption coefficient for electricity, then $\gamma^{(k)}(t)$ can be directly calculated by using the electricity balance in terms of kWh as shown in Table 6.3. In this case the rate of increase of demand for electricity for every sector can in the same manner indicate the rise in the rate of production for each sector. This puts the rate of increase of industrial production at –3.3 per cent in 1991, –8.4 per cent in 1992, –7.5 per cent in 1993, and –12.8 per cent in 1994. These annual rates put the cumulative decline for 1991–94 at 28.5 per cent, which is much smaller than the official decline (50 per cent). Even these simple estimates for industrial production are better than the official statistics since, in general, the activities of the industry and transportation sectors are technologically quite closely tied to electricity, particularly in Russia.

Simulation B: Let us next estimate the growth rates of industrial production, $g^{(1)}(t)$ by using the real sectoral output growth rates, $g^{(k)}(t)$, in Table 6.2, equation (2) and the distribution coefficients, $\alpha^{(k)}(t-1)$, in Table 6.3 (k=2,3,...,m). The distribution coefficients for the agriculture, construction and transport sectors for 1990–94 are directly given in Table 6.3. Furthermore, roughly put, the distribution coefficients for the trade sector at 0.033 for 1990, 0.043 for 1991 and 0.05 for 1992–94 by adjusting data given in Tables 6.3 and 6.4. We can then put those for the 'other services' sector at 0.101, 0.099, 0.099, 0.108, and 0.122 for 1990–94. Thus, it follows from equation (2) that the estimated figures of growth rates of industrial output are –0.1 per cent in 1991, –6.3 per cent in 1992, –7.4 per cent in 1993, and –13.2 per cent in 1994. In this case, industrial production shows a 24.7 per cent cumulative decline for 1991–94. When we assume that the distribution coefficients for 1995 are the same as those for 1994 and that exports and imports of electricity in 1995 show the same declines as in 1994, we obtain the estimate of industrial growth rate for 1995 as –0.2 per cent.

Simulation C: Let us here attempt to calculate the rate of increase in production of the final demand sector (consumption plus exports) on the basis of the following assumptions: (1) use the official statistics in Table 6.1 for the rate of increase in electricity production, and (2) use the figures in Table 6.4 for the distribution coefficients for 1991. Goskomstat revised its figures for 1992's real growth rate in retail sales drastically upwards, from –35 per cent to –3 per cent, in its *1993 Annual Report* (published in 1994). Bearing this in mind, we can compute the growth rate for production for 1992 for 'trade plus other material branches' at about 0 per cent. Employing the official statistics of production of other non-industrial sectors given Table 6.2, we can obtain $\gamma(2)(1992) = -15.1$ per cent for the non-industrial production sector. If, in this case, we use the official growth rate for production for industry, –18 per cent, as $\gamma(1)$, $\gamma(3)(1992)$ for the final demand sector reaches an unrealistically high level 35.4 per cent. Moreover, if we attempt to adjust figures for $\gamma(3)(1992)$ in a more appropriate direction, the industrial production growth rate falls at worst to the –10 per cent range (in fact probably to the –3 per cent to –6 per cent range). In the case of 1993 as well, the figures in Table 6.5 (those changed from SNA to MPS) are used for the distribution coefficients for 1992, while growth rates of production of electricity remain Table 6.1's official figures. If we use the figure of –4.5 per cent as $\gamma(2)$ for the production growth rate in the non-industrial sector, which reflects the revised figure of +2 per cent of the official statistics on the real rate of retail sales growth, then the production growth rate in industry is better than –11 per cent.

Figure 6.2 displays the growth figures given by *Simulation B* which are regarded as our reference estimate of Russian industrial output growth in the early transition. As can be seen, industry's decline in 1991–94 was far less severe than the official statistics. Of course, a 25 per cent decline in industrial production is still a grave matter. However, it should be emphasised that the official statistics have exaggerated the declines in industrial production and, furthermore, to point out that revising the downward bias in the statistics reveals the vast range of activity taking place in the shadows of Russia's transition to a market economy.

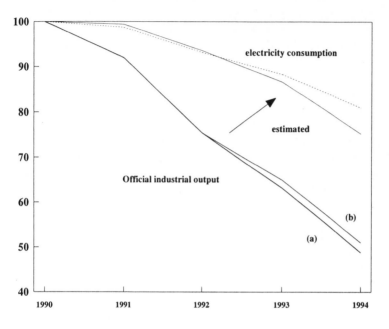

Figure 6.2   Industrial output and electricity consumption.

Our estimates assumed that electricity input coefficients for all sectors and consumption coefficients were stable. The electricity input coefficient for industry $a_{e,1}(t)$ in nominal terms was 0.022 for both 1990 and 1991, according to the 1990–91 input–output tables at producers' prices. Comparing input coefficients in nominal terms over periods can be affected by relative price fluctuations, but this does support the hypothesised stability. The final public consumption coefficient was also the same for both years at 0.017. Although the electricity input coefficient of the trade sector dropped sharply from 0.021 to 0.010, the electricity input coefficient of the non-industrial sector as a whole was stable.

The input coefficient of the industrial sector, $a_{e,1}(t)$ is quite stable at 0.019 for 1990, 0.018 for 1991 and 0.020 for 1992, according to the 1990-92 I-O table at purchasers' prices (in 1992, it was changed from an SNA-type to an MPS-type table). The consumption coefficient is also stable because of the large share of public consumption at 0.020, 0.018 and 0.020 in 1990, 1991 and 1992, respectively. The electricity coefficient of the trade sector was unstable in these three years at 0.022, 0.010 and 0.030, but was stable for the non-industrial sector as a whole.

The estimates given here were not derived from analysis of the direct and indirect relationships between the production of electricity and production in all other sectors. Therefore, we would like to amend our estimates by showing the results computed for the output inducement effect of one particular product. The data used here are taken from the 1989 I-O table (MPS non-competitive import type at producers' prices). Let us assume that output change in the sector does not result in any change in final demand for the other sectors.

Let the n-th sector be the selected sector. Assume that this sector's output X_n changes only by ΔX_n. Then the output changes in the other sectors induced by ΔX_n amount to:

$$
\begin{bmatrix}
\Delta X_i \\
\cdot \\
\cdot \\
\cdot \\
\Delta X_{n-1}
\end{bmatrix}
=
\begin{bmatrix}
b^d_{1n}/b^d_{nn} \\
\cdot \\
\cdot \\
\cdot \\
b^d_{n-1,n}/b^d_{nn}
\end{bmatrix}
\Delta X_n
$$

where $(b^d_{ij}) = (I - A^d)^{-1}$ and A^d is a matrix with elements of inputs domestically produced needed to produce one unit of each gross domestic output.

Using the above equation, we can compute the magnitude of the decrease in electricity output induced by a unit decrease in production for each sector, as shown in Figure 6.3. From this figure, it can be seen that the decreases in the output of the chemical, construction material, non-ferrous metal, and oil and gas sectors induced relatively greater decreases in electricity output. On the other hand, decreases in the output of the MBMW and light industry sectors induced relatively smaller decreases in electricity output.

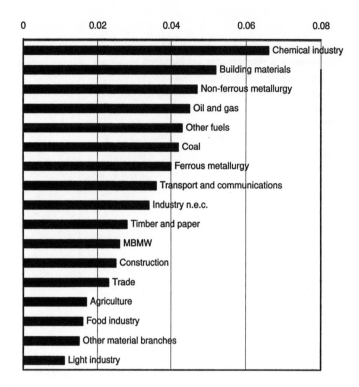

Figure 6.3 Electricity output drops induced by one unit drop of each output

According to the official industrial statistics, the MBMW and light industry sectors contributed strongly to the overall reduction in industrial output. Furthermore, the above input–output analysis suggests that the output decreases in the MBMW and light industry sectors were associated with relatively low decreases in electricity output. I do not dispute these findings; nor do I dispute the finding that the decreases in electricity consumption could be much less than the reductions in industrial production: our estimates indicate the same results. But it should be noted that the above findings in no way confirm the accuracy of the official statistics.

Figure 6.4, whose values are calculated using the above equation, shows the decline in production of each sector induced by a unit

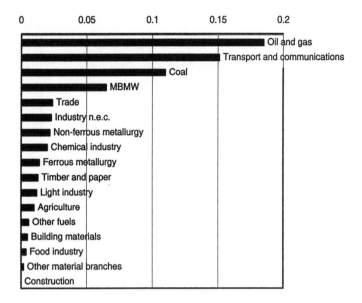

Table 6.4   Output drops induced by one unit drop of electricity output

decrease in the production of electricity. It also shows that relatively strong inducement effects are felt in the oil and gas, transport and communication, coal, and MBMW sectors. This implies that the oil and gas and MBMW sectors cannot function without electricity.

Alternative Estimates of Real GDP Growth Rates for 1991–95

The collapse of the Soviet Union led to the breakup of the traditional centralised system of statistics and inspection which, along with vast under-reporting or non-reporting of information by enterprises seeking to evade taxes, brought about marked downward biases in officially measured output, consumption, exports and imports. In order to resolve these biases, Goskomstat, at the beginning of 1994, first revised data on retail sales and paid services for 1992. However, Goskomstat did not then perform a systematic revision of GDP data, even though, in general, the household consumption component of GDP is directly related to retail trade and paid services and constitutes a major part of GDP. Gavrilenkov and Koen (1994) – hereafter referred to as G-K – presented alternative GDP growth figures for 1991–94 in November 1994. Their estimates, shown in Table 6.8, were derived by considering a downward bias of output and adjusting consumption figures based on revised data of retail sales, paid services and other factors. They concluded that the Russian GDP dropped not by half as then officially reported, but by about one-third. In October 1995, almost one year after the first G-K estimate of real GDP growth rates appeared, a joint Goskomstat-World Bank team published revised GDP estimates, also shown in Table 6.8, which are close to those given by Gavrilenkov and Koen while the joint team's results were mainly derived through the production approach (Goskomstat and World Bank (1995) and *Russian Statistical Yearbook for 1995*).

Table 6.8 Official and estimated figures for GDP growth, 1991–95

	1991	1992	1993	1994	1995
	Annual growth rates (per cent)				
Official data prior to revision	–12.8	–19.2	–12.0	–15.0	–
Official data after revision	–5.0	–14.5	–8.7	–12.6	–4.0
Estimated by Gavrilenko and Koen (G-K)	–6.4	–14.0	–7.5	–9.1	(–6.8)
Estimated by Kuboniwa (K-1)	–6.3	–13.4	–7.8	–11.0	(–3.0)
Estimated by Kuboniwa (K-2)	–3.3	–8.9	–5.6	–8.9	(–2.7)
	Index (1990 = 100)				
Official: prior to revision	87.2	70.5	62.0	52.7	–
Official: revised	95.0	81.2	74.2	64.8	62.2
Estimated by Gavrilenko and Koen (G-K)	93.6	80.5	74.5	67.7	(63.1)
Estimated by Kuboniwa (K-1)	93.7	81.1	74.8	66.6	(64.6)
Estimated by Kuboniwa (K-2)	96.7	88.1	83.2	75.8	(73.8)

Note: The figures in parentheses are preliminary estimates given by the authors, based on the corresponding methods.

Sources: Goskomstat RF, *Statistical Year Book 1995*; *Monthly Report*, 1995, No. 12; Gavrilenkov and Koen (1994, 1995); and Kuboniwa (199a, 1995b).

It should be noted that Goskomstat did not revise the official index of industrial production along with the revision of GDP figures. In recalculating real GDP growth figures, Goskomstat employs growth rates of industrial production which are almost equal to the official growth rates of industrial production shown in Table 6.1 (except for the figure for 1991). The department of national accounts of Goskomstat independently recalculated the annual growth rates of industrial production at –6 per cent, –18 per cent, –15 per cent and –21 per cent for 1991–94 while the department of industrial production of Goskomstat provided the official figures shown in Table 6.1, namely – 8 per cent, –18 per cent, –14 per cent and –21 per cent for the same years.

Kuboniwa (1996) computed the GDP growth rates for 1961–95 by employing a production approach which is similar to but simpler than the Goskomstat and World Bank method (the indicators used in deriving the GDP estimates given in the paper are given by Table 6.2). Part of these computational results is shown as K–1 in Table 6.8 where the official industrial production indexes (series (b) in Table 6.1) were faithfully used. On the other hand, K–2 in the table provides an alternative estimate of GDP growth figures where the estimates of industrial output growth presented in this paper were used.

As shown in Figure 6.5, the cumulative fall of GDP for 1991–94 in the revised official figures and the estimates G–K and K–1 converge on

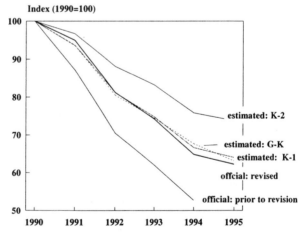

Figure 6.5   Official and estimated indexes of GDP growth in Russia, 1991–95 (1990 = 100)

around 35 per cent, while the estimate K–2 based on an upward revision of industrial production shows the smallest drop in GDP for the period, namely 27 per cent.

Micro-economic Aspects of Downward Bias of Industrial Output

Let us next consider the micro-economic foundations of the downward bias of industrial output. First, this downward bias is based on the presence of hyperinflation, which is characterised by a predominance of speculative behaviour along with a marked fall of productive investments on the part of private agents and by an acceleration of the inflationary process despite the efforts made by the government authorities.

With price rises of over 6 per cent per month (yearly 100 per cent), a firm with a relatively long cycle of production would earn rather higher profits in terms of the enterprise accounts than in the industry production account without inflation. However, taxes are levied on this nominal profit at a high rate of over 30 per cent. Using after-tax profits, the firm then has to compensate for the loss due to the inflation of material input prices. Let us show this by a simple formal analysis.

Assume that for the production, $x(t)$, in the t-th period the firm has to buy a material input, $k(t-s)$, in period $(t-s)$ at a price of $q(t-s)$. Letting $p(t)$ be the price of the firm's output, then the enterprise accounts record for the t-th period:

$$\text{Production} - \text{Materials used} = p(t)x(t) - q(t-s)k(t-s) \ (= Z); \quad (5)$$

whereas the production account of the industry without inflation is:

$$\text{Production} - \text{Intermediate inputs} = p(t)x(t) - q(t)k(t-s) \ (= Z^*) \quad (6)$$

Then the loss due to the inflation of material inputs amounts to: $q(t-s)k(t-s) - q(t)k(t-s)$. If taxes are not levied on the profit, Z, the firm can compensate for the loss by the extra profit due to the inflation, which amounts to:

$$Z - Z^* = q(t)k(t-s) - q(t-s)k(t-s) \quad (7)$$

However, if taxes are levied on profits at a rate u, and hyperinflation prevails, then the firm can not fully make up for the loss. The difference between the after-tax profit in the enterprise accounts and that in the production account of the industry amounts to:

$$(1-u)(Z - Z^*) = (1-u)[q(t)-q(t-s)]k(t-s) \qquad (8)$$

Therefore, as a result, the deficit for compensation of the loss amounts to $u[q(t) - q(t-s)]k(t-s)$. The greater the tax rate and inflation rate are, the larger this deficit becomes.

Thus, with proper functioning of the taxation system, hyperinflation is a threat even to the simple reproduction of the firm.[2] In order to survive, or to retain more of its own profits, the firm would need to send to the public authorities underestimated reports of its production and pre-tax profits. Indeed, manufacturing firms with rather long production cycles (firms producing watches, for example) complain of these inflation taxes and government tax policy, while firms with very short production cycles (firms producing chocolates and the like) do not suffer so much from this kind of inflation tax.[3]

Second, not only firms with long cycles of production but also other firms suffer inflation of durable equipment prices and relative price distortions such as a higher increase in prices of fuels and transportation. Every firm also has to deal with a marked increase in wages. In order to cover increasing costs and prepare for the expected difficulties, firms would like to avoid taxes as much as possible. Thus underestimated reports of outputs become a nation-wide phenomenon owing to inflation.

Third, the Russian Federal Government (the central government) has needed to increase revenues as much as possible under the decentralised system in order to repay the external debt burden accumulated in the former centralised system, and to meet the needs of the social safety net and demands for support from industry and agriculture. Under the prevailing decentralised taxation and budgetary

2. In fact, however, much of this problem really concerns the proper definition of profits under conditoions of rapid inflation, which most tax codes do not handle very well. [Editor's note]
3. Based on the author's interviews with managers of the 'First Watch Factory', the 'Second Watch Factory' and the 'Red October Chocolate Factory' in Moscow at the end of 1993.

system, local governments also needed to increase revenues to meet local needs. Under hyperinflation a high rate of profit tax apparently reduces the possibility of investment. However, the tax authorities do not rely on the Goskomstat statistics. Furthermore, they can easily collect a large amount of taxes from large-scale industrial firms, while they face serious difficulties in collecting taxes from a great number of new or small firms in the service sector. Thus the tax authorities continue to maintain a high profit tax policy. Firms, in turn, continue to try to evade taxes. This game between the general government and the firms cannot end until hyperinflation ends and the financial infrastructure develops sufficiently to meet the preconditions for a reasonably well-functioning market economy.

Lastly, it should be pointed out that firms' reports for industrial production statistics can be used for other purposes, including taxation, in Russia. In Japan, by contrast, by law the tax offices do not have access to firms' industrial output reports sent to MITI (the Ministry of International Trade and Industry of Japan) so that MITI can compile indexes of industrial outputs reflecting the actual production level in a well-defined manner.

Concluding Remarks

When we consider the micro-economic foundations of the Russian macro-economy, we need, first of all, a better understanding of its macro-economic performance. In this chapter, we have described the actual situation of the macro-economy, investigating the inconsistencies in the official statistics and the behaviour of economic agents. By performing this preliminary task we are better able to reconcile various different perceptions of the Russian economic situation: that the Russian economic performance is much better than indicated by the official figures, and that the general situation is far from good; or a perception that relies heavily on the macro-economic stabilisation policy, and another that makes much of structural reforms.

In conclusion, we would like to mention some remaining issues. First, this chapter did not deal with the factors contributing to a downward bias in output as officially measured in the Soviet era – namely, the effects of the so-called informal sector on the official output statistics for the period which was studied by Professors Grossman, Treml, Belkindas and others. Second, it did not check for consistency between the rapid growth of the service sector (material and non-material services) and our estimate of industrial production in the early transition. Third, it may be necessary to study how changes in industrial organisations have affected the statistics of electricity in physical terms, which is related to the treatment of internal consumption of electricity within an organisation in a dynamic context.

References

Cohen, D. (1994), 'Economic Transformation in Russia,' *Economics of Transition*, Vol. 2, No. 2, pp. 259–62.

Gavrilenkov, E. and V. Koen (1994), 'How Large Was the Output Collapse in Russia?,' *IMF Working Paper*, November.

—— (1995), 'How Large Was the Output Collapse in Russia? Alternative Estimates and Welfare Implications,' in IMF, *Staff Studies for World Economic Outlook* (Washington, DC).

Greenslade, R. (1972), 'Industrial Production Statistics in the USSR', in V. Treml and J. Hardt (eds), *Soviet Economic Statistics* (Durham, NC: Duke University Press).

Kornai, J. (1980), *Economics of Shortage* (Amsterdam: North Holland).

Kuboniwa, M.(1995a), 'From Upward to Downward Bias of Industrial Production,' *Financial Markets*, Jan.–Feb. pp.6–11.

—— (1995b), 'Al'ternativnaya otsenka tempov spada promyshlennogo proizvodstva v Rossii na osnove modeli "zatraty-vypusk"', *Finansovye rynki*, January–February.

—— (1996), 'Economic Growth in Postwar Russia' *Discussion Paper Series* B-11 (Tokyo: Institute of Economic Research Hitotsubashi University).

Kushnirsky, F. (1989), *Growth and Inflation in the Soviet Economy* (Boulder, CO: Westview).

Makarov, V. (1994), 'Dual Economy in Russia Today', *The Economic Review (Keizai Kenkyu)*, Vol. 45, No. 2, pp. 117–25.

Sapir, J. (1994), 'What's Going On in Russia', *Economics of Transition*, Vol. 2, No. 2, pp. 255–9.

Seliunin, V. and G. Khanin (1987), 'Lukavaya tsifra', *Novyi mir*, No. 2.

Shmelev, N. and G. Popov (1989), *The Turning Point: Revitalizing the Soviet Economy* (New York: New York University Press).

Treml, V. (1988), 'Perestroyka and Soviet Statistics', *Soviet Economy*, Vol. 4. No. 1, pp. 65–94.

Winiecki, J. (1995), 'The Applicability of Standard Reform Packages of Eastern Europe', *Journal of Comparative Economics*, Vol. 20, No. 3, pp. 347–67.

Part II

Country Studies

7 Polish Economic Reforms in Japanese Historical Perspective

Ken Morita

Introduction

It has been suggested that there are no superior strategies for the East European transition because 'There is no significant difference in the output decline of the countries implementing shock and gradual treatments. ... one can't say that countries in favour of a gradual approach (as Hungary and the Ukraine) are more successful than those preferring shock treatment'.[1]

This chapter sheds some indirect light on this controversy by showing that the policies adopted in Poland and other transition states were neither sufficiently stringent nor pro-competitive to have generated the efficiency gains achieved by the Japanese with their mixed use of shock therapy and gradualism.

High-speed Economic Growth in Postwar Japan

The standard authority on postwar Japanese economic transition and growth is Komiya (1975a and b). According to these sources, Japan's average annual growth rate of real GDP over the decade 1950–60 was 9.5 per cent, higher than experienced by most other industrialised countries including West Germany at 7.7 per cent, Italy at 6.0 per cent, France at 4.2 per cent, Canada at 3.7 per cent, the US at 3.3 per cent, and the UK at 2.8 per cent. This superior performance was propelled by high rates of savings and investment. The ratios of gross domestic

---

1. Stanley Fisher, early 1993, cited by Kiss (1993), p. 69.

saving to GNP in the industrialised countries during the decade 1950–60 were as follows; Japan 29.9 per cent, West Germany 26.0 per cent, Italy 20.5 per cent, France 18.4 per cent, Canada 22.5 per cent, USA 18.3 per cent, and the UK 15.5 per cent. The ratios of gross domestic investment to GNP during the same decade were Japan 28.9 per cent, West Germany 23.3 per cent, Italy 21.0 per cent, France 18.4 per cent, Canada 24.4 per cent, USA 17.6 per cent, and the UK 15.7 per cent.

Postwar Japanese marginal capital coefficients were also low, implying a very high efficiency of the newly-invested capital. The crucial factors in achieving this were as follows: (1) labour-intensive industries had a major share of industry as a whole; (2) postwar labour conversion from the military sector and excess labour in rural areas made the prices of labour (that is, wage rates) relatively cheap; (3) Japan rapidly transferred and diffused foreign technology; (4) market structures were mostly competitive; and (5) the distributions of income and assets became more equal, facilitating the achievement of economies of scale.

These supply-side opportunities were complemented by the high rates of domestic savings which obviated the need for foreign investment. Why did people save so much? Savings shares in the decade 1950–60 were as follows: private savings 37 per cent, depreciation allowances 26 per cent, government net saving 21 per cent, and corporate net saving 16 per cent. Private savings obviously played the major role. Government and corporate net savings as shares of GNP were actually lower in Japan than in other industrialised countries, as were depreciation allowances. But the ratio of private savings to GNP was much higher: 10.9 per cent, compared with West Germany's 8.7 per cent, Canada's 5.2 per cent, France's 4.3 per cent, the USA's 5.2 per cent, and the UK's 1.9 per cent. This high propensity is attributable to the unincorporated business sector. Although the exact propensity to save varied from year to year, figures for 1955 show that the ratio of saving in the unincorporated business sector was 25 per cent before tax (the agricultural sector's ratio was 10 per cent and the employee sector's was 8 per cent). About 38 per cent of the unincorporated business sector's saving was accumulated as investment in new business equipment. The ratio of their transient to overall income was higher than that for employees, who seemed to save money largely as a precaution.

Postwar Japanese Economic Reforms

Radical stabilisation versus gradual stabilisation

Japan lost 25 per cent of its capital stock during the Second World War and had more than 10 million jobless workers (more than 30 per cent of the total labour force) in late 1945, most of whom were transferred from the military sector. This is comparable in some respects with the Russian and East European economies, which have experienced 40–50 per cent declines in real GNP since 1990, with unemployment rates of 15–16 per cent or higher.

However, in Japan the unemployment rate had already decreased to 1.1 per cent, by 1947, with real GNP growth rate reaching 8.6 per cent, enabling per capita real GNP to recover to 55.3 per cent of the 1934–36 level (by 1949 the recovery had reached 68 per cent) (see Table 7.1).

Table 7.1 Main economic indicators of Japanese economic performance

Year	Real GNP growth %	Inflation (WPI) %	Unemployment rate %	Gross capital (1934–36 = 100)	Trade balance US$ million
1946		364.5	4.0	120.4	–238
1947	8.6	195.9	1.1	124.8	–267
1948	12.7	165.6	0.7	139.9	–285
1949	2.1	63.3	1.0	135.0	–195
1950	11.0	18.2	1.2	139.8	34
1951	13.0	38.8	1.1	145.4	–291

Sources: Ministry of Finance (1978); Morita (1993).

As far as the Engel's coefficient is concerned, this was 67.8 in 1946 and 60.1 in 1949, both higher than the 32.5 recorded for 1931. (Engel's coefficients for Poland for various labour categories were: employee 52.3, farmer 51.8 and pensioner 57.9 in 1990; employee 39.2, farmer 51.8 and pensioner 43.8 in 1993). How was full employment restored so quickly? The main reason seems to be the inflationary 'Ishibashi fiscal policy' of the first Yoshida cabinet, begun in May 1946, which caused prices to rise by 364.5 per cent in 1946 and 195.9 per cent in 1947, despite the Emergency Financial Measures Ordinance of 16 February 1946, introduced by the Shidehara cabinet. Under this programme, all deposits were frozen. Old currency greater than 5 yen could not be circulated and only 100 yen could be changed into the new currency by each individual. Money circulation decreased by 50 per cent following these measures, and cash plus non-frozen deposits diminished by 70 per cent. Moreover, on 3 March 1946, a new property tax (with rates between 25 and 90 per cent) was imposed, and was expected to absorb 9.2 per cent of nominal GNP in 1946.[2]

The Ishibashi policy lingered on until 1949, when it was replaced by the shock therapy of the Dodge Program, aimed at improving economic efficiency. Although employment was already 21 per cent above the level of 1930, production was still only 39 per cent of the 1930 level. Also, the money supply had drastically increased from 173 billion yen in February 1947 to 413 billion in February 1948, and the trade balance was in huge deficit, with exports covering only 30 per cent of imports.

Faced with excess money expansion, low labour productivity and low exportability, Dodge imposed a tight policy, forcing firms and workers to be self-sufficient and reducing Japanese dependence on US assistance, which reached 5 per cent of Japanese GNP in the years 1946–49. These goals were accomplished by eliminating the budget deficit, terminating loans issued by the Reconstruction Finance Bank, establishing the US Aid Counterpart Fund Special Account, and setting a unified exchange rate. Reconstruction Finance Bank loans were un-sterilised, and stopping them automatically decreased the money supply. The US Aid Counterpart Fund Special Account promoted efficiency by ending the practice of using US Aid commodities receipts to subsidise firms and institutions. Multiple exchange rates also provided hidden subsidies through the undervaluation of yen exports and the overvaluation of yen imports.

This sharp policy change provoked a debate over the comparative merits of shock therapy and gradualism, that is, 'one-shot radical stabilisation versus intermediate gradual stabilisation'. The shock therapists insisted that radical monetary reform was the elixir of sustainable

2. See Kosai (1995), p. 20.

rapid growth, while the gradualists emphasised improved resource allocation through a policy such as the 'priority production system'.[3]

The specifics of the gradualist proposals are interesting, because they showed a shared concern with the shock therapists for monetary stabilisation, but added a greater concern for industrial policy. The programme called for the absorption of the monetary overhang within six months, followed during the succeeding year by a full-scale, staged deflationary initiative, supplemented over the next three–four years with a concerted development programme.

Structural Reforms

The key feature of the Japanese reform strategy was the elimination of anti-competitive barriers to efficiency including: (1) deconcentration policies, such as the dissolution of the Zaibatsu, the Law for the Elimination of Excessive Concentration of Economic Power, and the Anti-Monopoly Law; and (2) Agricultural Land Reform Policies which led to a more equitable distribution of income and assets.

It is very difficult to prove scientifically the relationship between deconcentration policies and competitive market structures.[4] However, we could say there have been some connections between the two. According to Nakamura, these policies worked: 'In most industries, the concentration ratio particularly of the largest three companies was lowered. And it helped to make the conditions for keen competition which was the feature for postwar Japanese industries' (Nakamura, 1989, p.153). Comparing concentration ratios in 1937 with those in 1950, the ratios of the largest three firms in particular sectors of industry were reduced as follows: in the pulp industry, from 65.2 per cent to 39.5 per cent; in the caustic soda industry, from 55.1 per cent to 33.8 per cent; in the marine transportation industry from 29.8 per cent to 18.1 per cent.

The agricultural land reform policies – the redistribution of land ownership rights from landlords to tillers – were drastic. They were decided by the General Headquarters of the Supreme Commanders for the Allied Powers (GHQ) and approved in the Diet on 11 October

3. Such an assertion, insisting on the importance of industrial policy, is sometimes maintained by Central and East European economists who are quite knowledgeable about the Japanese economy. See, for example, Bakos (1994).

4. See, for example, Miwa (1993).

1946. They caused the share of tenanted land to decrease dramatically from 46 per cent in 1941 to just 13 per cent in 1949. During the period of high rates of inflation, agricultural land values decreased. 'In 1939 the price of 1 tan [= 0.099 hectares] of good paddy land was equivalent to over 3,000 packs of cigarettes or 31 tons of coal. In 1948, however, it was equivalent to only 13 packs of cigarettes or 0.24 tons of coal' (Kawagoe, 1993, p.195), facilitating peasant ownership.

The results of these efforts were successful, although it might not always seem so because of the high concentration ratios in many Japanese industries. For example, according to the World Bank (1993), the concentration ratio of the largest three companies in Japan in 1980 was 56 per cent (averaging across sectors), far higher than in Taiwan, the USA, Brazil and Argentina. None the less, competition among firms in the same industry has been keen and contributed significantly to Japan's postwar economic growth. Apparently, the potential for new entry keeps firms competitive.

This suggests that the post-communist transition states might be well advised to pay attention to their industrial policy, especially since some of them continue to resist effective monetary stabilisation. Pro-competitive programmes, following the Japanese example, would obviously be desirable, as might more directive policies of the sort championed by MITI as long as they promote infant industries capable of being – or becoming – competitive without entrenching other, inefficient firms. MITI attempted to master this juggling act by applying income elasticity and productivity tests,[5] which will suffice when they happen to correspond with the more demanding Mill and Bastable criteria.

According to Bastable, infant industry assistance is justified when the (present value of) social benefit exceeds (present value of) social cost. The cost has two components:[6] (1) tariffs normally reduce consumption and (2) the opportunity costs of importable substitutes are too high. These aspects can be illustrated with the aid of Figure 7.1.[7] The horizontal axis plots quantities, the vertical axis prices,

5. Concerning the tests, see Komiya (1984).
6. See Grubel (1966).
7. If we adhere strictly to the MITI criterion on elasticity, Figure 7.1a should be used in place of Figure 7.1, implying that, as the income level increases, the demand curve shifts from DD to D'D', and a more elastic demand gives rise to a more rapid demand increase towards q_w starting from q_d. Readers should re-read

showing the international price level p_w and domestic price level p_d. The equilibrium quantities corresponding to p_w and p_d are q_w and q_d respectively.

The first social cost, a decrease of consumers' surplus, is indicated in Figure 7.1 as the area of the triangle BAC, because with decreased consumption, from $0q_w$ to $0q_d$, consumers' surplus decreases by BAC. And the second social cost, due to distorted resource allocation, is shown by the rectangle $p_w p_d AB$ because, given the cost of domestic importables, the quantity $0q_d$ defines the import opportunity cost rectangle $0p_d Aq_d$. Deducting the import payment $0p_w Bq_d$ from the cost $0p_d Aq_d$ results in a net allocational inefficiency loss indicated by $p_w p_d AB$.

The total social cost attributable to government protection is the trapezoid $p_w p_d AC$.

Infant industry subsidies are justified if the total (present valueof) social benefit exceeds the total (present value of) social cost. This may occur when (i) the domestic price level p_d falls towards the international price level p_w, and/or (ii) q_d rapidly approaches q_w. (i) may hold when productivity is increasing sharply and (ii) when demand is elastic. Both these conditions are considered to have held in the post-war Japanese case and could apply selectively in Eastern Europe.

Polish Economic Reforms: The Current Situation

Poland began experimenting with shock therapy on 1 January 1990, when it adopted the Balcerowicz Programme. The goals of the programme, influenced by the IMF and World Bank were: (1) disinflation, (2) the eradication of shortages, (3) a sound national currency, (4) privatisation and structural reform. 'From January to March in 1990, a 50 per cent decrease of the money stock in real terms took place' and the programme led 'to the appearance of excess supply and the development for the first time in 45 years'.[8] But these gains were accompanied by unexpectedly severe depression.

Figure 7.1 in the text, not as describing a movement from A to C along the same demand curve DD, but as a demand curve shift from DD to D'D' and then moving from A to C.

8 . National Bank of Poland (1990), p. 7.

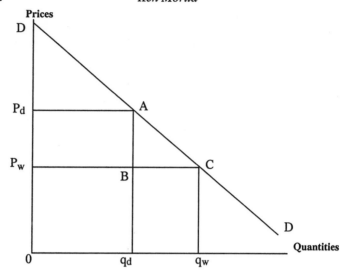

Figure 7.1a

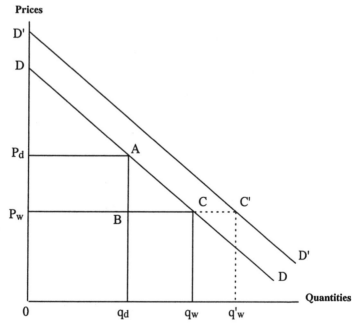

Figure 7.1b

Several years later the debate over the wisdom of the Balcerowicz Programme continues. The real GNP growth rate turned positive after 1992 and inflation followed at a moderate rate 30–40 per cent annually, evaluated from the standpoint of other transition states. However, inflation is hardly negligible and the unemployment rate was approaching 15–16 per cent by the middle of the decade. The inflationary overhang persists. Queuing for goods in short supply has been eliminated by raising prices to clear the market.[9]

The evidence on privatisation and structural reform is likewise mixed. The main purpose of the Balcerowicz Programme was to purge the economy of its inefficiency. Few in Poland believe this has been accomplished, despite the evidence in Table 7.2 showing a rising rate of aggregate growth in the vicinity of 5 per cent per annum and industrial production expanding (from –11.9 per cent in 1991 compared with the previous year) to 3.9 per cent in 1992, 6.2 per cent in 1993 and 11.9 per cent in 1994.

Table 7.2 Main economic indicators of Polish economic performance

Year	Real GNP growth %	Inflation (CPI) %	Unemployment rate %	Change in investment (year to year)	Trade balance (convertible) US$ million
1990	–11.6	585.8	6.1	–10.0	2214
1991	–7.6	70.3	11.8	–4.0	51
1992	2.6	43.0	13.6	0.7	512
1993	3.8	35.3	16.4	1.0	–2293
1994	5.0	32.2	16.0		–836

Sources: Morita (1993); World Economy Research Institute (various years).

Scepticism, however, is in order because real monthly income in Poland is shrinking, the income and assets distribution have been extremely inegalitarian,[10] and official statistics are suspect. For example, the official unemployment rate in Poland stood at about 15 per cent in the mid-1990s, but if involuntary pensioners are counted the number of unemployed workers increases to 11.5 million and the effective

9. According to Kornai (1993), the same thing occurred in Hungary.
10. See, for example, Bożyk (1992) and WERI (1994).

unemployment rate to 40 per cent.[11] Also, monopolistic market structures remain entrenched, particularly in large-scale manufacturing industries, and privatisation has been half-hearted, amounting to only 10 per cent of the potential in the industrial sector five years after the start of the reforms.

To sum up, institutional reform has been feeble and income and assets redistribution perverse. For this reason, it is hard to believe that Poland's growth path of over 5 per cent a year will prove to be sustainable.

Polish Economic Reforms in Japanese Historical Perspective

The Polish and Japanese postwar transition strategies have elements in common. Both used shock therapy to dampen inflation and spur efficiency, bolstered by structural reforms. The differences, however, are equally stark. In addition to variations in timing, Poland's shock therapy was less stringently implemented and its structural reforms have been limited. As a consequence, inflation remains pronounced and efficiency gains have been meagre, casting doubt on Poland's long-term modernisation potential.

The Japanese example demonstrates that Poland might have done much better with a firmer stabilisation programme, and stronger pro-competitive policies, perhaps including a MITI-type infant industry nurturing strategy. The same conclusion holds for a gradualist strategy since we have seen in the Japanese case that this did not preclude monetary stabilisation. The central lesson of this comparison, therefore, is that neither shock therapy nor gradualism mean much if the underlying policies do not do enough to create competitively efficient markets.

References

Bakos, G. (1994), 'Hungarian Transition after Three Years', *Europe–Asia Studies*, Vol. 46, No. 7.

Bożyk, P. (1992), *Kto Winien?* (Who Is Responsible?) (Warsaw: PAE).

11. See, for example, Bożyk (1995).

—— (1995), *Polityka Gospodarcza Polski 1985–2000* (Political Economy of Poland 1985–2000) (Warsaw: PWSH).

Grubel, H.G. (1966), 'The Anatomy of Classical and Modern Infant Industry Arguments', *Weltwirtschaftliches Archiv*, No. 97.

Kawagoe, T. (1993), 'Land Reform in Postwar Japan', in J. Teranishi and Y. Kosai (eds), *The Japanese Experience of Economic Reforms* (New York: St. Martin's Press, and London: Macmillan, pp. 178–204.

Kiss, K. (1993), *Western Prescriptions for Eastern Transition* (Budapest: Hungarian Scientific Council for World Economy).

Komiya, R. (1975a), 'Sengo Nihon no Shihon Chikusekiritsu' (Capital Formation Proportions in Postwar Japan), in R. Komiya (ed.), *Gendai Nihon Keizai Kenkyu*.

—— (1975b), 'Kojin Chochiku no Kyokyu' (Personal Saving Supply), in Komiya (ed.), *Gendai Nihon Keizai Kenkyu*.

—— (1984), 'Jyosho' (Introduction to Industrial Policy in Japan), in R. Komiya et al. (eds), *Nihon no Sangyo Seisaku* (Industrial Policy in Japan) (Tokyo: Tokyo University Press).

Kornai, J. (1993), 'Transzformacios visszaeses' (Transformational recession), *Kozgazdasagi Szemle*.

Kosai, Y. (1995), *Yen no Sengoshi* (Postwar History of Japanese Yen) (Tokyo: NHK).

Ministry of Finance (1978), *Showa Zaisei-shi* (The Fiscal Policy of the Showa Era) (Tokyo: Toyo Keizai Shinpo-sha).

Miwa, Y. (1993), 'Economic Effects of the Anti-Monopoly and other Deconcentration Policies in Postwar Japan,' in J. Teranishi and Y. Kosai, *The Japanese Experience of Economic Reforms*.

Morita, K. (1993), 'A Comparative Analysis between Postwar Japanese Economic Reforms and Current Polish Economic Reforms' in Hans-Georg Fleck and Ryszard Lawniczak (eds), *Alternative Models of Market Economy for Transition Economies* (Poznań: SORUS Press).

Nakamura, T. (1989), *Nihon Keizai – Seicho to Kozo* (Japanese Economy – Growth and Structure) (Tokyo: Tokyo University Press).

National Bank of Poland (1990), *Annual Report 1990* (Warsaw).

Teranishi, J., and Y. Kosai (eds) (1993), *The Japanese Experience of Economic Reforms* (Basingstoke: Macmillan).

World Economy Research Institute (1992), *Poland: International*

Economic Report (Warsaw: Warsaw School of Economics).

—— (1994), *Poland: International Economic Report* (Warsaw: Warsaw School of Economics).

—— (1995), *Poland: International Economic Report* (Warsaw: Warsaw School of Economics).

World Bank (1993), *The East Asian Miracle* (Oxford: Oxford University Press).

8 Theories of Disintegration of the USSR

Hillel H. Ticktin

Introduction

The question of why the Soviet Union disintegrated has become more controversial as the time from its disintegration increases. Most Sovietologists did not expect the USSR to come to an end but they subsequently tried to recoup and discover reasons for its demise. As a result there is now a whole variety of viewpoints.

I will outline five popular attitudes, which are more or less representative, and then go on to criticise them and discuss possible alternative theories. Michael Ellman,[1] among others, has argued that the introduction of the Law on the State Enterprise of 1986 was the crucial change that brought about the end of the Soviet Union. The view that Gorbachev somehow became General Secretary and then changed the system, largely on his own, is another variant of this view.[2] Professor Abel Aganbegyan, along with many Western economists, has argued the intensive–extensive thesis: he takes the view that the USSR reached a point of diminishing returns in respect of the extraction of raw materials, in the use of labour and in the utilisation of machinery. The popular economists' and journalistic view is that all state enterprises were bankrupt. Thus *The Economist* journal certainly appears to

---

1. See Michael Ellman and Vladimir Kontorovich, *The Disintegration of the Soviet Economic System* (London and New York: Routledge, 1992). Michael Ellman has correctly pointed out that I exaggerated his viewpoint. He does provide a number of significant conditions for the decline of the Soviet Union. I am still left with the feeling that he sees Gorbachev and his actions as absolutely crucial.
2. See Archie Brown, *The Gorbachev Factor* (Oxford: Oxford University Press, 1996). The whole book is devoted to this hypothesis.

give the impression that planning, state holdings and the monopoly of foreign trade were all responsible for the decrepitude of the Soviet economy. Boris Kagarlitsky, on the other hand, has a more or less empirical description of the last days of the Soviet Union but he also seems to think, along with Alexander Buzgalin,[3] that the Soviet elite decided to bring an end to the Soviet Union in order to maintain and extend their power and privileges. Alexander Dallin has summarised various attitudes[4] in a useful analytical article. He argues that there was no single cause but a series. His multifactor approach is effectively a fifth viewpoint. These five approaches can be described as the accidental, the economically necessary, non-market illegitimacy, the elite's subjective desire, and multifactoral. Dallin has spoken of the essentialist and non-essentialists which is another divide. I do not agree with any of these and will outline my own viewpoint after disposing of the rest. The two that I will deal with first are the illegitimacy argument and then the one of a multiplicity of factors.

The Market Viewpoint: The Illegitimacy of the USSR

The market viewpoint is widely accepted in academia, advisers to the countries of the former Soviet Union, and right-wing publications. They argue that the USSR contravened the laws of economics and hence foundered. This view is based on the attitude that the market is eternal. From this it would follow that planning is impossible. It is argued that the economy may be organised for a time but it will be incapable of raising productivity to international levels. As a theoretical approach it has often been discussed over the past two hundred years and refuted. To assume that any existing system is eternal is simply a mode of supporting the status quo. There is no logical reason to assume it. Capitalism is so obviously a failure in terms of supplying basic necessities to the majority of mankind that, at the most minimal level, it would be difficult to assume that mankind would not find an

---

3. A. Buzgalin and A. Kolganov, *Tragediya sotsializma* (Moscow: Ekonomicheskaya demokratiya, 1992), p. 156. The authors write of an evolutionary transformation from an authoritarian–bureaucratic system to a *nomenklatura* capitalism, which was speeded up by the failed *putsch* of August 1991.

4. Alexander J. Dallin, 'Causes of Collapse of the USSR', *Post-Soviet Affairs*, Vol. 8 (October–December 1992).

alternative. A society which prides itself on mass unemployment, increasing polarisation of incomes and billions living on the brink of starvation, when so-called rich countries are destroying their food surpluses, has no justification, except the one which concerns this chapter: that there really is no alternative. The Soviet Union was worse, it is argued, and this proves that the only alternative to capitalism is a better capitalism.

It is clear that the arguments on the nature of the disintegration of the USSR do not take place in an ideological vacuum and each viewpoint has a political outcome. In the end, each viewpoint or theory must take a position on the nature of the period of transition to capitalism. For some countries the transition will be difficult but successful while for others it is a transition to nowhere.

Indeed, to argue that the market is the best possible of all alternative worlds, there has to be a powerful reason or series of reasons. The usual reasons are little more than ideological justifications for a system of inequality put forward by its beneficiaries. It is to be expected that the British periodicals *The Economist* and the *Financial Times* would take a pro-market position, given their ownership, staff and audience. Equally, since academic appointment and promotion are controlled to a greater or lesser extent by governments, even if indirectly, we could not expect a professor to oppose the market. This is not to say that arguments ought not to be refuted on their own terms. It is only to say that the unqualified support for the market is methodologically primitive even if it is mechanically sophisticated.

Conditions for a Successful Theory of Disintegration

Arguments based on the alleged superiority of the market ought therefore to be set aside as primitive teleology. The source of the failure of the USSR has to be sought in the nature of its political economy. Looked at from this point of view there are only a limited number of possibilities. First, there may never have been a mode of production, that is, a particular form of extracting the surplus product, with accompanying laws. In non-Marxist terms it could be argued that no socioeconomic system had gelled. There were rulers and ruled existing in the only empirical way that they could. In the second place, the USSR may have disintegrated because it had a new mode of production which had exhausted itself. In the third place, it could be held that the USSR was capitalist but that it was totalitarian and it could no longer maintain its totalitarian nature, for a particular reason. This is the theory of all those who held that it was either totalitarian or state-capitalist. They hold that the USSR was an inferior capitalism and had to give way to a superior form. In the fourth place it can be argued that the USSR disintegrated for accidental reasons and hence no theory is required for its disintegration. A theory must, however, be provided to explain how such a society could succumb to an accident. Paul Sweezy has advanced a different and fifth argument: that the USSR disintegrated because socialism was victorious in a part of the world where it could only be weak. Therefore, it could not compete with modern capitalism.[5]

For a theory to be successful it has to fulfil certain conditions. It must be able to link categories, such as labour, to a mode of change. It must show how the form of the category could no longer be maintained. Thus, it can be argued that labour in the USSR was atomised, which led to low productivity, which led to increased levels of discontent and eventually to an absolute barrier in production. In short, the theory must be able to show why the USSR came into existence, why it industrialised the country and why that could not be maintained. In theoretical terms, every category and form comes into being, matures and declines, and a theory must demonstrate the way in which its categories and forms have evolved over time.

It should be noted that a hypothesis is not the same as a theory. Empiricists tend to provide speculative reasons for occurrences and then call them hypotheses. If a number of predictions and so-called facts confirm their speculation they conclude that they have a theory. Put another way, a theory is not a model. A model is essentially static, predictive and empiricist. A theory must provide an explanation and hence an understanding of change between social groups over time.

The accidental viewpoint clearly will not fit into this characterisation. It does not constitute a theory. Hence any discussion of it must be

5. Paul Sweezy, 'Socialism: Legacy and Renewal', *Monthly Review*, January 1993, pp. 2–6; see also Paul Sweezy, 'Preface for a New Edition of Post-Revolutionary Society', *Monthly Review*, July–August 1990, where he argues that the Soviet Union was not socialist, so that socialism had not failed. None the less, he appears to see the Soviet Union as having certain achievements which are to be offset against its failures.

of a different form. It must discuss the relative stability of the USSR and where the Soviet Union was heading so that an accident could throw it off course.

What Is Disintegration?

Distinctions

It is necessary at this stage to make a distinction between the *trigger* for the disintegration and the disintegrative process itself. The final act of political disintegration occurred at the end of 1991 when Ukraine refused to continue in the Soviet Union; but this was merely the final act or trigger which brought the Soviet Union to an end. There is another distinction to be made – between the immediate cause and the underlying process. Thus Gorbachev passed a series of decrees which clearly assisted the process of disintegration, but the disintegration itself already existed before Gorbachev came into office. The decision of the elite to move to the market – a decision implemented by Gorbachev – was itself motivated by the fear which the disintegrative process had aroused in the elite.[6] It is necessary, therefore, to look at the driving cause, the immediate cause and the final event which brought the system to an end.

It is also important, at the outset, to make a distinction between *breakdown* and disintegration. From one point of view, the Soviet Union dissolved into its constituent national parts by the end of 1991 and so disintegrated politically. It did not break down as in Yugoslavia, where the constituent parts went to war. Yet, the Soviet Union as such ceased to exist and so reached a natural terminus, but it was a political terminus. The society did not break down, although Stalinism ceased to rule. The worsening and precipitate malfunctioning of the economy was largely the result of the reforms. Although the economy was in dire straits before, it had not collapsed. Soviet political economy was

6. 'The real reason for perestroika 10 years ago was to preserve a system that was breaking down on its own', says Yevgueni Nemets. 'Since then there have really been two layers of change – official change, which has mostly been geared toward preserving the old power centers, and the spontaneous changes that are the result of the old system breaking down and haphazard reforms': quoted in Therese Raphael, 'Russians Raise Their Expectations', *Wall Street Journal*, 9 July 1996.

disintegrating over a period of ten to twenty years but it could have continued disintegrating for longer. In the period 1988–91, it came as close to an economic breakdown, by most social and economic indicators, as is possible for an industrialised economy. The breakdown, however, was the result of a long period of disintegration which was brought to a head by Gorbachev's measures. I would argue that the political disintegration and disappearance were a consequence of this process.

The relative economic figures are well known and undisputed in these terms. (The problem with them is that their absolute numbers remain a matter of contention, for which reason there is no need to cite them.) The point, however, is that industrial rates of growth had become low to negative by the late 1970s, while agriculture effectively stagnated, and this decline can be shown to be part of an earlier pattern. In itself, an economic decline does not necessarily lead to change, of course, but the Stalinist regime had come to rely on industrial expansion and, under Khrushchev, raising the standard of living, as one of the bases of its stability.

This chapter is not concerned with the final end of the Soviet Union or the immediate trigger, which in principle could have been a series of unpredictable events, but the process which made the trigger possible.

Disintegration defined

Put into a more general perspective we can regard disintegration as a process which occurs when supersession cannot take place or, in non-Hegelian terms, when the new society cannot replace the old society, when a new ruling class cannot replace the old, worn-out rulers. The poles of the contradiction governing the society cannot interpenetrate. They pull apart and hence all parts and sections of that society stand in antagonism to one another. Production stands opposed to consumption, agriculture to industry, town against country, heavy industry against light industry, workers against managers, and so on.

At the same time, the USSR was not capitalist, and it did not have the same laws or contradictions. Even those who argue that it did are obliged to argue that these same laws have to be reinterpreted or understood in a modified way. The point here is that the process of disintegration cannot be understood except in terms of the substance of that disintegration. At this point, only a view which sees the USSR as essentially unformed or the form of no form – that is, as a non-mode of production – can make sense of disintegration. The essential fact is that the USSR *disintegrated*: it was not overthrown from inside or outside. At this point, I have to go back to my own theory as expounded over twenty years ago.[7] We have to understand the USSR in terms of antagonistic laws: the law of organisation and the law of self-interest. It was the imposition of the organisation forms deriving from the first law which held the country together, but that was possible only under certain conditions of which the most important, in my view, was the flow of surplus labour. I shall return to this point. At this juncture I am arguing that the disintegration can be explained by observing the inherent instability of Stalinism and asking what held it together. The exhaustion of the factors of production approach does take this view indeed, and I discuss its weaknesses and strengths below.

Some Old Views

The standard constellation of views of the collapse of the USSR refers to the following features.

1. The Soviet Union had exhausted its ability to exploit labour, raw materials and machinery. Whereas for a time it could use these resources extensively, eventually intensive development was needed.
2. The modern Soviet and Russian argument is in terms of the new technological revolution which the Soviet Union could not surmount. Western theorists would tend to talk of hi-tech industries rather than a new technological revolution.
3. It was accidental in that the regime was squeezed economically by a fall in the price of gold and a fall in the price of oil.
4. It was accidental in that Gorbachev introduced a series of measures whose effect he did not understand or expect, as with Michael Ellman's or Archie Brown's views referred to above. It is true that Michael Ellman does see a number of more necessary reasons as playing a critical role.

7. See my original article, 'Towards a Political Economy of the USSR', *Critique*, No. 1 (Glasgow, 1973).

5. A new generation had come of age and it no longer agreed with communism. It therefore set about overthrowing the old system.
6. The West had succeeded economically whereas the Soviet Union had failed, and this undermined the internal ideology. No one supported the old regime and it crumbled.
7. National differences, which were aeons old, could no longer be suppressed. The empire could no longer be maintained.
8. It was caused by the Reagan squeeze.

The left has produced other arguments for the downfall of the old system. These reasons are more social, with the stress on the ruling group or class. They do not really address the question of disintegration as opposed to the ending of Stalinism. Hence they argue:

9. The Soviet Union succumbed to capitalism; counter-revolution finally succeeded after all its failures.
10. The old ruling class had exhausted its possibilities and preferred to transfer from state capitalism to capitalism.
11. The ruling caste found an opportunity which they had long sought to transfer to capitalism.
12. The *nomenklatura* were afraid to continue along the old road and sought to find a more stable alternative.

I will go through these arguments, taking what is valid in each case and discarding the dross. For this purpose, however, I will consider these views under more general headings. The economic arguments are closely interrelated and I will consider them first.

The Intensive–Extensive Argument

The intensive–extensive argument is the most important semi-theory but it rests on dubious grounds. If it means anything it must refer to the argument that at some late time the USSR used increasing volumes of its resources without an accompanying rise in productivity. It also relies on the diminishing returns to scale argument which is always insufficient. There is no automatic reason why greater use of capital (for instance) will lead to a decline in productivity. The fact that unemployment declines and workers may demand better conditions and higher wages and so cause a decline in returns to capital is not automatic but social. It is clearly true that Soviet raw materials were used wastefully and that some became more costly to extract or obtain over time. It is also true that the return to amounts invested had declined very considerably over time. There is a reason in each case, however. Returns to investment had often become negative because of the nature of the social relationships both within the enterprise and within the society. Negative attitudes to the introduction of new machinery and a refusal to reorganise production to cope do not have to do with investment but with declining forms of social control. Raw materials were extracted or grown on a massive scale in the USSR. At the same time, it is clear from the oil company scramble to buy into the former Soviet Union's energy resources that the Soviet Union continued to have massive quantities of oil and gas. The problem was that, on the one hand, large quantities were simply wasted because of the nature of the system, while on the other the Soviet Union was not able to use the most modern techniques to extract the raw materials because of the essential conservatism of the system. We are therefore driven, it seems to me, to the question of labour as the only resource which was crucial.

When discussing the disintegration of the USSR, it is necessary to explain the declining growth rates. I argued above that it was the shortage of labour which was crucial.[8] Orthodoxy has it that the problem lay in the need to move from the extensive exploitation of resources, which in their terminology includes labour, to intensive exploitation. The fact that the regime was indeed almost founded on that very precept seems to have passed them by. What, after all, were the Five Year Plans about if not the production and use of modern technology in order to exploit resources more intensively? The whole nature of the Five Year Plans lay in the introduction and building up of heavy industry in order to supply the machinery with which to replace labour and raise productivity.[9] The Soviet Union made more machine

---

8. I have argued this case in more detail in my book, *Origins of the Crisis in the USSR: Essays in the Political Economy of a Disintegrating Society* (Armonk, NY: M.E. Sharpe, 1995).

9. The accumulation of capital in the Soviet Union allowed many formerly unproductive workers to move out of agriculture into industry, and this certainly raised average productivity in the economy as a whole. It did not, however, lead to rapid or large increases in productivity within industry itself. [Editor's note]

tools than the United States. Workers did not work themselves to the bone. On the contrary, the usual elite view was that they did nothing. Raw materials were certainly extracted in a wasteful way, but not without machinery or without raising productivity over time. Labour, machinery and raw materials were all used in a wasteful way, but this is only to state that the system was wasteful. What, then, can be meant by a shift to more intensive use of resources? If it means a reduction in waste then that ought to be said directly. In short, the concept is derived from a functionalist social science which could not cope with regimes in process of rapid movement.

The upshot of this discussion is that the problem with the USSR was certainly socio-economic, but it was not because it had simply used up its resources that it collapsed. It is true that the USSR was not capable of introducing new technology rapidly and that the newest electronic technology was causing it particular problems. None the less, it had coped before, even if by copying the West and even if it was done slowly. The problem lay, therefore, in the particular form of electronics, which required high-quality production. That, indeed, was the real problem. Poor quality on the other hand was a consequence of the social relations of production, and hence we return once again to labour.

Ideology and its Alternatives

The argument that the old controlling ideology was no longer believed is dubious. The Stalinist system had a set of conflicting beliefs from anti-Semitism, Soviet nationalism and anti-egalitarianism to their exact opposites. Reality was always very different from the school textbooks and *Pravda*. Few could then have believed the official propaganda. The exact role of so-called Marxism-Leninism is another question. Only the very ignorant could actually have believed that the Stalinist regime was anything but the negation of a socialist society. Some Western discussions of this question are distinguished mainly by their own ignorance of Marxism, in that they discuss the Stalinist regime as if it were Marxist. There is no question of fanatical believers trying to implement an unnatural utopia which reached its inevitable ideological end. The Stalinist elite were always corrupt, pragmatic and profoundly anti-Marxist. The semi-Marxist slogans were used in the same way that Hitler employed the word socialism and corrupted socialist slogans. A genuinely Marxist or socialist regime would be distinguished by its attempt to move to the goals of a socialist society, namely egalitarianism, the elimination of the state, internationalism and hence antinationalism, and increasing levels of direct control from the workers or ordinary people.[10] It is doubtful whether the regime would ever have received a substantial positive vote in an open and contested election. In that sense the regime was always unstable, as it lacked any social base in the society. It was effectively rendered even more unstable by the patent collision of Soviet reality with Marxist goals, when they continued to pay lip service to Marx and Lenin.

Members of the society did not change their minds. On the other hand, both the intelligentsia and the workers became progressively less afraid of the regime over time. As the distance from the purges increased, and as shooting workers became more costly, the secret police lost their power over society. The totalitarian theorists, whom Dallin correctly criticises, never expected their 'pillars of the society' – the one party state, the repressive apparatus and the ideological control – to disintegrate. While repression was absolutely critical to an understanding of the society, that repression had itself to be understood and explained beyond a simplistic statement of evil gangsters or demented revolutionaries in control. In fact, it would now appear that even the totalitarian theorists underestimated the degree of repression. The critical political economic role of the atomisation of society consequent on that repression provided a key to an understanding of the evolution of the repression and atomisation of the Stalinist society and hence to its decline also.

Forms of Control and their Decay

Both intelligentsia and workers increased in numbers and relative strength. The potential power of the work-force grew considerably down to the time of Gorbachev. Concentrated in large factories and enterprises, with the major enterprises themselves concentrated in strategic towns, the workers had come of age. This had the dual effect

10. How do we know these would be the goals of a socialist society? [Editor's note]

of challenging the regime and forcing the regime to make concessions of a social-democratic kind. From Khrushchev onwards, the regime continued its old form of atomisation but it added a form of welfare state with free health and education, together with full employment and rising living standards. These rested in part on cheap transport, housing and utilities. This did not gain the regime general support but it meant that opposition was less militant than it might otherwise have been. Hence the intelligentsia complained bitterly about the passivity of the work-force. None the less, the work-force resisted in the only manner possible under the circumstances, through its control over the labour process. In turn, this meant that the low productivity, poor quality goods and backward technology increasingly stood opposed to the attempts to raise the standard of living or increase the surplus product in order to expand production.

As long as the work-force was increasing, this effect was masked by the use of the new labour flowing into production; but once that dried up, as it did in the mid-1970s, the regime was doomed. A series of effects then began to show themselves from the declining growth rates, declining standard of living, declining life expectation, increased number of strikes. These symptoms then reinforced the general attitude that the regime was finished and had to be replaced. In turn, the level of atomisation declined and the intelligentsia turned to Western ideologies to understand their situation.

It is important to note again , however, that the society disintegrated and was not overthrown. Such a phenomenon occurs when the old ruling group is too strong to be overthrown but too weak to maintain the old order. In that case, the old system disintegrates economically, socially and politically. Put more clearly, the old system fell apart because the old forms of integration could no longer function.

Accident and Immediate Cause

Was there a trigger or immediate cause? Some would see this in terms of the figure of Gorbachev himself, others point to the rise of national-ism, while still others talk of pressure from the West. There is no doubt that all three aspects played their role. None the less, we are left asking whether they were historical accidents or perhaps necessary features of a dying system. Even the pressure from the West can be seen as a kind of response to internal developments.

It is certainly difficult to imagine Gorbachev acting on his own. He came to power as part of the old Andropov–KGB faction. We know that Ligachev helped him take power. We must, therefore, conclude that the elite which put Gorbachev into power had some conception of what they wanted. Under conditions of stagnation and disintegration, it made sense for the elite to attempt to control events rather than be faced with a *fait accompli*. Gorbachev's reforms can then appear as conservative actions intended to preserve the old elite, within a disintegrating system. Indeed, I would argue that this is precisely what did happen.

The alternative argument is that Gorbachev unleashed forces which he did not expect and could not control and was then swept away by an unforeseen series of events. This is what underlies the series of 'accidental' arguments. It is obvious that Gorbachev understood little of the effects on society as a whole. None the less, he and his advisers were quite clear from early on that they had to go to the market, and their understanding of the market was unambiguous: they wanted capitalism. What they did not know was whether they could achieve their goal gradually or all at once. Gorbachev tried to go slowly and failed, while Yeltsin tried to go fast and also failed. Both, however, succeeded in holding the ring for the elite long enough to allow it to externalise itself and acquire title to property. In that sense Gorbachev and Yeltsin knew what they were doing, in strengthening the position of the old elite.

The Transition as a Form of Disintegration

They have both failed, however, to introduce capitalism. The former Soviet Union is today highly unstable and continuing its process of disintegration. On this point, orthodox Soviet or Russian and East European or Slavic Studies has again failed miserably. It was generally assumed that, whatever the costs, the former Soviet Union would transfer to capitalism within a finite time. Orthodox observers have now lengthened the time which they give to the former Soviet Union to transfer to capitalism: thirty years is commonly bandied about. The present transition process has come as a surprise, in which each new event or social occurrence appeared to be totally unexpected. Most old Sovietologists went along with the orthodox economic prescriptions, which involved so-called shock therapy, even if some wanted more therapy and less shock. They wanted a straight market-clearing price system, mass bankruptcies and mass unemployment. Indeed, these features were absolutely essential in order to introduce money, competition and control over labour. The fact, however, that such measures were totally contrary to the interests of the mass of the population never seems to have entered their heads, since they based themselves on the old prescription of 'no gain without pain'. The fact that Stalin's propaganda was in essence no different, in calling for the workers to sacrifice themselves for their children, also seems to have been overlooked.

History will no doubt judge these post-Soviet policies as beyond belief. The Sovietologists came of age when they became responsible for much of the policy followed in the Kremlin and elsewhere in the Soviet Union. Hence, the fact that the Russian and Ukrainian regimes could not implement their prescriptions led them to blame these regimes themselves rather than their own advice. The idea that the population would accept a massive decline in its standard of living as well as mass unemployment, which these policies entailed, never appeared realistic except to themselves. The departure of the advisers to the Russian Federation in 1993, after the parliamentary election of 12 December, was long overdue.

Few former Sovietologists have tried to explain the real failure of the move to the market or the new phenomena in this new 'transition' period. The rise and rise of criminal enterprise, the phenomenal growth in corruption, the increase in the bureaucratic apparatus of Russia, the continued disintegration of the socio-economic forces operating in the society, and the rise of a new kind of vicious anti-Semitism are just a few aspects of the society which require to be explained rather than just described. They have no explanation for any of these features beyond banal abstract statements. We are told that the new 'Wild West' in the East is understandable under conditions where society has broken down but it will gradually give way to a more genuine capitalism. In fact, society did not break down, although the old system did disintegrate. For criminals to play a crucial role in society there have to be criminals not only ready but also able to play such a role. They cannot come from some unknown underworld, although such people may take part in this new layer, because the old elite never lost control. In other words, they must come from the elite itself.

We can clarify the above by making a further distinction between the Soviet Union and its successor states. The old Soviet Union was the basis of the Stalinist system and Stalinism was effectively jettisoned or overthrown. Both the old form of political rule and the so-called planning system ceased to exist.

The Soviet Disintegration in a World Context

In one sense, the Soviet Union can be regarded as a failed counter-revolution. The elite preferred capitalism but could not get it. As a result, the laws of the society were neither socialist nor capitalist but derivative of a world in transition away from capitalism. The fierce antagonism between a centre bent on organising and holding together the society and multi-national entity and the individual units of the society which acted in their own interest in order to survive has its counterpart in every bureaucratic entity in the capitalist world. The workers' deliberate refusal to work at a faster pace, in a more productive way, has its counterpart in different countries and different firms throughout the world. Wherever the worker is alienated and not provided with an incentive to overcome that alienation, he will work as slowly and badly as possible. The money incentive is blunted wherever there is full employment, workers' control or high wages. The socialisation of production has meant that nationalised industries, large firms, monopolies and needs-based industries constantly hit the barriers of capitalist production. They need workers to act in the interests of that production, but they cannot achieve that goal without destroying capitalism itself.

In other words, the disintegration of the Soviet Union represents the dissolution of the control of the centre over the periphery, over the unit, over the individual, and its logic can lead only to further disintegration unless an alternative form of integration is introduced. At the same time the market which is held up as that alternative is also undergoing its own disintegrative process: indeed, the very disintegration of the Soviet Union implies that the global integrative process of the Cold War must end. We are now witness to the barbarism which is following the end of the Cold War. We can only understand that barbarism as a further step in the global disintegrative process heralded by the October Revolution itself. Either mankind takes a leap into the true socialist future where the individual is part of the society and controls that society rather than personal or impersonal forces controlling him, or the society will continue to pull apart.

Finally, I shall turn to the so-called left views of disintegration. If the Soviet Union was not socialist, or a workers' state, at least since 1923, then the argument that it failed because it was too weak applies only to the period down to 1923. This, however, is not what Paul Sweezy and others mean. They have a curious view that seems to imply that the non-socialist Soviet Union failed because it was too weak. This is in contrast with the more general view that socialism in one country is impossible.[11] They contrast, therefore, socialism in one strong country or a number of strong countries to socialism in a weak country. Whatever this explanation provides, it does not explain why the Soviet Union lasted for so long and why it came to an end.

Those who argued that the Soviet Union was a new bureaucratic mode of production now look foolish in that their mode of production hardly lasted 70 years. They have to explain the nature of the laws governing such a mode of production and the nature of the decline of those laws almost as soon as they came into being. There is little to be gained from such arguments. The state capitalist and capitalist arguments now look so worn or even worn-out that it is hard to take them seriously. Why should a capitalist country want to go over to capitalism? If one says that their capitalism was different from that of the West and that they wanted to go over from nationalised capitalism to privatised capitalism, then one is still left wondering why it should have wanted to do so and why they are failing so badly in this process.

It makes far more sense to discuss history in terms of epochs. We may regard the present as a transitional epoch in which there have been a number of transitional forms which could never become socialist,

---

11. The view that the Soviet Union had to collapse because of the impossibility of socialism in one country ultimately derives from L.D. Trotsky, of course, but neither Trotsky nor many Trotskyists expected that it would disintegrate, still less without any significant working class opposition demanding a left alternative: see *The Revolution Betrayed* (London: Faber, 1937), *passim.*

which came into being only through historical accident. Capitalism will necessarily develop through the socialisation of the forces of production. The resistance to the democratisation of the economic processes can lead only to further economic failures unless the working class takes power. Before that time, disintegration is inevitable. Capitalism is disintegrating over centuries rather decades, whereas the historic abortion which was the Soviet Union has disintegrated in a historically short time. None the less, we cannot understand the disintegration of the USSR without understanding that of the so-called West.

9 Political Problems of Economic Transformation in Post-Communist Russia

Vladimir Mau

Political Factors at the Outset of Radical Economic Reforms

The end of 1991 marked the beginning of a fundamentally new stage in the development of Russia, and it was not the beginning of just the next phase in the reform of Soviet society, which began in the mid-1980s. There had occurred two radical changes which had long-term and full-scale economic and political consequences. First, the policy of late-socialist reformism had been replaced with one aimed at solving post-communist transformation problems. Second, the centre of gravity of this process had shifted on to the level of the former Soviet republics, which had just become independent states.

Already in the autumn of 1991 all the responsibility for the state of affairs, including the situation in the national economy, fell on the shoulders of the Russian leadership. The situation was then catastrophic and was getting worse literally by the hour. This demanded prompt and decisive action on the part of the Russian Republic's leaders, which it was all the more difficult to do since, traditionally, the Russian government was incapable of conducting an independent policy: it had always passively followed the course prescribed by the USSR leadership, either unreservedly or, on the contrary (from 1990), bitterly criticising the same course.

But now there was no one to prescribe such a course. Hence the president of Russia had to make a crucial political choice, and there were two alternative courses of further action. First, it was possible to try to stabilise the economic situation by means of the extra-economic instruments traditionally used by the Soviet economic management mechanism: toughening the supply and marketing system, balancing prices by means of new price rises, resorting to full-scale rationing of consumer goods, which people could buy at socially acceptable prices, and so on. At the same time, a truly reformist government could start preparing measures and procedures to enable it to carry out a comprehensive social and economic transformation, including liberalisation of the economy and the introduction of institutional reforms. Such a scenario would actually have been the conservative variant, albeit with certain modifications: it would have been realised by a government more popular than the Gorbachev–Pavlov cabinet, and its long-term goals of gradual de-communisation of society would have been more definite. The logic of such a course could be expressed as follows: stabilisation of the economic situation must precede the implementation of the reforms. All the signs are that it was this course that was favoured by Grigory Yavlinsky in the autumn of 1991.

Second, there was the possibility of a rapid introduction of market reforms, which could themselves become a factor of economic stabilisation, with the simultaneous implementation of stabilising measures proper (such as limiting the budget deficit and carrying out a restrictive credit policy) – measures well known in international practice. In that case the main role would be assigned to liberalisation and macroeconomic stabilisation measures, gradually (in the course of working out relevant legislation) supplemented by measures of institutional transformation.

The first variant was more acceptable to the mentality of both the Soviet economic and political establishment and the population at large, who expected the authorities to take compulsory administrative steps (in the economic sphere, at any rate) and who, over the decades of the communist regime, had seen that it was precisely such steps that had invariably been taken in the past in order to overcome economic difficulties. However, any practical realisation of such a policy would come up against one problem: in the Russia of the 1980s–1990s there were no political and organisational mechanisms capable of carrying out 'administrative stabilisation'. There was no administrative top-down 'vertical' structure to issue commands, the coercive bodies had lost their former efficiency, and the law enforcement system had been considerably undermined. In a word, Russia (like the USSR in the last months of its existence) was a country with weakened government institutions. *The weak state was an objective reality, which had to be reckoned with when choosing the economic and political strategy to follow.* Russia had inherited from the USSR a weak state, and it had to build its statehood practically from scratch. This largely predetermined Russia's choice of its economic course.

The difficulties of the second variant were also quite easy to see. The country's population was not accustomed to such a policy and would find it difficult to grasp. This policy (regardless of its actual effectiveness) would be almost certain to tell adversely on the popularity of any politicians bold enough to start implementing it. In the shortest time possible it would transform the country's economy into a qualitatively new state, with none of the economic agents having any experience of how to behave in the new situation. It was clear that price liberalisation would inevitably entail sharply increased prices, the complicating factor being the high monopolisation of the Russian economy. At the same time, such a policy would resolutely put an end to many illusions characteristic of the period of the early reforms, above all to the illusion of the omnipotence of a democratic and popular government. From the very start this policy would be based on the recognition of the fact that Russia was a weak, albeit hypertrophied state, and its proponents proceeded from this fact in working out their economic and political goals.

After two months' hesitation, the Russian president chose the second variant and announced his decision at the Fifth Congress of People's Deputies of the Russian Soviet Federative Socialist Republic, held at the end of October 1991. In early November a qualitatively new government was formed, headed officially by the president, who took responsibility for the new economic policy.

Politically, this was a very dangerous period. Much depended on the initial reaction of both the managerial and political circles and public opinion. However, the situation was resolved satisfactorily thanks to at least three factors. First, Boris Yeltsin was at the height of his popularity, and his proposals generally met with full support of both the Supreme Soviet deputies and the population at large (see Table 9.1). Second, the most conservative and politically active pressure groups (the military–industrial complex and the collective and state farm

Table 9.1   President Yeltsin's popularity rating

1991	July	5.36
	October	6.01
	November	5.07
1992	January	4.54
	February	4.62
	March	4.90
	April	4.15
	May	3.86
	June	3.96
	July	3.97
	August	3.86
	September	3.77
	October	3.60
	November	3.69
	December	3.89
1993	January	3.91
	February	3.53
	March	3.66
	April	4.32

Note: Scores on a 10-point scale, 10 being highest.

Source: All-Russia Public Opinion Surveys Research Centre.

lobbies), whose leaders had been involved in the attempted coup in August 1991, were disorganised. (Besides, the managers of Soviet enterprises, brought up in the atmosphere of goods shortages and manufacturers' dictates, had no clear idea of the problem of low demand for their products and, therefore, believed that the liberalisation of prices and economic ties would give them an opportunity to sell their products freely at prices fixed by themselves or at excessive prices.) And, third, society had become somewhat socially fatigued, and this made any social destabilisation resulting from the price rises very unlikely. There existed no popular or populist mass movement of the Polish 'Solidarity' type and at the same time there were no high expectations of or hopes for an 'economic miracle'.

The acute economic situation, coupled with the defeat of the USSR leadership in its opposition to the Russian authorities, predetermined a certain change in the correlation of the economic and political problems. In late 1991 there was a feeling that the political struggle had mainly ended, that power had become concentrated in the hands of one person, and that the leader's principal attention should centre on carrying out economic reforms. It seemed that economics had ceased to be subordinate to politics and had acquired an independent or even overwhelming significance. This was partly true: the political future of Russia's leaders depended on the success or failure of their economic policy.

At this time, whether consciously or otherwise, an important political decision was taken: the reformation of the political system was practically halted, whereas in 1988–89 political reform had received the main attention of Gorbachev and his associates. Yeltsin decided to 'freeze' the situation, to preserve the status quo in the organisation of state power.

As further developments showed, this decision was wrong. The problem is not that no new elections to independent Russia's state legislature were held, as many political analysts wrote later. Such elections were hardly likely to produce qualitatively different representative bodies. What was needed was decisive reformation of the state power organisation from top to bottom, with the aim of introducing clarity and precision into this system. There were two obvious gaps in the Soviet constitutional system: no vertical, top-down distribution of authority among the institutions of power and no horizontal separation of powers. This was not important for the totalitarian system, based on the hierarchy of Party organisations. However, it was precisely the presence of these gaps that was so painfully felt soon after genuine economic reforms started.

However, it would be wrong to say that political problems had receded to the background compared with economic ones. In the implementation of the economic reforms the absence of a clearly defined political space for them became one of the major problems. The process of economic power seemingly concentrating in the hands of the Russian government encountered considerable obstacles. On the one hand, there was the continued formal existence of the All-Union leadership, already incapable of carrying out a rational economic policy but quite capable of taking decisions to destabilise the situation in Russia. On the other hand, there existed uncertainty about the relations between Russia and the other republics, whose economic decisions (often extremely populist in character) directly affected the efficiency of the course pursued by the Russian government. Attempts to regulate these relations on the basis of a collective agreement patently failed, and with the approaching liberalisation of prices this uncertainty was becoming increasingly intolerable (even because an incautious and ineffective fiscal policy in the situation of price liberalisation could push the country into the abyss of hyperinflation). Therefore, the Russian leadership, together with the leaders of Ukraine and Belorussia, decided to denounce the 1922 agreement on the formation of the USSR and took the initiative in forming the Commonwealth of Independent States. Russia assumed full control over the financial and monetary systems. However, this was only the first, albeit very important, step in Russia's gaining full economic sovereignty.

The political space of the economic reforms was becoming more or less definite. Of course, the situation was complicated by a complex of unsettled political and legal questions of relations between Russia and the former Soviet republics, the absolute 'transparency' of the country's frontiers, the inseparability of its monetary and credit system, and so on, but in any case certain parameters had been set and directions for deciding interrepublican relations chosen. From then on, the Russian leadership, and those of the other newly sovereign states, could fix the real geographical frontiers of their authority in the matter of economic and political reforms.

Economic Policy and the Dynamics of Social Forces

Strictly speaking, the history of the post-communist transformation of the Russian economy is in many ways a history of the formation and transformation of politically influential interest groups, their emergence and development, and their convergence or divergence. A distinctive feature of Russian public life in the period under consideration was the fact that the most influential political forces were economic agents: enterprises, their amalgamations, and financial and commercial structures. Having intimate connections with the institutions of power, possessing material, labour and financial resources, and being better organised than anyone else, they could directly influence economic decision making. Judging by everything, this is in general characteristic of societies whose economy is being fundamentally reformed. And politicisation of the economic subjects is all the more unavoidable when the social system itself is being transformed, when the old political associations have disintegrated and the new ones have not yet been formed: for in our case we are dealing with a transition from a totalitarian system, under which all the socio-political organisations other than the officially approved ones were simply outlawed.

Thus, for a certain time Russian enterprises directly participated in the country's political life. The future of economic reforms in no small degree depended on their position and their co-operation with the institutions of power. They were also becoming sources from which a number of new public organisations sprang up. How were their economic interests transformed and how did this affect economic policy?

The Russian government formed in November 1991 was new not only in form but in substance as well. It had no apparent and firm links with any interest groups in the production and managerial sphere. The goals which it set itself were dictated exclusively by considerations of economic expediency and were in fact a more or less standard set of measures capable of slowing down the crisis and averting economic catastrophe. The liberalisation of the prices of most goods and services, accompanied by price rises (a shock) coupled with a tougher financial, credit and monetary policy, was intended to produce results which could be regarded as a kind of litmus test. Such results would be a rapid slowing down of the growth of prices and the achievement of price equilibrium; the appearance of goods on the shelves in stores and overcoming commodity shortages; gradual stabilisation of the currency rate and abandoning multiple exchange rates; and activation of the structural transformation, beginning with the bankruptcies of inefficient enterprises and a perceptible growth of unemployment.

At the first stage the government acted without any apparent social support for its policies. Therefore it was free to implement unpopular but necessary measures, remaining equidistant from the various pressure groups. However, in practice it proved impossible to stay completely indifferent to their persistent lobbying.

Technically, the achievement of the above-mentioned goals was quite feasible. The chief problem of the anti-inflationary policy was its social price and the political opposition on the part of the recipients of government aid (in the form of subsidies, preferential prices, grants, and so on), the number of which, as the efficiency of the Soviet economy fell, kept increasing. That is why, after the price liberalisation, the inflation level became not so much an economic as an integral political indicator characterising the stability of the position of the government team of reformers, the state of Russia's political climate, and the prospects for the realisation of this type of market reforms.

Even the first steps of the government encountered bitter opposition, which initially had purely political forms. The vice-president, Aleksandr Rutskoi, and the chairman of the Supreme Soviet, Ruslan Khasbulatov, vigorously opposed any price liberalisation. Although the tone of their statements was quite serious, there were as yet no influential social forces to support them. So far, these political figures, strongly inclined toward populism, merely engaged in political games in the corridors of power.

However, in the spring of 1992 there appeared clear signs of consolidation of the social forces opposed to the government's firm anti-inflationary policy, which had by that time become identified with the name of Yegor Gaidar.

The growing non-payments crisis had provided a common platform for the opposition bloc, the core of which consisted of state-owned enterprise managers. Their mutual indebtedness seemed to put different enterprises on an equal footing, levelling out their more profound differences arising from their different adaptability to market conditions. So, both potential bankrupts and potential leaders found themselves in the same situation, without financial resources and with confused settlement arrangements with their suppliers and customers. The social equality of different producers was to a certain degree also 'solidified' by the presidential decree on bankruptcy, issued in June, under which practically any enterprise came under the formal definition of bankrupt.

Another reason which had compelled different groups of producers to unite quickly on a common political platform was the impending decision to liberalise fuel prices. The relevant announcement in the memorandum forwarded to the International Monetary Fund (March 1992) was probably the government's most serious political error. It was to some extent an attempt to repeat the favourably received advance notification of price liberalisation in the autumn of 1991. At that time such a measure had enabled people to prepare themselves psychologically for life in different conditions, while both manufacturers and distributors had been able to lay in stocks. Besides, before 2 January the managers of most state-owned enterprises had not yet realised how price liberalisation would affect demand. Many of them had regarded price liberalisation as an opportunity to improve their own situation at their customer's expense, having but a vague idea of 'limited demand'. However, by the spring of 1992 the situation had changed radically and the threat of fuel price liberalisation, coupled with the non-payments crisis and the looming threat of bankruptcies – so far only in the form of political declarations, it is true – played a consolidating role in the formation of a producers' 'interest group' – a powerful alliance of post-Soviet producers, which for a time united moderate and conservative politicians.

In April–May bizarre alliances of producers from different branches and spheres of the economy came into being, who had previously vied with one another for a bigger share of state budget resources. A particularly graphic example was the coalition of the leaders of the military-industrial and agro-industrial complexes: the former demanded credit injections not only for themselves but also for the agrarians, believing that the latter would use such credits primarily for the purchase of the agricultural machinery they produced, the demand for such machinery having sharply decreased in 1992.

At the same time, co-operation strengthened between the organisations uniting the state-owned enterprise managers and the traditional labour unions (left over from the communist system). Especially significant was the agreement between the increasingly powerful Russian Industrialists' and Entrepreneurs' Alliance (RIEA) and the Federation of Independent Labour Unions (FILU – the successor of the All-Union Central Trade Union Council), which was concluded in May 1992 and had a clearly anti-government character. The agreement envisaged the creation of a mechanism for co-ordinating the activities of its two participants in the 'tripartite commission', the third participant being the government. The purpose of the agreement was clear from the very beginning: both the industrialists and the labour unionists went out of their way to avert the danger of halting the inflation at the cost of real bankruptcies and growing unemployment. Already in March the FILU leaders and the leaders of the Moscow Federation of Labour Unions unequivocally declared that, from their standpoint, inflation was a lesser evil than unemployment (although in that context the question of the acceptable inflation level was not discussed or even raised).

In a word, by the early summer of 1992 a powerful pro-inflationary bloc had been formed, embracing various interest groups. This bloc held strong positions in the industrial sphere, among the legislators (as was graphically demonstrated by the decisions of the Fourth Congress of People's Deputies of Russia, held in April 1992), and in the mass media. Politically the bloc took shape at the end of May and the beginning of June, when the party superstructure of the Russian Industrialists' and Entrepreneurs' Alliance– the All-Russia 'Renewal' Union – was created. Soon the 'Civil Alliance' was formed, which included a number of centrist and left-of-centre parties and organisations.[1] All of this convincingly demonstrated that the post-Soviet 'interest parties'' disorganisation and demoralisation, which followed the *putsch*, had been overcome.

In the summer of 1992 the pro-inflationary bloc had become well organised and more powerful politically. The Gaidar government could not avoid responding to it, so one of the main party political gaols in June–August was tactical manoeuvring with the purpose of weakening the pro-inflationists. This demanded first, that the government should pay more attention to the creation (and broadening) of its own social base. Second, striking compromises and manoeuvring became inevitable if the opposition were to be split. Both the first and the second factors implied a certain retreat from the initially declared goals of achieving rapid stabilisation, slowing down inflation, and minimising the budget deficit. However, such a retreat was not unexpected: it was made inevitable by the radical character of the reform policy of the first months of 1992.

Radical reformers had to form an alliance with part of the industrialists – managers of state-owned enterprises, primarily those who believed that entering the market economy and functioning in the new conditions had a future. Such an alliance secured the support or at least the neutrality of a sizeable part of the engineers, technicians, and workers of the enterprise concerned.

The compromise was reached at the cost of a number of concessions

1. The main parties to the Civil Alliance (CU) were the 'Renewal' party (of Alexander Vladislavlev), the Democratic Party of Russia (of Nikolai Travekin), the People's Party of Free Russia (of Alexander Rutskoi), and the 'New Generation – New Names' group (a small, but very active faction in the Supreme Soviet).

in the monetary, credit and foreign trade spheres and it was sealed by the inclusion in the government of several important representatives of the management of enterprises belonging to the military–industrial complex (Vladimir Shumeiko and Georgii Khizha) and the fuel and energy complex (Viktor Chernomyrdin). The price of the compromise was an upsurge of prices in September–November (up to 5 per cent a week) and a plunge of the exchange rate of the rouble (by a factor of three in two months). The expected transformation of unemployment from the hidden into the open form did not materialise.

However, the compromises enabled the government to achieve a number of important political goals. First, in the autumn there already appeared signs of a split in the ranks of the industrial and agrarian opposition. A considerable part of the state enterprise managers started distancing themselves from the uncompromisingly anti-government and pro-inflationary statements which the leaders of the managerial lobby in the Supreme Soviet (Yurii Voronin, Yurii Kekht and others) and the leadership of the RIEA made, allegedly on behalf of the entire enterprise management. This polarisation of the economic agents' forces was sharpened by the process of privatisation, which also began in the autumn. The procedures underlying this process gave some managers a real opportunity to become the *de facto*, and later also the *de jure*, owners of their enterprises, which resulted in the radicalisation of the position of the managers, especially of those who were more efficient and active than others.

Second, the sharp deterioration in the economic situation in the autumn was a confirmation in practice of the fact that the government was right to have resisted any weakening of monetary and credit policy, although finally it had to give in to the joint forces of the enterprise managers. This demonstration of the direct connection between credit expansion and inflation proved to be an important experience, which was used in subsequent macro-economic decision-making. Before this happened, both public opinion and enterprise managers had been sceptical about Gaidar's warning that the growing budget deficit and the 'soft money' policy would inevitably produce extremely hard consequences for the country's economy.

In 1992–93 two distinct interest groups had emerged, prepared to support essentially different versions of Russia's economic policy. They had different opinions about the problem of the role of inflationary processes and the methods and possibilities of overcoming them. Precisely this problem became central to the political struggle waged around the economic reforms following the polemics about the administrative and liberal-economic variants of stabilisation policy.

On the one hand, there were committed pro-inflationists. The principal elements of the economic policy that they championed included massive financial infusions into the national economy (through the credit and budgetary systems) with the purpose of supporting economically weak and uncompetitive enterprises, attempts to 'strengthen the management' of the national economy by restoring the centre's administrative power over the enterprises belonging to the state sector, toughening the export and import controls, and rigid protectionism. The important components of such a policy were: the state's all-around participation in the structural transformation of the national economy, the creation (or re-creation) of a ramified infrastructure which would direct the economic agents' activities – either through the state's administrative bodies (ministries and branch committees) or through large monopolist structures (concerns, industrial-financial groups and so on) controlled by the authorities.

The advocates of such an economic policy comprised fairly diverse groups of economic agents. Some clearly gained from the inflation, earning huge profits from the continuation of the state's financial support, which would stave off their imminent bankruptcy. Most interested in the 'cheap money' policy were weak state-owned enterprises (although often with very large work-forces), which for some objective or even subjective reasons were unable to adapt themselves to competition and were doomed if a macro-economic policy based on tough budgetary restrictions were to be implemented. Besides, this policy was extremely advantageous to a considerable part of financial structures (banks): their economic well-being, and sometimes even their very existence, to a large extent depended on preferential credits and budgetary subsidies. Finally, inflation is an extremely profitable source of commercial and mediatory activities, and this fact predetermined the favourable attitude to this policy on the part of this business sector in Russia's economic and political spectrum. In other words, the inflationary policy would enable inefficient enterprises to survive and commercial banks and trade organisations to receive profits incomparable with those of the productive sectors.

On the other hand, during 1993 there emerged some supporters of the alternative economic policy which had been officially chosen as far back as the end of 1991 and more or less consistently implemented in 1992–93. Its main features were consistent liberalisation of economic activities, a tough financial and credit policy, and consistent privatisation. The essence of this policy can be described as anti-inflationism. The ranks of its adherents swelled as privatisation went ahead and some enterprises grew used to working in the conditions of a genuine market environment, which opened numerous opportunities for economic and social advancement to active managers and qualified personnel. It is clear that the economic structures most interested in a consistent anti-inflationary policy are those which have already realised their own economic strength, have good opportunities for selling their products in the conditions of competition on the domestic (or even the world) market, and are already prepared to carry out an active capital investment policy, which needs macro-economic stability above all else.

The redistribution of interests reflected a new and very significant tendency in the development of the social situation in the course of the implementation of reform. While previously economic agents' interests were determined by whether they belonged to the public or the private sector, now the form of ownership began losing its importance as a determinant (an 'interest-forming' criterion). An essential factor was economic agents' position in relation to the redistributive flow of 'cheap money' (the only thing which remained in short supply): the possibility for them to use it in their own interest. As a result, both private and state-owned enterprises found themselves on the same side of the 'economic barricades'.

For a number of political reasons, during 1993 the government's real economic policy was rather unstable. The level of inflation, ranging between 12 and 35 per cent a month, actually reflected the conflict between the interests of the alternative models of economic development. *Inflation was in fact the form taken by the solution of regenerating redistributive conflict between the different types of economic agents.* The absence or weakness of structural changes was an indicator of the strength of the positions of the pro-inflationary forces, which succeeded to varying degrees in reproducing the established economic structure by means of monetary injections. However, the preservation of the unstable situation by no means meant the preservation of the social *status quo*. In this respect two kinds of process were under way.

First, the political activity of the enterprises which had supported the anti-inflationary policy was weakening. Their hopes that inflation would soon be checked did not materialise, and consequently they had to adapt themselves to functioning under conditions of prolonged high inflation. This called for a new strategy and, objectively, made potentially strong enterprises modify their direct support of the anti-inflationary political forces (that is, of those who had initiated the radical market reforms and put them into practice).

Second, some of the active entrepreneurs had merged with the institutions of power. The weak state sought the support of the new, economically strong and influential domestic entrepreneurs. And so representatives of big business (no matter whether private or semi-public) found themselves in a congenial environment where, instead of struggling for survival in the market, they could lean on the institutions of power for support.

As a result of these processes, the debates on the principles of economic stabilisation and control of inflation had gradually lost their former political intensity. This was also partly due to the resolutions, adopted at the insistence of Yegor Gaidar, which seriously restricted the flow of cheap money into the national economy.[2] Instead of the problem of cheap money, political struggle had now centred on problems of the state's protection of domestic producers from foreign competition. This was a new phase of political struggle, which also transformed the economic policy alternatives faced by the state institutions.

In the autumn of 1993, the tough inflationist variant based on direct emission in its various forms was replaced with a 'soft inflationist' variant. The essence of the soft inflationist policy consisted in rendering massive, all-round assistance to domestic business by selectively supporting enterprises and industries worthy of such support (without, however, specifying any criteria); actively forming 'from above' powerful financial-industrial groups, which would effectively suppress competition in the relevant sectors of the national economy; consistent protectionism in foreign economic activity; and striving to slow down

2. Here we mean the abandonment, from 25 September 1993, of the practice of granting preferential credits.

privatisation and place it under the control of various departments and businesses connected with such departments. While stressing the support of domestic business (or, more precisely, business connected with the state), such an economic policy indisputably remained inflationary, since the emergent monopolist structures, closely connected with institutions of state power and reliably protected by their very status from their customers' possible complaints and from foreign competition on the home market, would have exceptionally good opportunities for getting access to public financial resources and for monopolistic price formation.

An alternative to this policy consists in reliably guaranteeing freedom of enterprises' foreign economic activities and supporting them in their competition on foreign markets, but not on the home market (that is, not at the expense of domestic consumers). These measures are supplemented by consistent privatisation of enterprises and maximally distancing their activities from those of the institutions of state power. Accordingly, in this case both the emergence and growth of financial-industrial groups proceed as a natural process 'from below', that is, as a process started by the enterprises themselves.

In a word, having gone through several phases in 1991–93,[3] the socio-political struggle over the state's economic policy assumed the form of the opposition between two clearly defined models of further socio-economic development. On the one hand, there was the model which envisaged the creation of a nationally confined and highly monopolised market economy, protected from the world market by tough customs and legal barriers (in a form resembling the former state monopoly over foreign trade). On the other hand, there was the model which envisaged a modern, open, market economy, which guaranteed increasing efficiency of the economy through international competition. It goes without saying that these two economic models needed radically different political regimes for their realisation.

---

3. Let us list these phases briefly:

    (1) choice between conservative and liberal stabilisation;
    (2) economic and political structures' uncompromising opposition to the government's liberal course;
    (3) polarisation of forces and struggle between the inflationary and anti-inflationary alternatives.

Economic Reform and Institutions of Power

Constant tensions in the relations between the institutions of state power, periodically leading to intensified conflicts and political crises, have been among the most typical features of Russian public life practically from the start of the radical market reforms. During 1992–93 the antagonism between the legislative and executive branches could be seen practically everywhere, at all levels. However, it reached its climax at the federal level, and took the form of opposition between most people's deputies, on the one hand, and the president and his government on the other. This opposition culminated in a political explosion at the end of September and the beginning of October 1993, which resulted in the dissolution of the legislature and changed the constitutional foundations of the Russian economic and political process.

However, the election of a new parliament did not at all lead to a weakening of the antagonism between the two branches, although it quite significantly transformed the space in which this antagonism developed.[4]

There are two factors that caused this antagonism, whose nature is, of course, far from personal. The first explains the socio-economic roots of the conflict between the people's deputies and the administration at different levels. The second helps to draw a number of important conclusions about the constitutional and legal problems arising from the implementation of the economic transformation.

The first relates to the character of the interests of the members of post-communist society. In the short term, people indisputably strive to lighten their share of the 'burden of the transformation', to preserve the *status quo* of their pre-reform (pre-*perestroika*) material well-being, and to secure the preservation of their enterprise or organisation, even though it may have absolutely no future from the market standpoint. At the same time there is a common realisation of the need to reform the entire complex of economic relations radically and to escape from the economic blind alley in which communist Russia had been trapped.

4. The Russian experience of implementing economic reform gives a wealth of material for elaborating problems pertaining to 'constitutional economics' as a special branch of economics. The impact of Russia's constitutional system on its economic policy and reforms is not only extremely vivid, but it has also demonstrated a number of new aspects of the problems concerned. All this demands a special analysis, which far exceeds the scope of this contribution.

This dual nature of the interests finds its institutionalised expression in the different positions of the deputies and the executive branch. Owing to their position in the democratic system, the deputies, directly linked with their electorate, cannot help being driven in their activities by certain populist motives. Even when realising the inevitability of social hardships and economic decline, they have to respond sharply to the day-to-day problems experienced by their electorate. The executive branch, headed by the president, is in a different situation. The head of state, elected by the entire nation, must first and foremost pay attention to the national interests, ensuring the realisation of long-term goals. It is precisely the president who bears responsibility for the major decisions which affect the country's life, and he can afford to take steps which are as necessary as they are unpopular.

This contradiction reveals itself when real reforms get under way. It is not fortuitous that it surfaced only in late 1991, when the 'tug-of-war' between the Russian and USSR authorities had ended and the new government started implementing measures aimed at the rapid dismantling of the communist economic system.

As noted above, it was precisely then that the political conflict inherent in the emergent economic reforms was underestimated. It was then that the end of the conflict between the Russian and USSR structures was taken by the Russian leadership as a reason for weakening, if not terminating, the political struggle between the institutions of power. However, the antagonism inherent in genuine economic reforms is far more acute, and it keeps growing as the reforms, affecting the interests of almost all the social groups and sections of society, get under way.

The second cause of the intensified struggle between the institutions of power was the flabbiness and frankly the weakness of the Russian constitutional system inherited from the communist regime. The system of institutions of power continued to be based on the 'All power to the Soviets' principle, and not on the ideology of the separation of powers and 'restrictions and counterbalances'. The principle of balancing the top state powers was practically ignored. The attempt, in the autumn of 1991, to mend the situation by granting the president some special powers, and the use of these powers by Yeltsin to speed up the economic reforms, resulted in a corresponding strengthening of the powers of the opposition forces in parliament, which launched a bitter campaign to limit the president's prerogatives.

The absence of a new democratic and consistent Constitution created conditions for repeated attempts on the part of the legislative power to interfere with the authority of the executive branch and even to subjugate the latter completely.

In 1992 this was repeatedly demonstrated in the sphere of economic policy. The parliamentary deputies made persistent attempts to strengthen their control over the Central Bank's activities; they did their utmost to make the State Anti-monopoly Policy Committee directly accountable to them; they set up powerful and virtually multifunctional financial institutions (the Pension Fund, the Social Welfare Fund), stressing their independence of the government's authority; and so on. Economic issues were debated without strict observance of the rules of procedure, even budgetary decisions being taken without previous expert examination.

In 1993 the situation worsened still further. The Supreme Soviet started adopting measures or issuing statements through its chairman, which ruined every chance of carrying out a sensible economic policy.

The following may serve as examples of such activities: the Supreme Soviet's attempts to increase the budget deficit by escalating budgetary expenditures; its advice to the subjects of the federation not to transfer tax revenues to the federal government if they had insufficient funds for their regional welfare and economic needs; its persistent attempts to revise radically the privatisation mechanisms (that is, to change the rules when privatisation was already under way) in order to adapt them to the needs of the economic agents working out their long- and short-term policy in the course of privatisation.

Thus, the activities of the legislative power went far beyond economic expediency and were determined exclusively by the logic of the struggle with the president, by the wish to undermine his political position and at the same time win the support of the regional authorities. It is easy to see that this in many ways resembled the events of 1990–91, when economic processes came up against political opposition.

An important feature of the parliamentary deputies of the 1992–93 issue was the fact that some of them formed managerial lobby groups, which immediately began playing a significant role in the decision-making by parliament, which was poorly structured politically (that is, along party lines). Especially active in this respect were such factions as the Industrialists' Alliance and the Agrarians' Alliance.

Russian parliamentary lobbyism had a number of specific features distinguishing it from its foreign counterparts. First, Russian lobbying was almost exclusively limited to the material production sphere. Russian deputies did not experience organised pressure from public, women's and veterans' organisations, consumers' groups, ecologists, and so on. Second, Russian lobbyists actually spoke on behalf of large monopolist formations, insisting on the preservation and reproduction of the traditional system of state monopolies closely linked to the public sector of the national economy. Finally, the Supreme Soviet lobbyists showed a rather narrow understanding of the interests of the state-owned enterprises. Seeing a real danger of bankruptcies of some of these enterprises, they concentrated their efforts not on seeking mechanisms which could alleviate the workers' hardships caused by the structural transformation, but on the maximum preservation of the industrial–economic structures themselves. This in no way increased the deputies' popularity among the electorate, especially of those who represented the agrarian–industrial lobby.

In the absence of a clearly defined system of separation of powers, lobbyism proved to be especially dangerous, since the centre from which pressure on the executive power was exerted was located in the highest and omnipotent state institution: parliament (the Congress of People's Deputies). And yet in Russia's real political life the people's deputies, who were most susceptible to pressure from organised lobbyism, bore the least responsibility for the economic consequences of their decisions.

All these features of the post-Soviet representative branch – its extremely wide powers, its domination by the narrow industrial lobby, its minimal and impersonalised responsibility for the country's state of affairs – made the Supreme Soviet the main source of populist decisions affecting economic policy. A unique situation had arisen in Russia, when the leaders of the executive branch supported the policy of reducing state expenditures, whereas the legislators, by contrast, went out of their way to increase such expenditures substantially, using their constitutional right to introduce amendments (not co-ordinated with the government) into the state budget and the fact that the Central Bank was formally accountable to the legislative power.

As a result, from December 1991, the government mainly acted as a force opposing the legislature. This situation remained unchanged no matter who headed the government – President Yeltsin himself, Yegor Gaidar, appointed by Yeltsin (June–December 1992), or Viktor Chernomyrdin, elected at the seventh Congress of People's Deputies (December 1992).

During 1992–93 the popularity rating of the executive power varied, but on the whole it was somewhat higher than that of the Supreme Soviet (see Tables 9.2 and 9.3) The greater support for the government was chiefly due to Yeltsin's political manoeuvring. However, the president's personal popularity was far from limitless and this naturally told on the effectiveness of the government's work, especially in 1992.

Table 9.2   Does the Russian Supreme Soviet, in your opinion, deserve trust and to what extent? (Responses in per cent)

		Fully deserves trust	Partly deserves trust	Does not deserve trust at all	Hard to say
1991	September	33	35	14	18
1992	January	13	37	17	33
	February	6	42	26	26
	March	10	37	26	27
	April	7	40	31	22
	May	4	33	41	21
	June	4	37	39	20
	July	5	38	35	22
	August	6	38	35	21
	September	3	35	38	24
	October	3	35	43	19
	November	3	36	43	18
	December	5	36	42	17
1993	January	6	37	31	26
	February	4	31	28	31
	March	7	29	35	29
	April	5	24	44	27

Source: All-Russia Public Opinion Surveys Research Centre.

*Table 9.3   Does the Russian government, in your opinion, deserve trust
and to what extent? (Responses in per cent)*

		Fully deserves trust	Partly deserves trust	Does not deserve trust at all	Hard to say
1992	February	7	37	30	25
	March	8	38	30	25
	April	9	39	30	22
	May	7	37	35	22
	June	6	43	32	19
	July	8	38	33	22
	August	5	41	33	22
	September	4	37	36	23
	October	4	33	44	19
	November	7	38	38	18
	December	7	37	34	22
1993	January	8	38	22	31
	February	4	34	25	37
	March	7	35	26	32
	April	12	33	24	32

Source: All-Russia Public Opinion Surveys Research Centre.

During 1992–93 quite serious changes took place in the government itself. While at the first stage it was mainly a cabinet of politically like-minded people (as regards economics, at any rate), from the summer of 1992 it became clearly a coalition government (see above).

Moreover, an interesting new feature of the organisation of the Russian institutions of state power made itself felt in 1993. It could be defined as 'parliamentarianisation of the government': the government was becoming a body whose structure mirrored the approximate correlation between the social forces existing in Russia at that time. Indeed, by the end of their term of office the deputies elected in 1990 could hardly claim to represent the interests of their electorates or those of the country's entire population. This was confirmed by the results of the April referendum.[5] But if any political system is to function

5. Voters were asked the following questions: whether they trusted the president, whether they supported the president's socio-economic policies of 1992–93 (that

normally, it must represent the interests of some influential forces. When representing such interests through purpose-designed institutions becomes impossible, the relevant functions are taken over by other institutions of power, generally by the most influential ones.

The Council of Ministers became such an organisation. However, at critical moments any genuinely representative body proves to be largely ineffective when a political course is to be chosen, and then its functions are usually taken over by a more homogeneous institution. Thus the Presidium of the government took on such a role. From early 1993 it was only the Presidium of the government that convened regularly (once a week), whereas full-scale meetings of the Council of Ministers were held only once every three months and the number of participants in such meetings (regional leaders, scientists, scholars, public figures) was large, which strengthened still further the Council of Ministers' functions of representing the interest groups existing in society.

Naturally, no government of this type could carry out consistent market reforms, but it was able to balance between various influential socio-economic groupings. It can be said that in the situation existing at that time the stability of the government was achieved at the expense of the instability of its economic policy. The government now toughened its macro-economic policy, doing its best to arrest the upsurge of prices, then softened it under the pressure from pro-inflationary forces. Moreover, during 1993 the executive was periodically tempted to lean on the moderately conservative section of the enterprise managers and pursue a pro-inflationary policy, which, by balancing precariously on the edge of hyperinflation, would allow it to stave off painful structural changes in the national economy. The appointment of Oleg Lobov as first deputy prime minister and minister of economics symbolised precisely such a policy. However, an important factor preventing such a choice was the realisation that the preservation of the existing structure and inflationism would strengthen the positions of the frankly

is, the period when liberal reforms were being introduced), and whether they considered re-election of the president and the Supreme Soviet to be necessary. In response, the majority said 'Yes' to the first two questions, most people said 'No' to the re-election of the president and 'Yes' to early elections to the Supreme Soviet. However, the last question failed to win the support of a majority of registered voters, as required by the Constitution. This gave the people's deputies formal grounds for staying on until the end of their term of office.

reactionary politicians in the Supreme Soviet and the pressure groups acting behind them.

In the end, three groups had emerged in the 1993 government, each supporting one of the three different variants of economic policy outlined above.

One group consisted of advocates of the frankly inflationary variant. It consisted of Oleg Lobov, the leadership of the State Committee on Industrial Policy, and the leaders of the sectoral industrial committees, plus the representatives of the agrarian and military–industrial lobbies in the Council of Ministers. These politicians' ideas found their most concentrated expression in the documents and proposals of the ministry of economics, submitted in April–September 1993. They included a resolution on the selective support of industries (April), a draft presidential decree on the ministry of economics (May), a draft law on indicative planning, an alternative concept of carrying out economic reforms (prepared for the enlarged session of the Council of Ministers in July), and two memoranda for the president: 'On the economic situation in the country and urgent stabilisation measures' and 'On the indexation of the value of the privatisation cheques and the revaluation of the capital assets' (August–September). Most of these documents had a programmatic character. They stressed the authorities' greater organisational and administrative activities and greatly increased financing of the branches of the national economy (disregarding the country's financial situation) in order to overcome the production decline and support the domestic industries which faced an internal crisis and potential foreign competition. They proposed indexation of all the financial and capital resources at the disposal of the government, the state-owned enterprises and the population (revenues, incomes, circulating assets, investments, savings, privatisation cheques). It was further proposed to make the indexation of investments mandatory by law. The ministry of economics insisted that a new, large-scale mutual cancellation of enterprises' debts be carried out; a system of 'enterprise support (sanitation) commissions' be set up; the instrument of preferential crediting of enterprises be actively used, with the simultaneous re-creation of the system of centralised planning (albeit for the time being it was called indicative planning); and the state controls over exports and imports be strengthened.

At the same time there had emerged a group of advocates of a course which we have called above 'a soft inflationary policy'. Oleg Soskovets, Sergei Glazyev and Andrei Kokoshin were important supporters of this policy in the government. This policy was most consistently formulated in the conception of economic policy, prepared by Soskovets in late August 1993. It envisaged a revision of the law on enterprises (with the aim of strengthening the role of government bodies in the management of enterprises), 'selective' financing of enterprises, some changes in the privatisation programme, and the restoration of the vertical (top-down) management structures, similar to 'self-supporting main administrations and trusts'. The most salient feature of this economic policy concept was protectionism, the striving for maximum protection of domestic commodity producers and banking structures from foreign competition. At the same time, while insisting on those measures, their supporters often stressed the top-priority task of fighting inflation and did not deny the need to carry out a tough financial and credit policy as one of the most important factors helping to cope with this task.

Finally, there was a group of advocates of a consistent anti-inflationary policy, which included the State Property Management Committee's chairman, Anatoly Chubais, the minister of finance, Boris Fedorov, and Yegor Gaidar, who returned to the government in September 1993. They concentrated their efforts mainly on toughening the financial and credit policy, and carrying out consistent privatisation and liberalisation of foreign economic activities. This is explained by both the critical importance of these goals for continued economic reforms and the positions these politicians held in the government. Their main achievements were: the agreement signed in May between the government and the Central Bank, which somewhat toughened the credit policy; decisive suspension of the system of preferential credits (in September); and the adoption of a package of measures in the sphere of 'budgetary federalism'. As the result, the inflation rate was periodically checked and the exchange rate of the rouble was somewhat stabilised. The general trends in the privatisation process were preserved in the face of bitter attacks from the Supreme Soviet and strong opposition within the government.

The fundamentally different positions of the leading members of the cabinet and its coalition character made themselves acutely felt in the course of the preparation for parliamentary elections in late 1993, when ministers and their deputies joined election blocs of different political orientations – from neo-communist to those staunchly supporting the market economy.

Social Stability

The tasks of overcoming an economic crisis, carrying out a stabilisation policy and simultaneously introducing radical economic and political reforms, which are always quite painful and produce positive results only after some time, require some degree of social stability. Such tasks have to be achieved immediately after the foundations of the old system have been thoroughly shaken. Quite different types of environment are needed for their achievement. While the destruction of an old social system requires a high level of socio-political activity on the part of a substantial section of the population, tackling the tasks of stabilisation and construction proceeds better in the atmosphere of a relatively balanced public mood – even of the people's fatigue, resulting from the political clashes of the past, and compensated for (in case of a favourable concurrence of circumstances) by their increased activities in the economic sphere, in the solution of problems of their own material well-being.

After the policy aimed at price and wage liberalisation was proclaimed at the end of October, the prevailing topic in the media was that of the expected serious social upheavals and mass protest actions before, during, or after the inevitable upsurge in prices. The situation was aggravated by the rapid collapse of the consumer market, whose degradation naturally made itself felt in November–December, since the manufacturers and market traders were unwilling to part with their stocks before 2 January 1992 (when price liberalisation was to begin).

In the public consciousness, fear of open inflation was combined with hopelessness born of chronic shortages, the absence of practically all goods in the stores, with many hours of queueing even for articles of prime necessity, and the new phenomenon of interruptions in bread deliveries to the shops. In December the consumers' market saturation indicator had reached its minimum.

Fear and pessimism were exacerbated by neo-communist groupings, which greatly increased their activities and were doing their utmost to use the transitional period (the menacing hyperinflation, with practically empty stores) in order to destabilise the political situation and block all progress towards market democracy. Their attempt to organise mass protests in mid-December under the general slogan of 'marches of the hungry' was most significant in this respect.

However, despite all the expectations of a social explosion, the general public mood in Russia was more favourable for the implementation of radical economic reforms than for other policies.

First, the popularity of the president, who had proclaimed the liberal economic policy, remained extremely high. Second, on the whole, at the preceding stage of dismantling the communist regime's institutions the population's socio-political activity was not particularly high (passions ran high only in Moscow and a number of large industrial centres) and did not show any tendency to rise. Political activity was obviously on the decline and, according to public opinion surveys, most people ruled out the possibility of mass anti-government actions in the near future. Finally, the perception of a rapidly approaching catastrophe itself made people tolerate the painful stabilisation measures. Moreover, there appeared in the public consciousness a very important shift away from paternalism and total dependence. From two-thirds to three-quarters of Russian citizens, who had no illusions about a possible improvement of the economic situation in the near future, did not connect their personal well-being with any government or public organisation: instead, they relied primarily on their own resources.

There were no signs of an approaching 'revolution of disappointed expectations' or of illusions born of 'seeing the light at the end of the tunnel' in society, when the first indications of an improvement in some spheres (industries, regions) gave rise to hopes of an early change for the better, and disappointment in these hopes often resulted in a sharp deterioration of the social situation. On the contrary, in the Russia of the end of 1991 hopes of an 'economic miracle' had practically evaporated: nearly two-thirds of the people did not believe that the crisis could be overcome without a 'temporary lowering of the standard of living'. This realisation of the inevitability of hardships in the course of the implementation of the coming reforms showed the presence of important stabilising principles in the consciousness of most citizens.

The effect of the unjustifiably pessimistic forecasts had also played a role. The end of 1991 gave rise to expectations of almost insurmountable difficulties, failures in the supply of basic foodstuffs and electricity, and the disruption of central heating and transport. According to the All-Russia Public Opinion Research Centre, 80 per cent of Russian citizens were preparing themselves for all these contingencies. However, the sombre forecasts did not come true,[6] and only four weeks after the price liberalisation there already appeared tangible indications of an improvement in the consumers' market. This became an important factor in the stabilisation of the public attitude, and it was not accidental that, according to the sociological services' data, from the spring of 1992 consistent economic reforms found support among many people, their number steadily growing in 1992 (see Tables 9.4 and 9.5) Understandably, in the spring and summer of 1992 the

Table 9.4   Do you agree that it would be better if everything in the country had remained as it was before 1985?

	Dec. 1991	April 1992	June 1992	Aug. 1992	Oct. 1992	Dec. 1992	Feb. 1993	April 1993
Number of respondents	1927	1600	1660	1650	1500	1799	1649	1644
Agree (%)	41	28	33	28	28	30	35	25
Disagree (%)	36	51	42	40	48	42	33	40
Hard to say (%)	23	21	25	32	24	28	32	35

Source: State Statistics Committee.

6. Incidentally, expectations of this kind of cataclysm had long haunted the imagination of some Russian economists. As an example, we will give here one quotation from Grigorii Yavlinskii: 'The winter of 1992–93 will be much harder than the previous winter: there will be shortages of electric power (primarily in the Baikal area and the Northern Caucasus), unstable prices for oil and oil products, a growing number of breakdowns in city heating systems, growing forage and feed shortages in most regions, and possibly food shortages as well' (G. Yavlinskii, 'O novoi politike pravitel'stva' (The Government's New Policy), *Voprosy ekonomiki*, 1993, No. 2, p. 114). What is interesting here, by the way, is that this alarmist forecast was made in autumn 1992, but it was published (probably for technical reasons) only in the spring of 1993.

Table 9.5 Should the economic reforms be continued or stopped?

	Mar. 1992	May 1992	Aug. 1992	Nov. 1992	Jan. 1993	Feb. 1993	Mar. 1993	April 1993	May 1993
Number of respondents	1579	1630	1656	1603	1603	1629	1649	1644	1553
Yes (%)	46	47	53	57	57	51	42	53	49
No (%)	26	21	20	19	17	18	19	15	20
Hard to say (%)	28	32	27	24	26	31	39	32	31

Source: State Statistics Committee.

popularity of the government and Yegor Gaidar personally kept rising, but later, when in the following spring it became clear that the goal of eliminating inflation had not been achieved, the relevant indicators went down (see Tables 9.6 and 9.7) However, by that time other social stabilisation factors had come into play.

The population's lowering political activity found its graphic expression in the numbers of people taking part in rallies and demonstrations, either in support of the reforms or against the government. During 1991–92 the number of participants in neo-communist rallies and demonstrations somewhat increased at the expense of the dispossessed sections of the population, while the number of participants in

Table 9.6. Yegor Gaidar, Acting Cabinet Chairman: popularity rating throughout Russia

	Sept.	August	July	May	April	March	Feb. 1992
Should resign (%)	45	38	29	31	29	34	28
Should continue in office (%)	32	38	49	49	50	30	39
Hard to say (%)	24	24	22	20	36	36	33

Source: Mnenie Public Opinion Surveys Service.

Table 9.7　Government of the Russian Federation: Popularity rating throughout Russia

	September	May	April	March 1992
Should resign (%)	25	16	17	23
Should continue in office (%)	43	64	62	48
Hard to say (%)	32	20	21	29

Source: Mnenie Public Opinion Surveys Service.

democratic rallies and demonstrations decreased (mainly at the expense of the same class of people). However, in general, such rallies and demonstrations were attended in Moscow by between a few thousand and several dozen thousand, with both their numbers and their emotive impact on the institutions of power declining steadily during the year.

The social structure of the rallies is revealing. Selective investigations carried out in December, February and November showed that both nationalist–communist and democratic rallies and demonstrations were dominated by retired persons (30–40 per cent) and employees of the state budget sphere (30–35 per cent). The share of manual workers never exceeded 9–12 per cent and that of young people was about 10 per cent. It should be stressed that the social structure of the demonstrations of either political persuasion was practically the same.

In implementing the package of painful economic reforms, a positive factor was the absence in Russia of popular mass working-class organisations (of the Polish 'Solidarity' type), which by their nature are easily attracted by populist slogans and promises. The official trade unions amalgamated in the Federation of Russian Independent Labour Unions largely remained alien to the workers, although their leaders went out of their way to portray themselves as champions of the working-class cause, and to speak on behalf of the people not only on issues of labour relations but on political issues as well.

The most active of the alternative labour unions was the Independent Miners' Union. It usually took a pro-government and pro-reform stand, and actively participated on the conservative side against the radical political opposition. Other labour unions did not attempt to influence the progress of the economic reforms.

There were also important changes in the character of the strike movement. From autumn 1991, the number of strikes began to decline substantially, this process continuing throughout 1992. Later on, the strike movement remained at a comparatively low level. (Exceptions were fairly short individual strikes, mainly of local importance.) There were three significant changes in the character of strikes and the composition of the work-forces on strike.

First, as early as autumn 1991, the centre of the strike movement had shifted from industry to the social sphere (primarily to the sphere of public education and, although to a lesser degree, the public health service). Thus, while in 1991 85.9 per cent of the working-time losses fell on industrial enterprises, 8.1 per cent on public education and 2.1 per cent on public health, in 1992 the figures were 17.1 per cent, 64.3 per cent and 15.5 per cent, respectively. The numbers of strikers changed in virtually the same proportions.

This situation is to a large extent explained by the low ability of the budgetary sphere to adapt itself to the conditions of a market economy and also by the government's insufficiently flexible budgetary policy. Since in Russia the agrarian–industrial lobby wielded exceptional political influence, it absorbed a considerable part of the public funds which should have been channelled into the branches financed from the budget (that is, the social sphere).

These conclusions are also confirmed by the regional strike movement statistics. Thus, for example, in the principal mining regions (Kemerovo province and the Komi Republic), where the number of striking enterprises had increased, the scale of the strikes had definitely shrunk and the number of working hours lost had dwindled. While in Kuzbass the number of striking enterprises increased from 440 to 654, the number of the strikers and the working time lost dropped by three-quarters (from 125,100 to 29,800 strikers and from 1,613,900 to 396,900 worker-days, respectively). Although the situation in the Komi Republic was not so clear, the trend was definitely the same: the number of striking enterprises grew, whereas the number of strikers dwindled, as did the work-days lost by each individual enterprise. This reflected the real development of the situation in the regions: the workers of the main industries (the miners and the metallurgists) had succeeded in winning substantially bigger wages, which in the conditions of free pricing had led to relative increases in the prices of consumer goods (primarily foodstuffs). But since in the Komi Republic the salaries of those employed in the budgetary sphere were indexed to the all-Russia scale, their material situation had seriously worsened, which drove them to take strike action. However, since the number of enterprises in the non-material sphere was quite substantial, while the number of the people employed in them was relatively smaller than in the industrial enterprises, the overall incidence of strikes had correspondingly declined.

The situation in a number of other Russian regions and in the country as a whole was the same. The average intensity of strikes (the length of one striker's walkout and the losses of working hours per enterprise) was obviously decreasing, which showed that the problem was growing less acute. Also characteristic of 1992 was the fact that during the entire year the losses of working hours from strikes in industry were lower than the corresponding figures for the sphere of public education alone (not to mention the social sphere as a whole).

Naturally, the shift of the centre of the strike movement to the social sphere showed that it was this section of society that was hardest hit by the reforms. From the political point of view this was an obvious setback to the reformers, since it was precisely the intellectuals employed in this sphere who were among the reformers' most important social mainstays and most active supporters of the ideas of democracy and the market economy. Objectively speaking, however, in the medium term such a situation might be more conducive to speeding up the reforms, since it shifted the vector of social discontent to the sphere which was the least influential politically and was in principle incapable of radically destabilising the general situation in the country.

Second, the strikes had become depoliticised. Demands for the resignation of the president and the government, so characteristic of workers' rallies and demonstrations during the last years of the existence of the USSR, had changed mainly to economic demands. Naturally, this trend was not absolute, and political demands resurfaced from time to time (especially between 1993 and 1994), but now they resulted from the government's failures to fulfil its promises, non-payment of wages and salaries, and so on.

Third, the strike movement in the Russia of 1992–94, as far as economic demands were concerned, was usually not caused by the relations between the workers and the employers, as was often the case in the period of the first strikes. (By employers we mean the management of the enterprises where the strikes were called, or the administration of the relevant ministries and departments.) At that time the principal economic demands had been increases in the remuneration of labour and changes in working conditions, including reciprocal responsibilities of the workers and the administration.

Privatisation has so far removed many of these problems or made available more acceptable procedures to solve them, since the workers became the owners of a certain share of the voting stock. Moreover, since in almost all cases voucher-based privatisation followed the second pattern, worker-stockholders initially gained considerable potential influence over firms' decisions.

Now, as the reforms continue, the strikers' main demands to the government are economic. The strike movement now mainly affects the branches dependent on budgetary revenues, that is, coal mining and partly the social sphere. Finally, a special reason for strikes is non-payment for the products (especially fuel and power) supplied to CIS countries, which after the Russian Central Bank's refusal to continue granting these countries technical credits, created additional difficulties for the oil and gas industries.

At the same time, the above changes in the nature of the strike movement (shifting the demands to the governmental level) has had another characteristic consequence. Unlike 1989–91, when workers mainly distanced themselves from the enterprise management, in 1992–93 there were many cases of joint action on the part of enterprises' work-forces and managers, the latter sometimes initiating strikes in an attempt to use them for securing additional cost benefits and thereby strengthening their own positions as administrators.

When analysing the strike movement as one of the most significant factors of the social stability (or instability) of Russian society, attention should also be paid to another phenomenon, which is an important characteristic of the economic transformation process. The implementation of the economic reforms in general, and privatisation in particular, has not yet led to the emergence of classical conflicts between labour and capital; that is, at the present time private (including privatised) enterprises possess much greater stability than the state-owned ones. This is explained by the higher wages and salaries paid in many of them, by their lower dependence on public financial resources,

Table 9.8 Unemployment and vacancies (thousands)

At end of year	Unemployed					Available vacancies	
	Unemployed	Registered unemployed	Receiving unemployment benefit	Undergoing retraining	Engaged in public work	Total number	Including manual workers
1991							
July	351	16	2	0	2	708	647
August	383	25	4	0	1	838	773
September	421	35	6	1	2	916	843
October	474	51	8	2	1	898	818
November	469	62	12	4	1	841	769
1992							
January	485	69	18	4	1	586	534
February	554	93	33	5	2	490	438
March	616	118	53	7	4	451	406
April	696	151	74	8	5	408	363
May	743	177	89	8	7	400	359
June	779	203	108	8	13	399	357
July	843	248	140	7	14	377	337

August	888	303	173	7	15	364	327
September	921	367	219	10	13	345	310
October	982	442	267	14	8	316	246
November	1011	518	317	20	6	295	260
December	982	578	371	18	3	307	270
1993							
January	1029	628	411	20	4	301	263
February	1080	692	461	23	4	311	269
March	1097	732	497	28	6	358	312
April	1101	751	514	29	10	404	355
May	1070	740	499	26	13	472	425
June	1003	717	471	19	26	519	465
July	989	717	459	14	23	511	459
August	979	714	456	11	17	511	459
September	969	706	449	23	15	496	443
October	994	728	462	33	8	453	402
November	1056	779	506	40	6	386	336
December	1085	835	550	40	5	352	304

Source: State Statistics Committee, Moscow.

197

and by the fact that they possess some new means of resolving possible conflicts (for example, through stockholders' meetings at joint-stock companies).

What are the main factors capable of seriously destabilising the situation in Russia in the course of implementing market reforms? It is logical to single out at least two such factors.

The social situation may be destabilised by the authorities' attempts to overcome the crisis and 'restore management' by resurrecting tough administrative regulation of the national economy (primarily over prices). This will inevitably re-create the situation of acute goods shortages, aggravated by the government's inability to organise direct, centralised distribution and redistribution of the necessary capital goods and articles of consumption. At the present time such a distribution system no longer exists and it cannot be re-created very quickly.

The other factor for instability may be rapidly growing unemployment. Although by 1994 public opinion had basically accepted the inevitability of this phenomenon (at least in the transition period), a massive rise of the number of jobless people may still prove to be very dangerous. In the first two years of economic reform no such rise occurred and the numerous pessimistic forecasts of 6–10 million unemployed within a few months, made since the spring of 1991, have so far remained unconfirmed in practice.

Having transformed inflation into an open form, the Gaidar government proved unable to realise the second part of its programme – transforming unemployment into an open form, for such unemployment must inevitably accompany a radical structural transformation. In principle, certain changes in this direction were taking place during 1992: the number of unemployed was steadily rising, the number of the jobless having exceeded enterprises' officially announced job vacancies. Similar processes continued in 1993–94 (see Table 9.8). Unemployment largely remains hidden, for example, in the form of prolonged unpaid vacations and short time. A steep rise in unemployment remains unlikely, although the beginning of business bankruptcies is a contributing factor.

Unemployment will be increasing gradually (probably slightly accelerating), and simultaneously public consciousness will be adapting itself to the new situation in the job market. A mitigating role will probably be played by the involvement of workers in the privatisation of their enterprises (at least while the latter avoid bankruptcy) and, with time, by the strengthening of a genuine private sector.

Considerable growth in social tensions due to the worsening situation in the job market is likely to be limited to certain areas, mainly to regions with potential long-term unemployment (especially regions where one particular industry operates). In this respect large industrial centres pose big problems, but there the tension will be mitigated by the diversification of the manufacturing complex and the outflow of the dismissed workers into the private sector. Conflicts among various work-forces may grow sharper, and the lumpenisation of part of the unskilled and semiskilled workers will be practically unavoidable.

Problems of Regionalisation and Separatism in the Economic Reform

The policy of radical economic reforms was proclaimed at a time when processes extremely unfavourable for maintaining Russia's statehood were developing on the regional and inter-regional levels. The situation was so tense that one of the key problems discussed by politicians and academics was whether Russia was facing the danger of disintegration, following the disintegration of the USSR.

From the very outset, the regionalisation of Russia's political life was a complex and involved problem, resulting from the interaction of numerous factors. From the very start, regionalisation contained two components which played an important role from the standpoint of the development of economic and political processes. On the one hand, as the reforms were making headway, Russia was bound to undergo transformation from a formal federation, which it was in the Soviet period, into a genuine federation, consisting of self-reliant, independent subjects. Without this, the establishment of a market democracy in a country of such enormous proportions and diverse geographic conditions was impossible. Preservation of Russia as a unitary state would have been tantamount to abandoning the whole idea of genuine economic reforms.

On the other hand, the regionalisation processes in Russia, as they surfaced in 1991, had clearly separatist overtones and had to a large extent been determined by the incipient economic crisis and the bitter political struggle, first in the USSR and then in the Russian Federation.

In this connection a whole complex of economic and political causes of regional separatism can be distinguished. Their removal will be tantamount to overcoming the centrifugal trends and forming federation. The most important of these causes are the following.

First, the economic crisis itself and the inability of the central government to supply the regions with the necessary manufacturing resources and consumer goods by using the traditional redistribution mechanisms. In this situation, survival (in the literal sense of the word) became the top-priority task of the local authorities, which coped with it by resorting to the one possible method in such a situation: namely, placing the material and natural resources located on their territory under their control. Since the centre was unable to cope with the problem of redistribution, the regions were forced to take over this responsibility. In some cases the situation was far from merely a local one, as when the regional authorities demanded that the mining of coal, oil and diamonds on their territory be placed under their control.

Another aspect of the economic crisis and the situation of acute goods shortages was the local authorities' attempts to control the situation at the regional market, limiting the access of buyers from other regions to it. As a result, by the end of 1991 the Russian economic space had been virtually disrupted: the regions, territories and republics making up the Russian Soviet Federative Socialist Republic went out of their way to set up controls – similar to customs controls – on their borders.

Second, the emergence of regional separatism was influenced by the bitter struggle, first between the state authorities (the USSR and the RSFSR) and then between the institutions of power of the Russian Federation. The participants in that struggle often appealed to regional administrations, promising them a considerable increase in their authority in exchange for their political support. In particular, it was precisely this consideration that lay behind Yeltsin's well-known appeal to the regions ('Take as much power as you can digest!'), made in the summer of 1991 – an appeal which later created not a few problems for the president of Russia.

Third, many problems were created by the very method of discriminating among the subjects of the Russian Federation (various national formations and purely Russian ones) and by their unequal rights (in favour of the former). This led to the emergence of strong nationalist overtones in the separatist tendencies in some regions (in the autonomous republics of the RSFSR) and to attempts by other regions to broaden their rights and equalise themselves with the national regions.

Finally, fourth, the difficulties of the initial stage of the radical economic reforms also made themselves felt, with a twofold effect. On the one hand, some regions began to apply the brakes on the reforms openly, by preserving administrative price regulation, attempting to interfere with the economic agents' activities directly, restricting the freedom of trade, and so on.[7] On the other hand, there were also attempts to mitigate the hardships of the initial period of the reforms within the framework relations; however, decisions taken to this end undermined the integrity of Russia's economic space.[8]

Nevertheless, as the economic reforms got under way, many of the regional problems grew less acute. In 1993 many of the problems were kept alive for purely political reasons, rooted in the opposition between the executive and legislative powers at the federal level.

First of all, the price liberalisation and the consequent end of goods shortages radically changed the nature of the functioning of the regional

7. A classic example of this is Ulyanovsk province, whose administration operated a policy of low prices on foodstuffs and barred 'alien customers' from the local market over a two-year period. The regional administration was able to carry out this policy largely because, for a number of subjective reasons, it was able to retain 50 per cent of the collected value-added taxes, while for most other Russian regions this figure was 20–25 percent. A similar policy was carried out by Tatarstan, whose leadership had actually introduced a 'one-channel' fiscal policy. Tartarstan's authorities also tried to put the brakes on privatisation, and they made an attempt to carry out a special credit policy, more lenient than that carried out by the federal authorities.

8. Thus, one of the most acute problems of the first months of 1992 was a cash shortage. Trying to resolve this difficulty, the administration of Nizhny Novgorod province issued municipal bonds. When there was no cash available, the Nizhny Novgorod Banking House was to sell these bonds to enterprises in a non-cash transaction to the sum which the enterprises owed their work-force. In this case the population could either wait for cash to arrive in the region or receive their wages or salaries in bonds, which circulated on the territory of the region alongside Russian banknotes. The administration would get a non-interest-bearing credit to the sum of the sold bonds. In other regions less sophisticated measures were taken. In Yakutia (Sakha), for example, the administration issued its own cheques to a sum of 14 million roubles. In Kemerovo province local lottery tickets were issued, each ticket equalling 250 roubles in the cash turnover.

markets. Now the main problem was finding customers, buyers of manufactured products, and the local administrations' control over the market had become absolutely senseless. In this way Russia's internal barriers affecting commodity trade tended to collapse by themselves.

Another factor bringing the regions closer together was monetary policy. Once the money shortages had been overcome, the rouble became, if not a quite sound, then at least an attractive means of payment. Everyone needed financial resources in general and cash in particular, and such resources were in the hands of the centre. The attempts to introduce local (or national) means of payment, announced in some regions, was not, and could not be, realised in practice.

By the end of 1993 the government had succeeded, to a greater or lesser extent, in unifying the taxation system. While prior to this period 'haggling' about how to distribute the taxes between the federal and local budgets had been one of the most painful problems in relations between the federal and local authorities, now this problem seemed to have been resolved in principle. The regions received sufficiently wide powers to carry out their own taxation policy – from a liberal one to the toughest possible.

Finally, after the sharp confrontation between the president and the Supreme Soviet had ended and a new Constitution of Russia had been adopted, there appeared a sufficiently clear legal and political system of distribution of power between the federal centre and the subjects of the federation.

Simultaneously, a number of important economic and political processes were taking place in the regions themselves, which promoted stabilisation in inter-federative relations. An obvious merger of economic and political elites could be observed in most Russian regions, this process being accelerated by privatisation and the redistribution of ownership relations. The merger of elites is, undoubtedly, a conservative phenomenon, since in this case regional political and economic leaders make greater efforts to stabilise the situation rather than to carry out radical reforms. However, since such a merger occurs as a result of the changes in the regional economies themselves, which have already been given a considerable political impetus, stabilisation of the political situation in the regions, even if it is achieved at the expense of a certain political conservatism, may have favourable consequences from the standpoint of the consolidation of what has been achieved within the framework of the country's post-communist transformation. Furthermore, regional political stability in principle promotes the central authorities' reformist policies, which is helpful if these are genuinely intent on such policies.

A characteristic feature of the above process is that in most regions the conflict between the representative and executive branches had perceptibly weakened or ceased altogether even before it was resolved at the federal level in September–October 1993.

The real social and economic problems which regional authorities have to deal with now also require the federal centre's support, and not only financial and economic support, but political support as well. The leaders of practically all the subjects of the federation must choose a long-term economic policy. In practically all the regions this choice may be defined as the solution of the redistribution conflict between economically progressive and efficient enterprises and weak structures, unable to survive on their own in a genuine market environment. However, not infrequently the latter represent extremely influential political and social forces at the regional (or even federal) level. (Moreover, the opposing enterprises do not necessarily belong to different sectors. In one and the same region both efficient and weak enterprises may belong to either the agrarian or the military–industrial sector, or to light industry, and so on.)

In this situation, regional leaders must decide whether, by using the budgetary and taxation mechanisms at their disposal, they will promote their regions' structural transformation and the growth of some enterprises while hastening the bankruptcy of others, or they will embark on the path of mitigating the incipient tensions and do their utmost to redistribute the available resources with the aim of supporting inefficient enterprises.

It must be borne in mind that in this situation regional administrations as such have minimal freedom of choice, since the outcome of the redistributive conflict is decided by the balance of forces of the social groups interested in one or the other variant of the development of events. But let us repeat: economically weak structures are quite frequently very influential socially and politically (they employ large work-forces and sponsor numerous establishments of the social sphere). In a word, in this respect there emerges a complex of problems in the solution of which authorities seek Moscow's co-operation.

The New Constitution of Russia and the Economic and Political Situation

The December 1993 elections and the referendum on the new Constitution marked the termination of the initial phase of the post-communist transformation of Russia. The omnipotence of the Soviets had been done away with and the political and legal framework of the country's future development had been clearly outlined.

A number of political results of the elections can be distinguished, which are important from the standpoint of their impact on the formation of a market economy in Russia.

First, the country received a Constitution, which provides a legal foundation for political stability. And it was precisely political stability that, by the end of 1993, had become one of the decisive factors for the development and reform of the economic system. As the upsurge of prices subsided, there emerged real opportunities for increased investment activity (including attracting foreign capital), and it was precisely the unstable political situation and unstable legislation (the procedural ease with which the Supreme Soviet revised the laws) that constituted one of the main stumbling blocks to the realisation of those opportunities. Today, the legal regime has become more definite – owing to both the precise distributions of powers between the authorities vertically (top–down) and horizontally and the introduction of clearly defined procedures for legislation activity. It is another matter that political stability has been achieved mainly in the legal sense of the term, which does not at all guarantee lower political risks of entrepreneurial operations in Russia – risks posed by the activities of extremist political groups, doing their utmost to come to power.

Second, there has taken place a *de facto* legitimation of political organisations professing extremism and nationalism, of both left-and right-wing varieties. The election results served as a serious warning to reform-minded politicians. True, this signal allowed a dual interpretation. On the one hand, it conveyed the need to speed up the reforms, to make them more decisive and consistent, which would make it possible to pass through the phase of economic hardship in the shortest time possible and arrive at the start of economic growth. On the other hand, it provided arguments in favour of slowing down the pace of reforms whose implementation demands too high a social price, thus protracting the reforms in time.

Third, the election results revealed a very significant polarisation of public feelings. The parties which declared themselves centrist suffered a crushing defeat. They either failed to clear the 5 per cent electoral barrier (as happened to Arkadii Volskii's electoral bloc based on the Russian Industrialists' and Entrepreneurs' Alliance) or cleared it by the skin of their teeth (as happened to Sergei Shakhrai's Party of Russian Unity and Concord, which stressed its moderate position and its links with the regional elites). Yet we believe that it was not a defeat of centrism as such. What suffered a defeat was centrism in the traditional Soviet interpretation, that is, a movement that camouflaged the lack of a distinct political position and political will by appeals for caution, which was almost tantamount to inaction. Such positions were indeed shared by part of the regional and industrial establishment and, proceeding from this, the leaders of centrist political blocs believed that they were guaranteed the support of certain work collectives and regions. However, this had not happened, and it could not have happened after several years of reforms.

As a result of the elections a new, more realistic concept of centrism has emerged – in politics in general and in economic policies in particular. It meant a break with extremism, and consistency and persistence in the implementation of policies fundamentally different from attempts to conserve the established system of economic and political relations.

Fourth, the character of the legislative power has changed substantially. A parliament has been formed which more or less faithfully reflected the balance of socio-economic forces and interests. Unlike the Supreme Soviet of the 1990–93 type, dominated by rather narrow group interests, the deputies of the State Duma are supported by relevant economic and political formations, and it will be more difficult to 'corrupt' them by political slogans, promises, and individual privileges (to be granted to individual enterprises). However, because the contemporary interest structure remains contradictory, the membership of the Duma has turned out to be quite 'motley' and consists of representatives of a wide spectrum of political persuasions.

Standing out among the Duma deputies is the inflationary political bloc. It includes representatives of the Communist Party of the Russian Federation (Gennadii Zyuganov) and the Agrarian Party (Mikhail

Lapshin), a considerable part of whose electorate are in a difficult economic situation and demand massive financial injections and privileges for their survival. It also includes representatives of the Liberal-Democratic party of Russia (Vladimir Zhirinovskii) and the Democratic Party of Russia (Nikolai Travkin), who are more inclined to speak in the name of protectionism and national-patriotic capitalism. The 'Russia's Democratic Choice' (Yegor Gaidar), 'Yavlinskii–Boldyrev–Lukin' ('Yabloko') and '12 December' (Boris Feodorov) blocs more or less consistently support the anti-inflationary measures. Finally, the centrist position is occupied by the Party of Russian Unity and Concord (Sergei Shakhrai) and the 'New Regional Policy' party (Vladimir Medvedev), the former gravitating more towards the anti-inflationists, and the latter towards the inflationists.

Taking into consideration the structure of the political parties and organisations represented in the State Duma, one can see the dominance in it of pro-inflationary forces. One can see the same if one examines the personal composition of the Duma: apart from the deputies' sufficiently distinct social leanings, a considerable part of them are directly linked with the interests of specific industries and regions. Represented more strongly than before are the interests of the new commercial structures, which were able for the first time to take part in the elections. Representatives of private business were included in nearly all the parliamentary factions. This becomes still more apparent if one takes into consideration the composition of the Council of the Federation, in which leaders of regional administrations and their direct representatives hold commanding positions.

At the same time, the political results of the elections have far exceeded the framework of macro-economic interpretation. The 'weightiness' of the Liberal-Democratic Party, which occupies openly extremist positions and threatens not only the basic values of market democracy, but also the preservation of Russia's internal and external peace, calls into question whether the democratic course will be followed through. At the same time, it shows that it is not restoration of the traditional Soviet (communist) system that alone poses a threat to the country's future peaceful reformation. The real threat is still posed by a policy based on the revival of totalitarianism, now under nationalistic (and not internationalist–egalitarian) banners, the allies of the Liberal-Democratic Party of Russia being left-wing nationalistic groups of the Communist Party of the Russian Federation type, which have thrown overboard the slogans of 'proletarian internationalism', and organisations whose economic platforms are overtly or covertly protectionist (for example the Agrarian Party and the Democratic Party).

As a result, the balance of forces in the State Duma is obviously tipped in favour of the conservative majority of communists and nationalists. True, the present Constitution, the membership of the upper chamber, and the president's prerogatives create sufficiently strong possibilities for blocking reactionary decisions of the lower chamber. The Russian government has basically retained its coalition character, which, given certain flexibility, creates conditions for comparatively uncomplicated relations with parliament, in which it can nearly always form a majority ready to support this or that government draft law.

Yegor Gaidar's and Boris Fedorov's resignation from the government made the leaders of the executive power take personal responsibility for the results of their economic policy. Viktor Chernomyrdin had to choose unequivocally between the alternative – inflationary or anti-inflationary economic policies. Before Gaidar's and Fedorov's resignations he had managed to avoid making this choice owing to the politically confused situation of 1993. The government had found it difficult to carry out a consistent inflationary policy, since its leaders more or less clearly understood what consequences such a policy would have. However, it has also found it as difficult, if not impossible, to choose the anti-inflationary variant.

After some hesitation, the prime minister chose the anti-inflationary policy, basically continuing, both in form and in essence, the tough Gaidar–Feodorov financial and credit course. True, he tried to carry out this policy in a disguised way, that is, accompanying the restrictive financial measures by lavish promises of additional monetary injections. At the beginning this helped ease the conservatives' and lobbyists' pressure on the Government, although this led to an accelerated decline in production and to the growth of mutual indebtedness of enterprises, waiting for the handouts of 'cheap money'.

At the same time, as the rate of inflation went down, two groups of problems demanded the authorities' urgent attention.

First, institutional and structural reforms moved to the foreground.

Here, too, the key factors are the transition to the privatisation-for-cash stage, the start of real bankruptcies, and the encouragement of investment activities and personal savings. The presidential decrees signed in May–June 1994 mainly dealt with those problems. Their practical solution was indeed urgently needed, yet a number of painful social consequences were likely to follow, above all the growth of unemployment. However, people's attitude towards unemployment is not now as uncompromising as it was a few years ago. Public opinion has accepted the view that economic revival is impossible without an increase in unemployment (similarly to public opinion's acceptance, during 1988–91, of the inevitability of an upsurge of prices and a balance between prices and demand).

Second, the slowing down of inflation for a time increases the danger that it could return and even turn into hyperinflation. For it is precisely at this stage that economic agents begin demanding that they be supplied with cheap money, insisting that they do so not only because of their difficult financial situation, but also because of the existing favourable macro-economic environment. Many countries' experience has shown that governments often yield to such demands and, as the result, they very soon lose control over the macro-economic situation. This is all the more dangerous as the governments themselves, lulled by the favourable inflationary trend (easing of inflation), may embark on the road of inflationary injections into the national economy and fail to see the perils lying ahead, since the moments when the financial and monetary policy is slackened and when prices begin to rise are separated by a period of several months. During this period the growing money supply is accompanied by decreasing monthly inflation, which creates the impression that the economic and political course being pursued will produce no adverse consequences.

By the end of 1994, as was the case after the 12 December 1993 elections, the government had to choose the direction of its economic policy, its choice being obviously a political one, too. When resigning in January 1994, Yegor Gaidar issued a warning that the government had nothing to gain from slackening its economic policy, making it consistent, and engaging in populist games with the communists and the nationalists. The only result of this would be the loss of yet another year and the postponement of the start of economic growth. Gaidar's words proved correct. The accelerated inflation in September–October

1994, the plunge of the exchange rate of the rouble on 12 October, the Central Bank's loss of a considerable part (more than half) of its foreign currency reserves, built up with great difficulty after January 1992, all demonstrated the fragility of the stablisation that had been achieved and its dependence on the consistency of macro-economic policy.[9]

Having yielded to strong pressure from the agrarians and the industrialists during the budgetary debates in April–May, the government raised public expenditures in the budget to an unrealistic level. Its subsequent attempt to delay payments naturally increased social tensions. However, the payments made under the lobbyists' pressure in July–August led to a sharp deterioration of the economic situation. And it was precisely the political groups which forced the government to make the fateful concessions that headed the campaign of denunciations against the executive power.

The October 1994 events made it quite clear that the economic and political changes of recent years were not at all irreversible. It suddenly became apparent that it was possible to return to the economy of acute shortages and the state's omnipotence (and in Russian conditions this means the power of omnipotent corrupt officials) literally in a matter of a few months. All that needs to be done 'to achieve' this is to comply with the nationalist and communist leaders' first demand, namely, to slacken the monetary and financial policy. What will follow is easy to predict. It will sharply destablise the currency market, and that will make the authorities realise the Russian latter-day left-wingers' next demand – to introduce the compulsory exchange rate of the rouble. This will be tantamount to a return to the situation when state officials apportioned hard currency, deciding (not without some profit for themselves) who is to get it and who is not. The pegged (overvalued) exchange rate of the rouble would immediately put an end to all consumer goods imports. But no matter how vehemently 'imports domination' is denounced, it is precisely imports that constitute the main price-restraining factor in the Russian market. Without competing with foreign-made goods Russian monopolist manufacturers will immediately raise the prices of their products. And that will leave the government no alternative but to realise their opponents' next demand

9. These and associated problems have continued, and even intensified, in the years since this chapter was written. [Editor's note]

– the restoration of state controls over prices. What will happen next is now cleat even to high school students: goods will disappear from the stores and Russia will once again find itself in the trap of a dislocated consumer market, acute commodity shortages, useless ration cards, and very long queues for all kinds of goods. In other words, Russia will return to the 1991 situation with all its problems, including the danger of the country's disintegration into 'self-sufficient' regions, separated by customs barriers. Unfortunately, this scenario is quite realistic.

The alternative to this is a cautious, carefully thought-out policy for extricating the country from its present situation by returning to a genuinely tough financial policy and striving to achieve stabilisation, which alone is capable of creating conditions needed for economic growth. All the post-communist states in which economic growth has started have achieved it *solely* by halting or substantially slowing down inflation. The almost indisputable law, repeatedly confirmed by practice, is that approximately twelve months after prices cease rising by more than 3 per cent a month, the country's economy begins to grow. Russia is no exception to this law. However, let me repeat: the people carrying out such economic policies must be highly qualified professionals.

10 Western Economists and the Transition Process in Russia

Bob Arnot

Introduction

A central question for analysts of Russia and the former Soviet Union is why Western Sovietologists failed to foresee the collapse of the former Soviet Union and the Eastern bloc. This chapter considers the role of the economists in this failure and, after suggesting some reasons for their difficulties, considers whether they have learned anything from their inability to predict the demise of the former Soviet Union. In particular the chapter considers whether the economic advice proffered to Russia, in the period from the fall of Gorbachev to the present, demonstrates any critical reflection on past analytical failures.

The Economic Analysis of the Former Soviet Union

For all bourgeois economists the former Soviet Union, from its revolutionary origins to its disintegration, posed particular problems. But with regard to the economists active within Sovietology there is a relatively straightforward answer to the question of why they failed to predict the demise of the former Soviet Union. The argument developed in this chapter is that mainstream economic analysis failed because the methodology of conventional, neo-classical economics, which predominated in Sovietology, was unable to comprehend at any time the dynamics of the former Soviet Union. It was based upon a methodology that utilised static, partial and ahistoric categories which precluded an appreciation of how the system evolved over time.[1] Moreover, the analysis was based upon a process of abstraction that removed from consideration precisely those socio-economic forces that shape the destinies of economic systems. As a consequence, it inevitably failed to identify the developmental and degenerative tendencies within the former Soviet system.[2]

In one sense this was not surprising, as the methodology utilised was dependent upon the same categories that have proved just as incapable of identifying the laws of motion of capitalism. It would have been more surprising if such a methodology had proved capable of providing a deeper understanding of a different social formation. Furthermore, it is an analysis that is underpinned by a mechanistic and technicist view of socio-economic processes. It is as if the economic can be segregated from the political or the sociological and examined in isolation. Questions of the economy then become technical questions and not socio-economic questions.[3] This methodological approach was also underpinned by an implicit view of the 'normal' functioning of all economic systems and in contemporary economic analysis the dominant view is that the market is normal, natural and eternal.[4] As a consequence, there is no vocabulary or methodology that can deal with

1. There is a wide range of literature that provides a methodological critique of bourgeois economics. See, for example, M. Campbell, *Capitalism in the UK* (London: Croom Helm, 1981), pp. 9–30, for a useful, brief critique; F. Green and P. Nore (eds), *Economics: An Anti-Text* (London: Macmillan, 1977); S. Bowles and R. Edwards, *Understanding Capitalism* (New York: Harper & Row, 1985); J. Schwartz (ed.), *The Subtle Anatomy of Capitalism* (Santa Monica, CA: Goodyear, 1977).
2. For an excellent account of the weaknesses of 'economic science', see Homa Katouzian, *Ideology and Method in Economics* (London: Macmillan, 1980). His conclusion regarding the problems faced by economics is worth repeating: 'It is the preoccupation with little abstract puzzles as opposed to great and real problems; the parochial vision combined with technological formalism; the uncritical commitment to existing theories and methods; the discouragement of alternative approaches and views ... [which results in] ... the ever-increasing complexity of its formal edifice and the never-ending poverty of its substantial achievements' (p. 210).
3. See, for example, T. Buck, *Comparative Industrial Systems* (London: Macmillan, 1982).
4. See, for example, Ed Hewett's comments in Keith Bush (ed.), *From the Command Economy to the Market* (Aldershot: Dartmouth, 1991), p. 106. Hewett argues the following: 'I don't think you so much need to explain markets as you need to convey to people that ... this [is] ... the only way to go'.

ideas such as decline, decay, transformation or change of the 'eternal' market system. Since there is no recognition of the operation of a historico-economic process, there is no need for the conceptualisation of such a process! Indeed, if such questions could have been asked of the opposing system it would have posed the possibility of the creation of a methodology that could have been turned against capitalism itself, denying economics its function as a set of apologetics for capitalism.

Within this general methodological approach, economic crises are particularly difficult to analyse. For bourgeois economics the predominant concept remains that of equilibrium, and crises, which are fundamental to the operation of the system, are viewed as endogenous to its essential nature.[5] As a result the location for disturbances must be sought outside the 'normal' operation of the system. The consequence of this kind of approach was that the majority of Western economists writing on the former Soviet Union were well able to identify specific problems in agriculture,[6] in industry,[7] in consumption,[8] in technology and R&D,[9] in military expenditure and a whole host of other specific sectors of the economy. However, the underlying methodology and compartmentalism of the discipline precluded a systemic view that located these features as part of a fundamental crisis of the system as a whole. In fact those who took such a view were often seen as madmen on the fringes of both the discipline and sanity. To suggest that the

5. For an excellent brief survey of this question, see Anwar Shaikh, 'Crisis Theories in Economic Thought', *Thames Papers in Political Economy* (London: Thames Polytechnic, 1977).

6. See, for example, S. Hedlund, *Crisis in Soviet Agriculture* (New York: St. Martin's Press, 1984); D. Diamond, L. Bettis and R. Ramsson, 'Agricultural Production', in A. Bergson and H. Levine (eds), *The Soviet Economy: Toward the Year 2000* (London: George Allen & Unwin, 1983).

7. See, for example, Joseph S. Berliner, *Factory and Manager in the USSR* (Cambridge, MA: Harvard University Press, 1957); David Granick, *Management of the Industrial Firm in the USSR* (New York: Columbia University Press, 1954).

8. See Philip Hanson, *The Consumer Sector in the Soviet Economy* (Evanston, IL: Northwestern University Press, 1969); Alec Nove, *The Soviet Economic System*, 2nd edn (London, George Allen & Unwin, 1980).

9. See, for example, Ronald Amman and Julian Cooper, *Industrial Innovation in the Soviet Union* (New Haven, CT: Yale University Press, 1982); Ronald Amman, Julian Cooper and R.W. Davies, *The Technological Level of Soviet Industry* (New Haven, CT: Yale University Press, 1977); Joseph Berliner, *The Innovation Decision in Soviet Industry* (Cambridge, MA: MIT Press, 1976).

Soviet system could not survive or would not survive was to attract opprobrium and ridicule.[10]

Therefore, the starting-point of this chapter is to suggest that the failures of 'Sovietological economics' in the past can be explained by reference to the underlying methodology adopted. However, it could be argued that the economic analysis of the former Soviet Union reflected two general tendencies that were conditioned by the confidence shown by Western economists in the nature of capitalism itself. The two tendencies could be described as 'impossibilism' and 'reformism'. The proponents of both schools of thought would ultimately have agreed on the benefits of the market, the necessity of hierarchical social relations of production and, in the final analysis, the economic superiority of capitalism.[11] But their analysis of the Soviet Union differed in certain key respects.

The first tendency arose as a consequence of the debates in the early part of the twentieth century.[12] From the outset the attempt to undertake a revolutionary overthrow of capitalism and establish a socialist system of production was derided as an impossibility. For von Mises the early period of Soviet rule represented nothing more than

> a picture of the destruction of an existing order of social production ... all branches of production ... are in a state of entire dissolution. What is happening under the rule of Lenin and Trotsky is merely destruction and annihilation.[13]

The prospects were also necessarily bleak because no rational economic

10 . See, for example the responses to Andrei Amalrik, *Will the Soviet Union Survive Until 1984?* (Harmondsworth: Penguin, 1980), suggesting that his work was co-written with the KGB!

11. For example, the coupling of Alec Nove and Friedrich von Hayek as opposite poles in the market debate in an IEA pamphlet is somewhat disingenuous. The distance between Nove and von Hayek is not as great as might at first seem to be the case. Nove, rather than arguing (as his book title suggests) for a 'feasible socialism', always argues for a 'feasible' and humane capitalism: see Alec Nove, *The Economics of Feasible Socialism* (London: Unwin Hyman, 1983), and *The Economics of Feasible Socialism Revisited* (London: HarperCollins, 1991).

12. See F.A. von Hayek (ed.), *Collectivist Economic Planning* (London: Routledge, 1935). As well as von Hayek and von Mises this collection includes E. Barone's article, 'The Ministry of Production in the Collectivist State', as an appendix.

13. Ludwig von Mises, 'Economic Calculation in the Socialist Commonwealth', in von Hayek, op. cit., p. 125.

system could emerge under socialism.[14] When the Soviet Union industrialised, von Hayek[15] pointed out that this was in no way evidence of
the superiority or efficacy of the system, as the absence of 'rational
economic calculation' made it impossible to assess the worth or economic usefulness of the accumulation of means of production. For von
Mises,

> A socialist management of production would simply not know whether or
> not what it plans and executes is the most appropriate means to attain the
> ends sought. It will operate in the dark ... squander the scarce factors of
> production both material and human. Chaos and poverty for all will
> unavoidably result.[16]

With regard to the Russian experience what it showed was

> a very low level of the standard of living of the masses and unlimited
> dictatorial despotism.[17]

By the end of the Second World War the analysis of the former
Soviet Union advanced by the 'impossibilist' economists had been
partially eclipsed as a consequence of two new forces which gave rise
to the second tendency in mainstream economic analysis.

Firstly, the confidence of bourgeois economics was clearly shaken
by the experience of the inter-war depression and the apparent successes of the former Soviet Union.[18] The ability of Stalinist central
planning to industrialise an economically backward country (no matter
how brutal its methods) and, after a disastrous start, to contribute to the
defeat of fascism in the Second World War, convinced many economic
commentators that not only was 'socialism' possible but that it contained elements that could be adapted and incorporated into economic
policy in the capitalist West.

The supposed Keynesian revolution in economic policy in the West

14. Ibid., p. 130.
15. F.A. von Hayek, 'The Present State of the Debate', in ibid., pp. 204–5.
16. Ludwig von Mises, *Socialism: An Economic and Sociological Analysis* (London:
    Jonathan Cape, 1936), p. 585.
17. Ibid., p. 589.
18. As Maurice Dobb argued, the USSR seemed to be 'a simple country of progress in
    a crisis-stricken world': Maurice Dobb, *Soviet Russia and the World* (London:
    Sidgwick & Jackson, 1932), p. 12.

and the neo-classical–Keynesian synthesis in Western economics maintained some continuity with the von Mises and von Hayekian view of the difficulties in the micro-economics of central planning but simultaneously – and crucially – admitted the possibilities for state intervention to assist capitalism to overcome its tendencies to stagnation. At the same time, a similar argument was advanced that the predominantly micro-economic problems of the former Soviet Union were potentially amenable to resolution via the judicious addition of elements of the market mechanism to assist the operation of the central planning mechanism.[19]

Secondly, the practical analysis of the former Soviet economy was conditioned by the new needs of the cold war. What was now apparent was that the Soviet Union needed to be presented as a formidable enemy that not only was able to exist but was capable of considerable economic and military strength. This led to the cold war view of equal but opposite superpowers and gave rise to a particular economic view which was partially based upon the principle of 'know thine enemy' but which also sought to confirm the universal and generalisable nature of bourgeois economic theory. This was particularly reflected in the comparative economic systems literature and it was through this that thousands of economics students in the West received their education about the nature of the Soviet economy.[20]

The justification for this study was well explained by Bornstein, who argued that

> The comparison of systems enriches the analyst's understanding of his own system, sharpening his appreciation of its merits and demerits and suggesting organisational and operational changes to improve its performance.[21]

Methodologically, the questions to be asked about the Soviet

19. There is an enormous literature on market socialism: see Alec Nove and Ian D. Thatcher (eds), *Market Socialism* (Oxford: Blackwell, 1995), for a selection of key readings.
20. Even the best of the comparative economics texts suffers from this: see, for example, Paul Gregory and P. Stuart, *Comparative Economic Systems*, 4th edn (Boston, MA: Houghton Mifflin, 1992).
21. Morris Bornstein, 'The Comparison of Economic Systems: An Integration', in Morris Bornstein (ed.), *Comparative Economic Systems: Models and Cases*, 3rd edn (Illinois: R.D. Irwin, 1974), p. 18.

economic system were those questions familiar to any first-year economics undergraduate. The system in general was defined in terms of
'rules and order' that governed the interaction of participants involved
in the production, distribution and use of goods and services. The
familiar questions were: what to produce, how to produce, how to
distribute? In other words, the alternative system was faced by the
same problems but had its own peculiarities with regard to institutional
structure, incentive structures, and so on.[22] But even if the political and
institutional setting was different, since these questions were broadly
the same as those asked of capitalism the methodology of bourgeois
economics could be utilised to illuminate these problems. Once again,
this concentrated on a form of analysis that tended to eschew the study
of the nature of the system as a whole and focused instead on the
partial, descriptive and empirical.

This was, of course, perfectly appropriate for the positivist and
empiricist nature of bourgeois economics in this period. Many of the
studies undertaken provided significant insights into the day-to-day
operation of the system and the minutiae of its elements.[23] What was
absent however, was an integrative and historical approach that could
lay bare its laws of motion.

Perhaps the apogee of this reformist methodological approach was
the 'theory of convergence'.[24] This took the superficial similarities of
the contending systems and argued that there was a process of convergence evident in all industrialised economies that forced similar
problems to be addressed with similar solutions. The net effect of this
process of learning and 'rational' adjustment to similar problems would
be an 'optimal system' that would exhibit the positive features of both
systems.[25] As later critics pointed out, this view was superficial and

22. See Gregory and Stuart, op. cit., Chapters 2–3; J. Elliot, *Comparative Economic
    Systems* (Wadsworth: Belmont, 1985), Chapter 1.
23. This is not to suggest that interesting and illuminating work did not emerge: see,
    for example, the classic USAF-funded output from the Harvard Project, in
    particular Raymond A. Bauer, Alex Inkeles and Clyde Kluckholm, *How the Soviet
    System Works* (New York: Vintage Russian Library, 1956).
24. For a recent critical review of the idea of convergence, see B. Dallago,
    H. Brezinski and W. Andreff (eds), *Convergence and System Change* (Aldershot:
    Dartmouth, 1992).
25. See, for example, J. Tindbergen, 'Do Communist and Free Economies Show a
    Converging Pattern?', *Soviet Studies*, Vol. XII, No. 4 (1961).

partial, ignoring, among other things, processes of divergence that were just as evident over the period of the twentieth century.[26]

What the convergence debate did show, however, is the logical outcome of this second tendency within bourgeois economics. This considers that economic systems are capable of rational reform and that neither capitalism nor its polar opposite at this time, the Stalinist form of central planning, had any essential features. The economic system was simply a technical mechanism solving a technical problem. Social relations of production and relationships of power are wholly absent. The struggle to be understood in all cases is the struggle between 'man and nature' not 'man against man' or 'class against class'. The failure to grasp the essential features of capitalism and its laws of motion, and the inability to theorise the nature of the former Soviet Union adequately, led to the vacuous convergence hypothesis.

If it is accepted that Western economic analysis, because of its underlying methodological weaknesses, has proved itself conspicuously unsuccessful in understanding the origins, development and eventual degeneration of the former Soviet Union, a further question remains for the future: has anything been learned from this experience?

Western economists in the main have drawn the conclusion that the demise of the former Soviet Union and the collapse of the East European economies has finally answered the question regarding the possibility of a non-market form of economic organisation.[27] However, the further conclusion that should be drawn is that their analysis proved incapable of predicting this outcome, nor was it capable of adequately identifying the forces that led to the demise of these economies. In fact

26. See, for example, Michael Ellman's comprehensive critique, 'Against Convergence', in Michael Ellman, *Collectivisation, Convergence and Capitalism* (London: Academic Press, 1984), pp. 291–310; see also G. Roland, 'Tindbergen's Convergence Thesis: A Post-mortem Criticism', in Dallago et al., op. cit, pp. 39–47.

27. For Williamson, the reason for the transition arose because 'socialism failed to provide an effective alternative way of organizing an economy': see J. Williamson, *The Eastern Transition to a Market Economy*, Centre for Economic Performance, Occasional Paper No. 2 (March 1992), p. 3. For Sir Alan Walters the question is clear: 'socialist and communist systems have failed to deliver (in a literal sense) anything like the standard of material advance so often promised' and the superiority of the market is clear: see Sir Alan Walters, 'The Transition to the Market', in C. Clague and G. Rausser (eds), *The Emergence of Market Economies in Eastern Europe* (Oxford: Basil Blackwell, 1992), p. 99.

Western economists were suggesting, right up to the final demise of Gorbachev, that he could continue to muddle through.[28]

Furthermore, as Western economists have participated in the 'Great Trek to the East'[29] one of the casualties along the way has been the scientific claims of 'positive economics'. All the reams of print and hours of lecture-time spent explaining to first-year students that economics is a value-free, positive science, which can only evaluate what is and can say nothing on what ought to be, have been shown to be the sham they always were. The same Anglo-American professors who wrote the textbooks of 'positive economics' now espouse the virtues of the 'only system' or describe themselves as 'teachers of capitalism'. The ideological veneer of the positive science disappeared almost as quickly as the Berlin Wall once the initial breaches were made.[30]

Despite their poor record in evaluating the nature of the former system and identifying its laws of motion, Western economists have not been particularly modest with regard to proffering advice to the countries in transition.[31] Hewett's comment that 'western economists

28. Anders Åslund, writing in 1991, argued that it was truly remarkable that Gorbachev had been able to destroy the Soviet system in only six years but 'the problem is that when he had exhausted his destructive programme, there was no mechanism to eject him'(!): see Anders Åslund, *Gorbachev's Struggle for Economic Reform* (London: Pinter, 1991), p. 226. In Åslund's account no mention is made of the miners' strike of 1989 nor of the wave of labour unrest from that period onwards. For the significance of this labour unrest, see W. Moskoff, *Hard Times: Impoverishment and Protest in the Perestroika Years* (Armonk, NY: M.E. Sharpe, 1993), pp. 183–233.

29. This phrase comes from Williamson, op. cit., p. 2.

30. See, for example, Åslund, op. cit., pp. 229–33. In this section Åslund outlines a series of obstacles to economic reform which must be overcome. This is a curious blend of assertion and wishful thinking. As a consequence, 'Marxism-Leninism *must* be defeated' (p. 230); the government *has to* accept 'private ownership as an ideal' (p. 230); 'people *seem* to stand a lot of suffering' (p. 231); 'massive privatisation *is required*' (p. 232); 'socialist forms of ownership' (e.g. workers self-management) *must* be avoided (p. 232); 'relations between republics ... *are bound* to be better, the earlier a full-blooded market economy is introduced' (p. 233) (my emphasis).

31. See, for example, Williamson, op. cit., who concludes his paper with advice for Eastern Europe to 'hang tough where a bang (i.e. shock therapy) has already happened and to grit their teeth and take the plunge in those places where it has still not occurred' (p. 46). This advice should be tempered by his comments earlier in the paper, admitting to 'the absence of any background specialist knowledge of the region or any ability to understand its languages' (*sic*).

know a great deal about how to manage a market economy, but very little about how to create one'[32] suggests the need for some humility in the advice that they offer, but the proponents of the neo-liberal Washington consensus have been particularly vociferous and have not been slow in offering advice.

The Neo-Liberal Approach to the Transition in Russia

The Russian populace, like much of the rest of Eastern Europe, has received very little real assistance from the West but has been given massive amounts of 'advice'. This has come from many institutional quarters, but in the main has been dominated by the neo-liberal *laissez-faire* views of the IMF, the World Bank and the Anglo-American economics profession in its many guises. These views have led to shock therapy approaches to economic reform that have little to do with the requirements of the domestic populace and everything to do with the attempted integration and subordination of these economies to the world capitalist system.[33]

It should be noted that the demise of the centrally planned economies and the overthrow of the rule of the communist parties in the eastern bloc countries coincides, in the period from the mid-to-late 1980s, with a period of optimism about the nature of capitalism. Everywhere the supposed alternatives were in retreat. In the UK, for example, the Thatcher government was busily destroying the post-war welfare-state consensus and, with its rhetoric of free markets and free individuals, was rapidly privatising state property and seeking to marketise as many social relationships as possible. This strategy was also exported extensively into continental Europe and to the

---

32. Ed Hewett, 'Is Soviet Socialism Reformable?', in Alexander Dallin and Gail Lapidus (eds), *The Soviet System from Crisis to Collapse* (Boulder, CO: Westview, 1995), p. 313.

33. The IMF's view was clearly articulated by the Managing Director of the IMF, Michel Camdessus, in an address to Georgetown University School of Foreign Service, *Economic Transformation in the Fifteen Republics of the Former USSR: A Challenge or an Opportunity for the World?*, IMF, 15 April 1992. The integration was seen as the most important task of the IMF and full membership for these republics would 'make the IMF at last a virtually universal institution –something we have looked forward to since our establishment'!

less-developed economies. Equally in the USA, the effects of Reaganomics were providing, for the wealthy at least, some optimism about the future of capitalism.

So it was a 'bullish' strategy of market reforms and shock therapy (or attempted shock therapy in Russia's case) that predominated in the early economic advice provided to the economies in transition. This strategy was not simply freely chosen by Eastern European economic policy makers but was often a precondition for financial assistance.[34] The shock therapy advice rested upon a primitive economic view that was derived from neo-classical economic analysis, with all the short-comings noted above and the experience of policy interventions in Latin America.[35]

All that capitalism needed in order to flourish was the correct eco-nomic environment which would be provided by macro-economic stabilisation, liberalisation and privatisation.[36] It was assumed that the agents necessary to make the transition would spring from the old order and, once the framework was provided, would act as the rational economic 'man' of the neo-classical fantasy. After all, if capitalism is the only way, is the natural order of economic organisation and is consonant with human nature and so forth, this should prove, once the fetters are removed, unproblematic. Naturally, there were disputes between the contending policy advocates over the question of sequencing and the precise nature of the strategy, whether gradualism,

34. See, for example, the conditions attached to the IMF loan to Russia in mid-1995. This involved policy actions prior to disbursements coupled with monthly reviews by the IMF's Executive Board to monitor policy progress in addition to the normal quarterly reviews: *IMF Survey*, 17 April 1995, p. 116.

35. Williamson, op. cit., p. 15, suggests that the origins can be traced to the Erhard Programme of 1948, via the Bolivian policies of 1985 and then through the intermediation of Jeffrey Sachs (who had been an adviser to the losing candidate in the Bolivian elections of 1985) to Poland in the latter half of 1989. He observes that the strategy is attempting to end 'the biggest failed social experiment in history'.

36. It is not my intention to go into the details of the shock therapy programmes, since there is already a copious literature that provides both a description of the strategies, a justification for the pain involved and an explanation that there was no other alternative: see, for example, C. Clague, 'The Journey to the Market', in Clague and Rausser (eds), op. cit., pp. 1–22; Anders Åslund, *Post-Communist Economic Revolutions: How Big a Bang?* (Washington, DC: Center for Strategic and International Studies, 1992), Chapters 3–5, provides a useful summary of the elements of the strategy plus a defence of rapid change.

minimum bang or the 'big bang'.[37] Moreover, differences emerged regarding the time period over which it would be necessary to maintain the financial and budgetary stringency of the transition process; but beyond this there was a broad consensus.[38] Since all the participants in this debate agreed that the market was the only solution, and since their institutional support was funded by governments with a clear political agenda concerning the market domestically and internationally, this consensus was hardly surprising.

In many respects the policy advice harked back to the earlier era of von Mises and von Hayek, reflecting a degree of confidence in capitalism and the neo-classical view of the system.[39] It was ironic, however, that the supposed virtues of capitalism as a spontaneous system of economic control necessitated a government-led plan for its implementation!

The Impact of the Neo-Liberal Programme in Russia

The record of the transition process is, of course, different country by country.[40] Some of the smaller countries, with a shorter period of

37. See for example, Gur Ofer, 'Stabilizing and Restructuring the Former Soviet Economy: Big-bang or Gradual Sequencing?', in M. Keren and G. Ofer (eds), *Trials of Transition* (Boulder, CO: Westview, 1992), pp. 83–106; R. McKinnon, *The Order of Financial Liberalization: Financial Control in the Transition to a Market Economy* (Baltimore, MD: Johns Hopkins University Press, 1991); T. Rybczynski, 'The Sequencing of Reform', *Oxford Review of Economic Policy*, Vol. 7, No. 4 (1991); A. Kővés, *Central and East European Economies in Transition* (Boulder, CO: Westview, 1992), pp. 17–36.

38. Williamson, op. cit., p. 21, points out that the consensus included the IMF, World Bank, OECD, EBRD, EC, and various advisers including Åslund, Dornbusch, Fischer, Layard, Sachs, Summers, Blanchard, Krugman and others. He concludes: 'The profession for once seemed to have reached timely agreement on some novel and pretty fundamental issues of momentous import' (*sic*).

39. It is perhaps worth noting in passing that the level of argumentation offered by many participants has rested not on rigorous understanding but on a series of similes and metaphors. The old system has been viewed as an apple completely eaten away inside by parasites but maintaining its external glossy skin; the transition process has been viewed as a leap across a chasm of unknown depth and width; the assistance offered by the West has been likened to building a bridge between two mountains, and so on.

40. A useful comparison of country performance (1990–94) with regard to real GDP and inflation was provided by the *Financial Times*, 7 March 1995, p. 19.

Stalinist planning and already having elements of market institutions in place, have fared less badly than, for example, Russia and the former Soviet republics. Here the record has been pretty bleak.[41]

In economic terms, the elusive stabilisation sought since January 1992 has still not been achieved.[42] Inflation is still far from under control[43] and the budgetary position fluctuates as a consequence of political events, such as the Chechen war, and economic pressures, such as the demands for increases in the minimum wage and pensions. The decline in industrial production and GDP has been precipitate and shows signs, even several years into the transition, of continuing.[44] The fundamental problems of the domestic economy are well illustrated by the enormous outflows of funds that were estimated to run to $1.0–1.5 billion a month in the mid-1990s.[45]

The impact of the reform process on the majority of ordinary Russians has been extremely negative. Shortages have not been solved but disguised by attempted marketisation. Moscow shops may well be full of foreign consumer goods, but Moscow homes – never mind those in the provinces – are not. The impact on living standards is further

41. This, of course, is not the view of the Western advisers or the IMF: see, for example, Ernesto Hernandez-Cata, *Russia and the IMF: The Political Economy of Macro-Stabilisation*, IMF Paper on Policy Analysis and Assessment, September 1994, who identifies in Russia 'impressive achievements' in the area of structural reform as opposed to the elusive nature of success in macro-stabilisation, or Anders Åslund, 'Russia's Success Story', *Foreign Affairs*, Vol. 73, No. 5 (September–October 1994), pp. 58–71.

42. For an account of the early period, see Bob Arnot, 'The Continuing Disintegration of the Russian Economy', *Critique*, No. 26 (1994), pp. 11–55.

43. The government had hoped to reduce inflation to 1 per cent per month but by May 1995 it still stood at 7.9 per cent per month (*Izvestiya*, 6 June 1995) and in June and July was only just under 7 per cent (*Interfax*, 28 July 1995).

44. According to *Interfax*, 17 and 25 January 1995, the decline in GDP, industrial output, capital investment and agricultural output was greater in 1994 than in 1993. Prime Minister Viktor Chernomyrdin, in a speech to the Duma on 19 July 1995, reported that the decline had slowed in 1995 but from September 1994 to March 1995 per capita national income had declined by 25 per cent: *Interfax*, 19 July 1995. Particular pessimism was noted in the consumer goods sector but also machine building and construction continued to show rapid decline: *Finansoviye Izvestiya*, 1995, No. 48.

45. *Rossiiskaya gazeta*, 4 July 1995. The total for 1994 alone was been estimated at $50 billion (*AFP*, 12 February 1995) and a report by Interpol suggested that the figure for the period 1991–94 may have exceeded $80 billion (reported in *Monitor*, 2 May 1995).

amplified by the decline in domestic production of consumer goods: in the first six months of 1995, light industry output contracted by 38 per cent.[46]

It is all very well for Western advisers to proclaim the end of the queue and to herald the assortment of goods available in the shops; but the disparity between average wages and prices suggests that living standards for the majority are continuing to decline.[47] There is a continual problem with the non-payment of wages and estimates suggested that up to 12 million workers were not receiving wage payments in 1995.[48] The evidence on poverty suggests that it is endemic[49] and growing income differentiation highlights this problem.[50]

As a consequence of the poverty, the level of food consumption and the assortment of food goods consumed has deteriorated and agricultural output continues to pose problems, even though this is one area where it might have been expected that market signals would have had a swift impact.[51] For example, by early 1995 meat consumption had

46. *AFP*, 12 July 1995.
47. In the first half of 1995, inflation rose nearly twice as fast as incomes, according to an Economics Ministry spokesman: Moscow *Echo Radio* report, in *Monitor*, 29 June 1995. Furthermore, 20 per cent of Russians were unable to earn enough to buy even basic foodstuffs and 45 per cent spent virtually all their income on food, according to *Interfax*, 30 July 1995.
48. *Trud*, 14 July 1995. [This problem has continued in subsequent years – Editor's note].
49. Comparative figures suggest that in 1993, 30–35 million persons were below the poverty line but in 1994 the figure was only (*sic*) 24 million: *Segodnya*, 10 September 1995. However, a more recent figure suggested 47 million below the poverty level in mid-1995: *ITAR-TASS*, 27 June 1995. These figures need careful consideration and it should be noted that the poverty level has been redefined many times and is set, by Western standards, at an unimaginably low level. Furthermore, many of those whose incomes take them above the poverty level are so close as to make no difference.
50. According to the then labour minister, Melikyan, the richest 10 per cent of the populace earn 15 times the poorest 10 per cent: *Interfax*, 28 February 1995. This should be compared with 1991, when the differential was a factor of 4, and 1993–94, when the factor rose from 8 to 11 times: *Interfax*, 29 January 1995. This disparity in incomes is what is officially recognised, but the reality is probably worse than officials admit. In part this is because the ministry of labour can only guess at the very highest incomes, and since many are illegally obtained these are outside the statistics. What is certain is that the disparities are growing.
51. Goskomstat figures reported by *Segodnya*, 23 June 1995, suggest that food

fallen to the level of 1970, butter consumption was at the level of the late 1970s and the consumption of milk products was down to that of the 1960s.[52]

The reform process has not only lowered living standards but also had a profound impact on a wide range of social problems. In Russia for the first time in the post-war period an absolute decline in population has occurred.[53] This has been caused by a combination of a sharp drop in the birth-rate and increasing mortality. Disease and infant mortality, particularly in the first year of life, are heading back to levels that were normal at a lower level of economic development.[54] At present, the mortality rate is 1.7 times the birth-rate and two-thirds of the deaths are due to accidents, crime and sudden deaths.[55] The reduction in life expectancy[56] can be directly linked to the collapsing social infrastructure, the social strains of the transition, and the reappearance of diseases that were thought to have been eradicated.[57]

A further consequence of the marketisation process and the resultant economic collapse has been that enterprises are economising on safety.[58] In 1993, 7,600 workers died at work, an average of 21 per

industry production of staple goods had fallen by an average of 12 per cent in the first five months of 1995.

52. *Nezavisimaya gazeta*, 8 February 1995.
53. *AFP*, 11 July 1995, reported that total population fell by 1.7 million in 1993–94.
54. Infant mortality in 1994, for example, reached 19.9 per thousand in comparison with rates between 7 and 9 per thousand in the West: *AFP*, 28 February 1995. Furthermore, the number of women who die during childbirth has risen significantly: *Interfax*, 24 June 1995.
55. *ITAR-TASS*, 7 February 1995.
56. In early 1995, average life expectancy in Russia was 58 for men (down by 7 years since 1987) and 64 for women (down 2 years since 1987). These rates are similar to Kenya and Indonesia but well below Western Europe where the comparable figures are 72 for men and 78 for women: *ITAR-TASS*, 7 February 1995. By July 1995 the male figure had declined further to 57.3: *AFP*, 11 July 1995.
57. For example, through the summer of 1994 a cholera epidemic raged in parts of Russia as a result of poor drinking water hygiene and collapsing sewerage systems. The incidence of diphtheria has increased by 20 times in only three years and typhoid fever and anthrax have reappeared: see Boris Kagarlitsky, 'Spread of Cholera Mirrors Social Decay', *KAS–KOR* (Moscow), Summer 1994; in 1995, the incidence of diphtheria doubled over that experienced in 1994: *Interfax*, 20 June 1995.
58. R. Clarke, 'Accidents in Russia: The Cost to Workers and the Environment', *KAS–KOR* (Moscow), Summer 1994.

day; in 1994 this average increased to 30 per day and in the first five months of 1995 – even though employment and production continued to fall – more than 3,000 died.[59] Furthermore, 14,000 people a year become disabled through the fault of their employers.[60]

Finally, the economic crisis has exacerbated an old problem: according to a British Medical Association study, alcoholism has reached 'pandemic proportions'.[61] The authors record more than 26,000 people per year dying from alcohol poisoning compared to 12,000 deaths at the start of the decade. Pure alcohol consumption has increased from 10.7 litres per capita in 1987 to 14 litres in 1992. The problem of alcohol consumption has been worsened by price distortions in the process of liberalisation and problems of food shortages. Whilst in 1984 a bottle of vodka cost the equivalent of two kilograms of sausage, a decade later it cost approximately the same as half a kilogram of sausage. As well as alcoholism, there is evidence that drug consumption,[62] suicide rates,[63] juvenile crime[64] and marital violence have all moved sharply upwards in the reform period.

The much-vaunted liberalisation of the economy has other effects that are far from positive, as it has meant that old forms of control have been removed, simply to be replaced by the criminalisation of the economy.[65] High-profile problems of criminal activity – drugs,

59. *Interfax*, 28 June 1995.
60. *TASS*, 7 September 1994.
61. British Medical Association study reported by *AFP*, 10 March 1995.
62. According to one report, one family in six has a problem with drug use: *Interfax*, 16 July 1995. Drug use is also related to an increase in crime and *ITAR-TASS*, reported a 60 per cent increase in drug-related crime in 1994 compared with 1993.
63. According to *Vechernyaya Moskva*, 6 June 1995, Russia has the third highest suicide rate in the world; in 1990, 39,150 persons committed suicide, and this rose to 56,136 in 1993; according to *Komsomolskaya pravda*, 25 July 1995, this rose to 62,000 in 1994.
64. Juvenile crime is estimated to have increased by 50 per cent over the period 1990–95. The 14–18 age group accounts for 8 per cent of the population but carry out 16 per cent of the reported crime. For example, teenagers committed 60 murders in Moscow in 1994: *Radio Rossii*, 2 June 1995, reported in *OMRI Daily Report*, 7 June 1995.
65. According to the Trade and Industry Chamber of the Russian Federation, one business in four pays protection money, while almost half of all businesses had contact with the mafia in a single year: *Moscow Radio*, 12 July 1995, reported in *Monitor*, 13 July 1995.

prostitution and the murder of economic targets[66] – have been extensively reported in the West, but every level of economic activity offers the possibility for criminality.[67] The low pay, or lack of pay, of minor officials has meant that the incentive to abuse bureaucratic power has increased. The privatisation process has offered a wide range of opportunities for criminal activities and official statistics suggest that over 40,000 commercial entities are directly controlled by criminal groups. At a more mundane level, the combination of inter-enterprise debt and non-payment from government, coupled with the non-payment of wages and the impoverishment of workers, has provided an enormous spur for theft from enterprises.

There is a pernicious instability that today pervades Russian industry. Enterprises do not receive payments either from other enterprises or from government; as a consequence workers do not receive wages and cannot buy commodities; production declines and revenues to the government decline and the vicious circle begins again. This has been the net result of the attempted marketisation of the Russian economy.

Liberalisation has also had an effect on trade flows and capital movements. As noted above, the reform process has led to large-scale outflows of funds. The liberalisation of trade has reflected and reinforced the inherent instability and growing dependence of the Russian economy. Exports are dominated by raw materials:[68] 90 per cent of Russia's hard currency revenue is derived from raw material exports.[69] In January 1995, for example, while production of oil fell by 8.4 per cent from the previous year to 25 million tonnes, exports of oil outside the former USSR rose by almost 50 per cent to 7.9 million

---

66. *Interfax*, 11 July 1995, reported that the level of crime in Moscow had grown by over 7 per cent in the first half of 1995, with murders and 'banditism' in particular increasing dramatically. The Moscow police reported that one murder occurs every five hours in Moscow oblast and one gang attack every six hours: *Moskovsky komsomolets*, 29 June 1995, in *OMRI Daily Report*, 29 June 1995.

67. A report on criminal earnings by the interior ministry (MVD) has suggested that at least $16 billion 'dirty dollars' are in circulation in Russia and that 40 per cent of the money in circulation was obtained through criminal operations both within and outside the country: *Interfax*, 4 February 1995.

68. For example, in 1994 exports of crude oil and oil products rose by 11.3 per cent and 10.6 per cent, respectively: *Interfax*, 8 February 1995.

69. *Finansoviye izvestiya*, 1995, No. 6.

tonnes.[70] At the same time, imports are dominated by consumer goods and food. The net impact has been that Russia's external debt has continued to grow.

For the IMF and the Western advisers, liberalisation is a key element in the reform process. However, liberalisation is the mechanism through which Russia and the other republics of the former Soviet Union are tied into a subservient position in the international division of labour.[71] The growth of dependency for the vast mass of the population is offset for the ruling group by the access it provides to Western consumer goods and its integration into international finance capital.

The advice of neo-classical economists, far from providing economic benefits, has led to a profound contempt for their advice and for the market.[72] Their response has taken a number of evasive strategies. The first approach has been to talk up the 'successes' of the transition and avoid the obvious negative impacts on the domestic population.[73] This strategy has had little success in convincing potential Western investors,[74] has not staunched the outflow of funds, and has had little impact on the domestic populace.[75] A second approach has been to

---

70. *Segodnya*, 10 February 1995, in *Analytica Moscow Economica Weekly*, Vol. II, No. 6 (11–17 February 1995).

71. This was admitted by Yeltsin's economic advisor, Aleksandr Livshits, who argued that any growth that does occur in the short term will be of the wrong kind (interviewed on Russian television, 25 July 1995, reported in *Monitor*, 27 July 1995).

72. Numerous public opinion surveys suggest a large degree of scepticism with regard to the benefits of the market and democratisation. This is reflected in the jaundiced view ordinary people have with regard to the 1995 elections. Surveys in the middle of the year suggested that over 80 per cent had not made their minds up whether to vote or not; 50 per cent believed it was not worthwhile; and 56 per cent trusted no political leaders; the majority saw the market reforms and democracy as simply opening the way for crime and corruption: *Izvestiya*, 26 July 1995. Furthermore, when asked what they saw as the most important problems, respondents cited soaring prices (76.5 per cent), crime (59.2 per cent), unemployment (49.6 per cent), economic crisis (48.4 per cent), and social differentiation (32.2 per cent): *Kommersant*, 18 July 1995.

73. See, for example, M. Camdessus, *IMF Survey*, 23 January 1995, pp. 21–4; Åslund, 'Russia's Success Story'.

74. According to Chernomyrdin, the foreign investment in Russia in the first half of 1995 was less than $500 million: *Kommersant*, 4 July 1995.

75. For example, an opinion poll reported in *Sovetskaya Rossiya*, 8 June 1995, showed that 70 per cent of respondents said that things were getting worse; 69 per cent thought it would be even worse that year than in the previous year, and

claim that the reason Russia has struggled, in comparison with some of the other Eastern European economies, is that the reform process has been half-hearted – not enough shock and too little therapy! This argument is unconvincing. Neither Yeltsin nor Gaidar was half-hearted in his approach to the reform process in 1992. The programme intended the full shock therapy treatment but it was a question of *realpolitik* that led to the amendment of the therapy by mid-1992. As Gaidar argued, 'we had looked into the abyss and pulled back'.[76] The threat of a major social explosion and the ebbing away of the minimal support they enjoyed caused Yeltsin and Gaidar to withdraw from the full implications of the programme and opt for a more pragmatic, populist approach.[77] Equally, critics of the form that privatisation has taken in Russia fail to recognise that Gaidar's room for manoeuvre was severely limited by prevailing attitudes to private property and speculative activity.[78] A third argument has been to suggest that the reason why the transition has been so problematic in Russia is that the problems created by the old system were so deeply entrenched that the transition was bound to be more difficult. This assertion has some validity in that the economic psychology of the Russian populace is clearly not easily adapted to the requirements of a market economy. But if this is the case why has the strategy advice not reflected these deep structural difficulties? Is it because the advisers had little appreciation of the nature of the problems faced, or is it that the model they attempted to transport was not a universally generalisable form of human social organisation but one that requires particular cultural and historical prerequisites which were absent and not easily created? In other words, the market and the requirements of the market are historically contingent and not a reflection of human nature or other fantasies of neo-classical economics.

Ironically, the failures in the transition process in Russia have also coincided with a period of uncertainty and lack of confidence in

80 per cent thought Yeltsin's economic policy was failing (teported in *OMRI Daily Report*, 10 June 1995).

76. Interview with Yegor Gaidar, *FNS*, 10 January 1993.
77. See Arnot, op. cit., pp. 29–31.
78. In a press conference Gaidar admitted that the second option, under which most of the privatisation had taken place, was forced upon the government. and they had reluctantly acceded to it as a way of making sure that the principle of privatisation was at least accepted: *FNS*, 2 June 1993.

capitalism on a global scale.[79] Dissatisfaction with this neo-liberal approach has caused a reaction to occur amongst Western economists who recognise the limitations and problems involved.[80] These responses come from a predominantly neo-Keynesian (or left-Keynesian) perspective and are a throw-back to the earlier 'reformist' tendency noted above. But the question has to be posed: is their policy advice any more appropriate than that offered by the neo-liberals whom they criticise; and if put into practice would it be any more successful? The last section of this chapter critically assesses one typical set of proposals for Russian economic policy and evaluates their likely impact.

New Advice: A Radical Departure or More of the Same?

An example of the alternative proposals being offered by Western neo-Keynesian economists is the report of the American Experts' Group, delivered at a conference at Moscow State University in the summer of 1995.[81] The combined report had been prepared for the conference but was also presented to an economic committee of the Duma with the claim that it offered an alternative to the neo-liberal approach to transition.

The authors were very critical of both the 'Washington Consensus', that had led to the attempted shock therapy, and the economic policies of the Russian government in the period 1990–95. They sought to provide an innovative economic policy that was both politically and

---

79. It is difficult to find any of the major capitalist economies that is not experiencing difficulties. The Japanese 'bubble economy' of the late 1980s has burst; the USA continues to decline as an economic superpower; in Western Europe crises involving various types of corruption and sleaze have afflicted the UK, France and Italy; West Germany has experienced all kinds of problems absorbing the former GDR and labour militancy is on an increase.

80. See, for example, the articles on the possibilities of a 'social partnership' approach to economic development in *Voprosy ekonomiki*, 1994, No. 5.

81. The conference on economic transition at Moscow State University was held on the 13–15 June 1995. The American professors who delivered the report, giving themselves the modest title of the 'American Experts' Group', were Alice Amsden (MIT), Michael Intriligator (UCLA), Robert McIntyre (IPS/Bowdoin) and Lance Taylor (New School). The report was entitled *Strategies for a Viable Transition: Lessons from the Political Economy of Renewal*.

economically viable, and what they suggested as an alternative to neo-liberalism was a form of Western-style democratic corporatist capitalism.[82] Their solution was intended to be a more pragmatic view of contemporary capitalism that could replace the 'folk tales' of the neo-liberals. Nevertheless, it should be noted that their approach has the same fundamental objective – the introduction of the market – and to this extent, just as earlier reformists were not so distant from the impossibilists, they share the neo-liberal view.

What the American Experts suggested was a combination of an aggressive, Keynesian macro-economic policy intervention to boost domestic demand, coupled with a strong industrial policy geared to supporting viable enterprises and thereby developing the micro-economic structure; accompanied by wide-scale institutional change. In short, they argued for the necessity of a strong developmental state and the model for their programme is drawn from

> the constructive role of government intervention in the post-war rebuilding of Germany, Italy, Austria and Japan; the economic transformation of South Korea and Taiwan; and the recent restructuring of China and Vietnam.[83]

However, it could be argued that their approach is just as problematic as that of the neo-liberals. The path for reform in contemporary Russia that they offer may appear initially persuasive and attractive, but the parallel they suggest with Germany and Japan in the post-war period is misleading, with regard both to the preconditions necessary for this kind of strategy and to the likelihood that it would attract significant social support.

It is my view that the American Experts' programme mythologises both the process of development of capitalism and the outcome in the countries cited as examples. Implicitly it is assumed that the development of capitalism in those countries was a socially cohesive and consensual developmental process led by a neutral and benign state with a high degree of social support. However, in the first instances cited – Germany and Japan – the key precondition for the successful and early burst of capital accumulation after the Second World War, was that the labour movement had been destroyed.

82. Ibid., p. 14.
83. Ibid., p. 2.

In Japan in the immediate post-war period, there was a massive growth in both the size and the radicalism of the workers' movement. Trade union membership grew from practically zero in August 1945 to almost five million by the end of 1946.[84] But the new radicalism was soon defeated with the assistance of the occupying American forces, who banned a proposed general strike in early 1947. From 1949 onwards, there was a purge of 'leftists' in a wide range of occupations, left-wing newspapers were banned and managements were given 'either tacit or open approval to suppress independent union power'.[85] The strike waves of the early 1950s, particularly in the car, coal and steel industries, saw massive defeats for the trade unions after vicious pitched battles where a combination of police and gangsters defeated the trade unionists. This laid the foundation for the later economic miracle which was inspired, not by a general social consensus, but by the 'iron triangle' of 'conservative politicians, career bureaucrats and big business'.[86] As a consequence, by the late 1950s a combative, potentially independent labour movement had been broken and replaced by company unions, 'sweetheart deals' and slogans such as 'Those who truly love their union love their company'.[87]

Similarly in Germany, the mass workers' movement, on whom so many hopes had been pinned after the First World War, was destroyed politically and industrially (as well as literally liquidated) by Hitler in the 1930s. In the immediate post-war period, workers' committees and anti-fascist councils took over production and distribution in a number of areas, and politically the socialist and communist parties both re-emerged.[88] The basic policy of both the British and Americans towards the German labour movement was to suppress radical anti-fascist committees and to forestall the reorganisation of the trade unions and workers' parties. After a sufficient 'quarantine' period they would be allowed to reorganise but only in an acceptable form.[89] German trade unions were shackled by the British occupying forces who used

84. See W. Horsley and R. Buckley, *Nippon New Superpower: Japan Since 1945* (London: BBC Books, 1990), p. 26.
85. Ibid, p. 29.
86. Ibid, p. 39.
87. Ibid, p. 56.
88. P. Armstrong, A. Glynn and J. Harrison, *Capitalism Since 1945* (Oxford: Basil Blackwell, 1991), pp. 18–19.
89. Ibid, p. 35.

right-wing British trade union personnel to restructure the German unions on lines more functional for capitalism than for the labour movement.

These factors meant that both the German and Japanese workers were unable to act independently to defend their interests, labour was tamed, and the value of labour power was driven downwards. This process, directed and fostered by the state, gave favourable conditions for capital accumulation and provided the impetus for the post-war 'economic miracles' in both Germany and Japan.

A similar process has operated in the newly industrialised countries (NICs) of Southeast Asia. All these countries have used authoritarian control or denied basic trade union rights (or both – and in some cases denied basic human rights also) as the basis for their economic growth. Also, given their previous level of economic development prior to their experience of economic growth, there was no pre-existing labour movement. Semi-feudal and neo-colonial economies did not develop high levels of urbanised and organised workers or their political expression in the form of workers' parties.

In later years, in both Japan and Germany, some layers of the working population were incorporated into the 'economic miracles' by means of social expenditures and higher real wages, but this was only the case after labour was broken as an independent political and economic force. However, the benefits that accrue to labour should not be overstated.[90] The economic system that prevails in both Germany and Japan is still capitalism. It may be different from Anglo-American capitalism in terms of its structural and institutional forms but it remains capitalism. It still rests upon inequalities of income; social and economic exploitation of a domestic reserve army of labour (either in the home or in agriculture or in non-key sectors), or in the German case has required *Gastarbeiter* or the newly integrated former east Germans; it is still subject to economic cycles and it still passes that insecurity on to the poorest and least able to cope.[91] This says nothing about the exploitative relationship with the third world or the environment.

---

90. For a graphic account of how workers pay for the 'miracle', see Satoshi Kamata, *Japan in the Passing Lane* (London: Unwin, 1985).

91. An interesting journalistic account of the insecurities of daily life in Japan is provided by Joe Joseph, *The Japanese: Strange but not Strangers* (London: Penguin, 1994).

If the precondition for rapid economic growth in both Germany and Japan was the destruction of the labour movement, or its non-existence in the case of the NICs, then what of Russia?

Clearly this precondition does not exist and if anything it is just the opposite. Labour in Russia is still to a high degree urbanised, homogeneous, industrial and organised. It should not be forgotten that almost 50 million workers are in trade unions affiliated to the Federation of Independent Trade Unions of Russia (FNPR, in its Russian acronym), covering 90 per cent of workers, and amalgamations of unions have if anything strengthened the structures.[92] Furthermore, labour is still capable of conscious, collective, defensive action in particular regions, sectors or enterprises, in order to achieve specific goals. In 1994 strike activity began to increase and in early 1995 the number of enterprises on strike increased each month,[93] and was 120 per cent up on the previous year.[94] Much of this strike activity, for example the one-day warning strike by miners in February 1995, has been in response to the continuing problems of delays in wage payments.[95] Also, in 1995 there were two major collective actions, on 12 April and 1 May, both of them related to a series of labour demands, and they were bigger demonstrations than similar actions in the previous year and gave rise to a more politicised range of demands.[96]

These positive forms of collective labour activity are a testimony to

92. Kirill Buketov, *Organised Labour in Russia: Trade Unions in the Russian Federation, January–June 1995*, unpublished manuscript (Moscow, July 1995), p. 7.
93. In January 1995 strikes occurred in 92 enterprises, by February 249 enterprises and by April 513 enterprises: *Vesti FNPR*, 1995, Nos 2, 3 and 4, cited in Buketov, op. cit., p. 2; by June the figure had reached 829 enterprises: *Goskomstat*, 1 August 1995.
94. *Trud*, 25 July 1995.
95. It was estimated that by July 1995 more than 36,000 enterprises owed wages amounting to more than 6.5 trillion roubles: *Trud*, 25 July 1995. For details of the miners' strike, see Renfrey Clarke, 'Russian Coal Strike Opens Mass Political Campaign', *KAS–KOR*, 15 February 1995. [Strikes, particularly among miners and other key groups of unpaid workers, have continued in subsequent years – Editor's note.]
96. The 12 April 'Day of United Action' was called by the FNPR, and an independent research agency estimated that about 6.7 million workers participated in some form of action; although the FNPR tried to keep the demands limited to economic issues, participants called for the resignation of both the government and the president: Buketov, op. cit., p. 9.

the fact that the labour movement retains a capacity for action to impose its solution on events. Perhaps more important, however, is the negative control that labour can still exercise. What this means is that the potential threat of adverse labour reaction acts as a constraint on the actions of government. For example, the continual populist turns in the economic policy of the Russian government, often imposed on reluctant economic ministers by Yeltsin himself, reflect the fear of adverse public reaction.[97] The inability of the Russian government to follow the logic of the neo-liberal programme, with widespread restructuring, closures and mass unemployment, is further evidence of the negative impact of potential labour response.

This is not to suggest that either the labour movement generally, nor the trade unions through the FNPR, can forge economic policy unambiguously in their own interests.[98] The FNPR, for example, is riven internally by conflicts between unions in different sectors, different regions and with different political allegiances. Furthermore, politically it is unable to deliver a solid trade union vote to any particular bloc. The discussions around the electoral alliance 'Trade Unions in the Election' amply demonstrated this.[99]

Whatever problems and divisions there are in the Russian trade union and labour movement, and there are no doubt many, it is not at the same level of underdevelopment as that in the Southeast Asian countries. Nor have the trade unions and labour been defeated as they were in Germany and Japan. But what exists is probably the worst of all worlds from the perspective of the American Experts' programme.

Firstly, the precondition of a defeated labour movement or no labour movement is absent. To attempt to create the precondition of a defeated labour movement either physically or legislatively, is to invite an immediate social explosion.

97. This was particularly the case in the run-up to the referendum of April 1993 and the elections for the Duma in December 1993: see Arnot, op. cit., pp. 29–30.
98. I have been criticised at two conferences (*Critique* conference in London, January 1995, and the ICCEES conference in Warsaw, August 1995) with regard to this idea of the negative strength of the working class in Russia. On both occasions it was pointed out that Russian workers were in a very weak position and the evidence for this was the collapse in living standards and the serious social problems they face. That life for Russian workers is difficult is indisputable (as I have written about in a number of places). Nevertheless, the regime is also in a weak position and this is precisely why the current impasse exists.
99. Buketov, op. cit., p. 17; *Segodnya*, 18 July 1995.

However, secondly, a non-defeated labour movement would inevitably react against and resist elements of the American Experts' programme. In particular, that programme requires an incomes policy and rapid accumulation of capital. This can only be achieved domestically and will require an attempt to suppress real wages and increases in the level of unemployment. In an environment that is already sensitised to increasing income inequality, with widespread poverty and the growth of vast incomes for a small elite, this would inevitably have an impact on the social support for the programme.

Thirdly, and somewhat ironically, the weakness of the FNPR's control over its constituent trade unions makes it extraordinarily difficult to incorporate the trade unions and labour movement into any corporatist economic strategy.

A failure to comprehend the real roots of the process of capital accumulation in the economies that they cite, coupled with a limited appreciation of the social relations of production in contemporary Russia, leads the American Experts to inappropriate policy prescriptions.

Perhaps better comparisons for the model they suggest are not the war-devastated economies of Germany and Japan or the NICs of Southeast Asia but the developed economies of Western Europe that attempted the Keynesian–corporatist approach to economic growth in the period from the early 1960s to the late 1970s. The reason why this comparison is more illuminating is that the level of economic development, and in particular the development of the labour and trade union movement, in these countries is more akin to that of contemporary Russia. A number of West European countries (to greater or lesser degrees Britain, France, and the Benelux and Scandinavian countries) and Australia and New Zealand attempted to stimulate economic growth within a capitalist framework while attempting to incorporate the domestic labour movement. Yet in each of these countries the model either failed dramatically or is in retreat.

The broad reason for these failures has been the fundamental incompatibility that lies at the heart of this approach. The corporatist and interventionist elements of the strategy hold out the prospect of conscious control over the vagaries of the market. However, the capitalist framework of the programme subordinates economic policy to the requirements of both domestic and international capital.

Consequently, social peace is short-lived and economic policy rapidly becomes highly politicised. The neutral state, an illusion from the outset, rapidly shows its true colours as the handmaiden of capitalism and pursues policies that are at variance with the requirements of labour. The result is that labour leaders who have been incorporated attempt to encourage their membership to accept policies that are clearly not in their interest and as a consequence lose their authority.

In Russian conditions, given the peculiar combination of a rapid and deep economic decline coupled with high levels of overmanning and enterprise obsolescence, against a background of extensive trade unionisation, the decisions to be made would be particularly harsh and the fragmentation of the corporatist coalition so much quicker.

The absence of this domestic precondition is supported by the absence of an external precondition that influenced the revitalisation of the German and Japanese economies. When their model of economic development was initiated, the world economy looked much different from how it appears today. The world economy is now more centralised, concentrated and globalised, and the scope for individual 'national' solutions is much narrower. But, more importantly, in the post-Second World War period the USA played a crucial role. Under its hegemony the individual national economies developed along their particular paths, but the US economy was so strong that economically it could oversee the rebuilding of world capitalism and politically it was compelled to do this in the face of fear of the Soviet Union and the potential spread of communism during the cold war.

However, where now is the hegemonic world power that wants to see this happen and has the economic and political motivation for the reintegration of Russia and the former Soviet Union back into the world economy? No individual nation-state has that kind of economic power. The United States, racked by huge budget deficits and external trade imbalance, no longer possesses that kind of economic power. Neither does the Japanese economy, where the 1990s have led to some considerable doubt about its continued economic strength.[100] The collapse of the so-called 'bubble economy' of the 1980s has seen growth rates contract from an annual average of 4 per cent in the 1980s to an

---

100. See, for example, Bill Emmot, *The Sun Also Sets* (London: Simon & Schuster, 1989). [This problem has sharply intensified since this chapter was written – Editor's note.]

average of less than 0.5 per cent in the early 1990s.[101] The EU
countries have specific problems of their own and no world power has
an interest in creating more economic competitors, nor do they have the
pressing political necessity of integrating the former Eastern bloc in the
same way that the USA did at the end of the Second World War with
Germany and Japan.

Having said all this, it is equally true that no world power would
necessarily want to see the former Soviet Union and Russia descend
into complete chaos, since that could be extremely difficult to contain.
Hence the logic of the present strategy. First, provide limited and
conditional support for the market reform process which ideologically
reinforces the idea of the impossibility of any alternative to capitalism.
Second, allow for the international integration of the Russian economy
to occur where it is desirable, particularly in the energy and raw
materials sectors of the economy. Third, allow this integration to be
determined solely by the commercial criteria of independent (mainly
multinational) companies. Fourth, in return provide for a very narrow
sector of the domestic population to enrich themselves, integrate them
into international finance sectors and allow them to enjoy consumption
levels similar to their Western counterparts. This is a coherent (if
somewhat risky) strategy for the West which precludes the possibility
of Russian re-industrialisation and the problems which that might
engender. This is quite a different context from that provided by the
United States to Germany and Japan in the post-war period and to the
NICs more recently.

The potential of the American Experts' programme is critically
weakened by these two elements: the internal element – the strength,
negative or otherwise, of the labour and trade union movement; and the
external element – the absence of either a hegemonic world power or a
co-ordinated desire on the part of capitalist economies to see the
revitalisation of the Russian and former Soviet economies. These are
the two key weaknesses but they are not the only problems with the
programme. As briefly mentioned above, the conceptualisation of the
role of the state in the programme is a further problem. This has both a
theoretical and a practical dimension.

Theoretically, the American Experts see the state, and indeed all the
institutional forms necessary for the operation of a market economy, as

101. *Financial Times*, 31 July 1995, p. 13.

neutral. The state should act as a neutral arbiter, able to take a dis-
passionate overview of the social and economic processes at work,
evaluate alternative courses of action and make rational and necessary
decisions. In their view the state presides over a social consensus
which has an agreed developmental and transitional goal. Conflict is
apparently absent from their understanding of the transition process and
indeed from social processes in general.

But this seems exceedingly naive. The role of the state reflects
underlying economic interests and class forces and cannot be viewed as
an independent arbiter.[102] The same is true of other institutional forms.
In their verbal contributions to the Moscow conference at which the
programme was presented, one of the authors gave the example of the
accountancy and insurance industries as essential institutions for the
functioning of the market system. While this may be correct, these are
not simply functional, technical activities but reflect the underlying
forces and structures of interest within the wider social system. The
idea that institutions are neutral ignores the questions of why they take
the particular forms that they do, why they act in the manner they do,
and why and how they develop.

The practical problem with the American Experts' programme in
this respect reflects the theoretical issues addressed above. In the
context of contemporary Russian society, who is to staff the necessary
institutions, who is to provide them with their *modus operandi*, what
principles must they adhere to etc.? Members of the old state apparatus
may be formally 'qualified' to fulfil many of the technical functions
involved but how can they be constrained to act in the manner required
by the programme? Given the immense growth of corruption and
misuse of bureaucratic office, how would the new state institutions
protect themselves from the corrosive influence of capitalism, whatever
the superficial form it takes?

A further problem, which is not unrelated, is the nature of corporate
governance envisaged by the programme. What form will the enterprise take and what will be the nature of owner–management–labour

102. For a useful comparison between neo-classical and Marxian views of the role of
the state see M.C. Sawyer, *The Challenge of Radical Political Economy* (Hemel
Hempstead: Harvester-Wheatsheaf, 1989). For more comprehensive accounts see
Ralph Miliband, *The State in Capitalist Society* (London: Weidenfeld & Nicolson,
1969), and R. Jessop, *The Capitalist State: Marxist Theories and Methods*
(London: Martin Robertson, 1982).

relations? The American Experts' programme refers to the enterprise as either state-owned enterprises (SOEs) or privately owned enterprises (POEs). But what will determine the division between the two and what will labour's position be in each?

In the examples the American Experts draw on from the past, this problem is broadly absent because the German and Japanese economic redevelopment built upon capitalist social relations of production which pre-dated the war, and, while they may have been subject to some amendment, they were not fundamentally questioned, challenged nor changed. This is clearly not the case in contemporary Russia and the former Soviet Union.

Conclusion

The basic argument of this chapter has been that mainstream economic analysis failed to understand the operation and eventual disintegration of the former Soviet Union because of weaknesses in its fundamental methodology. The inability to theorise the old system and its disintegration has continued into the present with inappropriate advice based upon a neo-liberal view of the economic mechanism. This has resulted in a collapse of living standards for the majority of the Russian populace and the degradation of economic life as criminality and corruption become endemic, while offering little prospect of improvement in the immediate future.

However, it has also been argued that a neo-Keynesian approach to the transition would be similarly flawed and inappropriate for contemporary Russia. The historical parallels drawn with either Germany or Japan after the Second World War or with the NICs are inappropriate. Neither the internal situation nor the international context will allow the corporatist Keynesian solution to work. It may have been an appropriate strategy for capitalist renewal at a particular point in the past, but does not seem to offer much hope to Russia in the present.

While the neo-liberals (reflecting their impossibilist precursors) naively presume that the market is natural and institutions and individuals will emerge to fill the vacuum created by over half a century of Stalinism, the neo-Keynesians (reflecting their reformist predecessors) consciously want to create the institutions but fail to address the question of the underlying social relations of production. Ultimately both approaches to the transition in Russia present a fetishised view of capitalism.[103] The inability or reluctance to recognise that capitalism is based upon a process of surplus extraction from the direct producers leads to idealised views that capitalism can be introduced in a consensual way. Historically the introduction of capitalism has always been a bloody process and the problem is amplified by the attempt to introduce capitalism into what was once an industrialised society.

The Russian ruling group and their supporters in the West may have successfully undermined the old Stalinist model of central planning but have been unable to replace it with a system of domestic capital accumulation that is both viable and self-reproducing. The introduction of a quasi-money economy may have been relatively easy to achieve but the logic of that process has never been followed through. The attempts at privatisation, rather than being an example of the strength of the transition process, are in fact the reverse. It is one thing to transfer the formal ownership of the enterprise but it is quite another to restructure the enterprise, undertake mass redundancies and close perhaps whole sectors of the economy. Nevertheless, the full re-introduction of capitalist social relations of production requires precisely that, so that labour re-emerges as a commodity. Neither the neo-liberal proposals nor the alternative neo-Keynesian view provides a solution to this fundamental question. Mainstream economic analysis, because of its methodological precursors, does not even ask this central question.

---

103. For example, Richard Layard, writing in Bush (ed.), op. cit., p. 143, argues that what is required is 'millions and millions of capitalists'.

11 Russia's Economic Recovery Potential to the Year 2000

Steven Rosefielde

Introduction

Russia's gross domestic product and standard of living have plummeted since it became an independent nation in December 1991, falling by more than 50 per cent (Intriligator, 1994; Winiecki, 1991). This catastrophe is partly explained by the severance of inter-industrial production links with the former Soviet Union and the disbandment of the Council of Mutual Economic Assistance (CMEA, or Comecon) (Van Selm and Dölle, 1993; Van Selm and Wagener, 1993). But dislocation is clearly only part of the story. Russia is in the midst of a hyper-depression nearly twice as intense as the great depression of 1929 in the United States which shows few signs of abating, even though the leadership has abandoned shock therapy and sought to preserve the stability provided by the old Soviet system. What went wrong?

A great deal has been written on the subject, emphasising grand transition strategy and macro-economics (transitology). Much of this literature is superficially instructive, but it is detached from the past, giving the misleading impression that, if a few things are set right, prosperity will be quickly self-generating (Åslund, 1994, 1995a, 1995b; Murrell, 1995; Rosefielde, 1994, 1995a, 1995b; Campbell, 1994). This chapter investigates the plausibly of this hypothesis. It argues that Soviet Russian accomplishments were less than met the eye, and that communism has bequeathed to Russia a poisoned legacy: an infungible capital stock, a degenerate production potential, and transmuted anti-competitive institutions that cannot be easily extirpated. Although there are no compelling reasons for believing that Russia cannot eventually prosper, the evidence suggests that the nation will be fortunate to recover before the year 2000.

The Illusion of Soviet Russian Growth

This assessment of the baneful effects of communism's legacy is at variance with past scholarly descriptions of Soviet Russian economic performance. Official statistics reported in Table 11.1 indicate that national income rose steadily throughout the postwar Soviet era, more than doubling between 1970 and 1990, and implying a concomitant rise in production potential.

Table 11.1 Soviet Russian national income growth, 1970–90 (1970 = 100)

1970	100
1980	164
1985	195
1986	200
1987	201
1988	210
1989	214
1990	204
Compound annual rates (per cent)	
1970–80	5.1
1980–85	3.5
1980–90	2.2

Sources: Narodnoe khoziaistvo SSSR, 1990, p. 12. *Narodnoe khoziaistvo SSSR za 70 let*, 1987, p. 123.

According to the Central Intelligence Agency the dollar value of the Soviet gross national product in 1989 was two-thirds that of America,[1]

1. The dollar value of Soviet GNP used here differs from the figure in CIA, *The World Factbook 1989*, CPAS WF 89-001, May 1989, pp. 274 which was derived by the agency from the geometric mean of its rouble and dollar size ratios misleadingly expressed in dollars. The 67 per cent ratio correctly compares the CIA's dollar estimate of Soviet GNP directly with America's. Soviet and America

and new fixed investment exceeded it by 6 per cent,[2] suggesting that
Soviet Russia's size-adjusted accomplishments were correspondingly
grand. Why, then, has Russia had such a hard time harnessing this
industrial prowess to maintain and extend its past achievements?

Roots of Self-Deception

There are four possibilities: authoritative estimates of Soviet Russian
production potential were exaggerated; the old production potential
cannot be adapted to the post-communist environment; prevailing institutions are anti-competitive, and the decline is a normal part of the
process of Schumpeterian creative destruction which will soon usher in
an era of sustained prosperity. The first three explanations imply that
post-communist Russian economic prospects are being shaped significantly by the dead hand of the Soviet past, while the fourth, favoured
by the G-7, suggests that the triumph of competitive markets over
residual forces of disorder and control is just around the corner.

Although these factors are not mutually exclusive, the G-7 explanation has tended to hold sway because many specialists are reluctant to
admit that their previous appraisals of Soviet economic performance
were wrong, or to acknowledge that socialist and related controls
survive the formal abolition of administrative command planning. The
first task therefore in understanding why the Russian transition has
faltered is to clarify the record by revisiting the issues of Soviet
performance and the mechanisms of socialist control.

GNP were respectively 2,500 billion dollars and 4,862 billion dollars. The
corresponding per capita figures were 8,700 dollars and 19,800 dollars valued in
1988 prices. CIA, 'The Soviet Economy Stumbles Badly in 1989', paper presented
to the Joint Economic Committee, U.S. Congress, Washington, DC, 20 April 1990,
p. A5. For a detailed discussion of the Agency's dollar sizing methodology see
Imogene Edwards, Margaret Hughes, and James Noren, 'U.S. and U.S.S.R.:
Comparisons of GNP,' in *Soviet Economy in a Time of Change*, Vol. 1, Joint
Economic Committee of Congress, U.S. Congress, Washington, DC, 1979, pp.
369–401, and *Consumption in the USSR: An Intentional Comparison*, Joint
Economic Committee, U.S. Congress, Washington, DC, 1981.

2. CIA, *Handbook of Economic Statistics in 1988* (CPAS 88-10001), September
   1988, Table 8, p. 32.

Production Potential

The most fundamental measure of any nation's economic capabilities is its production potential; understood as the maximum competitive value of goods and services producible from its capital, labour and natural resources if all factors are efficiently employed (Rosefielde, 1994, 1996). This magnitude for most countries is higher than its actual output because production is never fully efficient, and lower than it could be had its factories been equipped with the world's best technologies and its resources allocated optimally across the globe. Since production potential in any of these senses is difficult to estimate econometrically, per capita gross domestic product (GDP) statistics are often used as surrogates, on the assumption that most countries are equally inefficient (Bergson, 1953, 1963, 1978a, 1978b, 1987, 1989, 1994; Rosefielde, 1990). Table 11.2 displays CIA estimates of this sort for 1989 which suggest that the production potential of Soviet Russia was 68 per cent of America's, above all of Eastern Europe, and on a par with the Netherlands, Italy and the European Community average.

Table 11.2　Gross Domestic Product per capita, 1989

OECD[a]	
United States	100.0
Australia	72.8
Canada	87.7
Japan	76.4
Sweden	77.0
Switzerland	94.8
European Community	69.3
Belgium	72.2
France	77.4
Germany[b]	80.9
Italy	70.7
Netherlands	69.6
Russia	68.0
Spain	51.9
United Kingdom	71.1

Selected East European[c]

Bulgaria	25.9
Czechoslovakia	37.3
Hungary	29.8
Poland	22.1
Romania	17.6
Former Yugoslavia	24.8

Notes:

[a] GDP figures to compute these data were converted to US dollars by purchasing power parties calculated by the OECD.

[b] Western area only.

[c] See Table 11.7, notes c and d for an explanation of the methodology used to estimate GDP.

Russia's gross domestic product per capita is computed in three steps. First the CIA's dollar estimate of Soviet GDP in 1989 is computed by multiplying America's GNP in 1989 valued at 1991 prices by the CIA's dollar-size ratio of Soviet to US GNP, 67 per cent. (5,659.2 billion dollars) (0.67) = 3,791.7 billion dollars. Second, the Russian GDP in 1989 valued in 1991 dollars is calculated from its rouble share of Soviet GNP reported by the CIA. (0.609) (3,791.7 billion dollars) = 2,309 billion dollars. Third, Russian GDP per capita is calculated by dividing the figure from step 2 by the population in 1989 (2,309 billion dollars)/(147.6 million people) = 15,631 dollars per capita.

The size ratio of Russian GDP per capita to American GDP per capita is computed by dividing the former by the later (15,631 dollars)/(22,977 dollars) = 0.680. See CIA, *Handbook of International Economic Statistics*, CPAS 92-10005, September 1992, Table 7, 21, and 31, pp. 24, 38 and 59. A detailed explanation of the CIA's sizing methodology is provided in Imogene Edwards, Margaret Hughes and James Noren, 'U.S. and U.S.S.R.: Comparisons of GNP', in *Soviet Economy in a Time of Change* (Washington, DC: Joint Economic Committee, U.S. Congress, 1979), Vol. 1, pp. 369–401, and *Consumption in the USSR: An International Comparison* (Washington, DC: Joint Economic Committee, U.S. Congress, 1981). Detailed estimates for 1987 are provided in Table A1. The dollar parity for 1989 was computed from the CIA's statement that the geometric mean in 1989 was about 50 per cent. It is possible that the dollar parity was closer to 66 than 67: see CIA, 'The Soviet Economy Stumbles Badly in 1989,' paper presented to the Joint Economic Committee, U.S. Congress, 20 April 1990, p. A.5.

This placed Russia momentarily in the CIA's first tier of countries, with the world's second largest dollar-valued GNP,[3] although it dropped to

3. The top five GDPs in 1989 computed by the CIA in 1991 prices were: America 5,659.2; Russia 2,309; Japan 2,044.2; Germany (West only) 1,143.5; and France

the second tier as the Soviet Union began to disintegrate in 1990–91 (Table 11.3).

These data will surprise those who believe that administrative command planning was inefficient, especially allowing for Russia's late industrialisation and relative backwardness because its performance is not notably inferior to many developed Western European nations despite the competitive advantages of capitalism. This implausible result has prompted several scholars, including Igor Birman, and Anders Åslund to reject the CIA's ranking, arguing that they overstate Soviet production potential because the composite dollar–rouble ratios used to convert rouble values into dollars do not properly take account of the inferior quality of Soviet goods, and their unsaleability on world markets (Åslund, 1988; Birman, 1983). These criticisms have been parried in the usual way by denying that quality adjustments were inadequate and that saleability mattered.

Under ordinary circumstances such perfunctory rejoinders would be dismissed since the composite goods employed in the agency's calculations could not possibility be properly micro-adjusted, and non-competitiveness clearly diminished their value. But the CIA's position was supported by a set of specious theories which made it seem that these concerns were misplaced.

Abram Bergson contended in a series of seminal essays that while Soviet GDP statistics did not measure market competitive production, they did closely approximate to production potential in the sense that firms operated near their production possibilities frontiers, and transformed goods at opportunity costs which could be estimated with adjusted rouble factor costing. The CIA's adjusted rouble factor cost estimates on this interpretation validly measured production potential in an important technical way that encompassed most aspects of efficiency other than the responsiveness of assortments to consumer demand, and even here it was suggested production potential could be construed to reflect planners' preferences.

A corollary of this approach was that the distinction between production potential and value could be carried over to dollar estimates of Soviet per capita GDP, with these values interpreted as the American

993.7 billion dollars. See CIA, *Handbook of International Economic Statistics*, CPAS 92-10005, September 1992, Table 7, p. 24, and Table 11.2 in the present chapter. Russia's current GDP computed through the exchange rate in 1991 prices is 201 billion dollars, which is less than ten per cent of Japan's. See note 5.

Table 11.3   *Gross domestic product per capita, 1991 (in 1991 US dollars)*

More than $15,000

Australia	Finland	Liechtenstein	San Marino
Austria	France	Luxembourg	Sweden
Belgium	Germany	Monaco	Switzerland
Bermuda	Iceland	Netherlands	United Kingdom
Canada	Italy	Norway	United States
Denmark	Japan	Qatar	

$10,001 to $15,000

Andorra	Guam	New Zealand	United Arab
Aruba	Hong Kong	**Russia (Dollar)**	Emirates
Cayman Islands	Ireland	Singapore	Virgin Island,
Faroe Islands	Israel	Spain	British
			Virgin Island, US

$2,001 to $10,000

Algeria	Estonia	Mauru	Serbia &
American Samoa	Falkland Islands	Man, Isle of	Montenegro
Anguilla	French Guiana	Martinique	Seychelles
Antigua & Barbuda	French Polynesia	Mauritius	Slovenia
Argentina	Gabon	Mexico	South Africa
Armenia	Georgia	Moldova	South Korea
Azerbaijan	Gibraltar	Montserrat	Suriname
Bahamas, The	Greece	Netherlands Antilles	Syria
Bahrain	Greenland	New Caledonia	Taiwan
Barbados	Grenada	Northern Mariana Islands	Tajikistan
Belarus	Guadeloupe	Oman	Trinidad &
Bosnia &	Hungary	Pacific Islands, Trust	Tobago
Hercegovina	Kazakhstan	Territory of	Turkey
Botswana	Kuwait	Panama	Turkmenistan
Brazil	Kyrgyzstan	Poland	Turks & Caicos
Brunei	Latvia	Portugal	Islands
Bulgaria	Lithuania	Puerto Rico	Uruguay
Chile	Libya	Reunion	Uzbekistan
Cook Islands	Macau	Romania	Venezuela
Croatia	Macedonia	**Russia (Geometric)**	
Cyprus	Malaysia	St. Kitts & Nevis	
Czechoslovakia	Malta	St. Pierre & Miquelon	
Dominica		Saudi Arabia	

$501 to $2000

Albania	Colombia	Egypt	Iraq
Angola	Comorons	El Salvador	Ivory Coast
Belize	Congo	Fiji	Jamaica
Bolivia	Costa Rica	Gaza Strip	Jordan
Burma	Cuba	Guatemala	Kiribati
Cameroon	Djibouti	Honduras	Lebanon
Cape Verde	Dominican Republic	Indonesia	Maldives
China*	Ecuador	Iran	Marshall Islands

$501 to $2000 *continued*

Mauritania	Paraguay	Solomon Islands	Vanuatu
Mayotte	Peru	Swaziland	Wallis & Futuna
Micronesia,	Philippines	Thailand	West Bank
Federated States of	**Russia (Exchange**	Tokelau	Western Samoa
Mongolia	**Rate)**	Tonga	Yemen
Morocco	St. Lucia	Tunisia	Zambia
Namibia	St. Vincent & the	Tuvalu	Zimbabwe
Niue	Grenadines		
North Korea	Senegal		
Papua New Guinea			

Less than $501

Afghanistan	Gambia, The	Madagascar	Sierra Leone
Bangladesh	Ghana	Malawi	Somalia
Benin	Guinea	Mali	Sri Lanka
Bhutan	Guinea-Bissau	Mozambique	Sudan
Burkina	Guyana	Nepal	Tanzania
Burundi	Haiti	Nicaragua	Togo
Cambodia	India	Niger	Uganda
Central African	Kenya	Nigeria	Vietnam
Republic	Laos	Pakistan	Zaire
Chad	Lesotho	Rwanda	
Equatorial Guinea	Liberia	São Tome and Principe	
Ethiopia			

Notes:

* Estimates of China's per capita GDP range from $315 to more than $3,000. The wide discrepancy among the figures is in part due to the difficulty of assessing the size and rates of growth for various economic sectors as Beijing attempts to reform its socialist structure, and the poor quality of much of China's data. None the less, many studies have placed China's per capita GDP within the range $500 to $2,000.

Per capita Russian GDP in 1991 was $11,981 computed by adjusting the figure for 1989 in Table 11.2 for the negative growth 1989–91 shown in Table 11.4. The geometric mean pseudo dollar estimate is 0.50/0.67 ($11,981) = $8,941. According to Oxford Analytic Reports, Russian GDP in the first quarter of 1995 was $55 billion dollars; and 220 billion dollars annualised through year's end. The implied per capita GDP in current dollars is 1,472: see 'The Russian Economy-Stabilization at Last?', World Bank, *Transition*, Vol. 6, No. 5-6 (May–June 1995), p. 20. Russian GDP per capita further adjusted to 1991 dollars is 1,327: see note 5.

Source: CIA, *Handbook of International Economic Statistics*, CPAS 92-10005, September 1992, Figure 1, p. 10.

dollar factor cost of manufacturing outputs with Soviet characteristics assuming fungible technologies, given planners' preferences. In this way it could be acknowledged that dollar estimates of Soviet goods overstated their international market value, while asserting their validity in other senses – a point stretched even further by the use of composite dollar:rouble ratios in practical applications for calculating dollar estimates, which concealed qualitative differences between Soviet and Western products through aggregation.

It was impossible to persuade the profession that these arcane rationalisations drastically exaggerated the USSR's relative capacity to produce desirable goods and services while the Soviet Union existed because most economists were reluctant to concede the magnitude of the system's shortcomings. The collapse of communism has radically changed matters. With the cancellation of state contracts by the post-Soviet authorities, it has become clear that the manufactured products and the capital durables required to produce them have little value domestically and none abroad. Now that the planners are gone, the fiction that Soviet goods were valuable has been glaringly exposed, and with it the justification for pretending that the CIA's dollar and adjusted rouble factor cost estimates measure comparative international production potential.

The further issues of whether adjusted rouble factor costing renders Soviet prices proportional to marginal rates of transformation, and whether firms operate near their production possibilities frontiers, are less easily settled by post-communist events. However, it has been demonstrated mathematically by Rosefielde and Pfouts that adjusted factor costing cannot reliably have the properties claimed (Rosefielde and Pfouts, 1995). Likewise econometric stochastic production frontier studies, undertaken separately by Afanas'ev and Nowakowski, for multi-product firms and output at different states of production revealed that enormous inefficiencies afflicting Soviet firms were concealed by aggregation (Afanas'ev, 1996; Nowakowski, 1994). It therefore follows directly that the CIA's comparative production potential estimates for the Soviet Union are grossly exaggerated on all counts. Instead of Russia being in the first tier of the world's nations (Table 11.3) ranked by production potential, it actually falls in the fourth tier or below, as Åslund earlier claimed without providing adequate theoretical justification.

Growth

This reassessment which has been gradually gaining ground has not gone unchallenged. It has been counter-argued that, even if adjusted rouble factor cost prices do not reliably reflect opportunity costs, Soviet growth closely tracks the West European mean in a variety of prices, including official established roubles and dollars, indicating that physical outputs of all kinds (and therefore production potential) were steadily increasing. As always, estimates of per capita GDP may be imprecise, but the price insensitivity of Soviet growth rates, it is asserted, demonstrates that, whatever the Soviet Union's comparative production potential may have been initially, the command system was sufficiently efficient to enable it to keep pace with capitalist competitors.

Table 11.4 Real gross domestic product growth

	Average annual rate of growth						
	1971–80	1981–85	1986	1987	1988	1989	1990	1991
OECD	3.2	2.3	2.9	3.2	4.2	3.1	2.5	0.8
United States	2.8	2.5	2.9	3.1	3.9	2.5	1.0	-0.7
Canada	4.6	2.9	3.3	4.1	4.7	2.4	0.4	-1.5
Japan	4.5	3.7	2.6	4.1	6.2	4.6	5.6	4.5
Switzerland	1.2	1.4	2.9	2.0	2.9	3.9	2.2	-0.5
European Community	3.0	1.4	2.8	2.9	4.0	3.3	2.8	1.3
France	3.2	1.5	2.4	2.2	3.8	3.6	2.6	1.3
Germany								
Eastern	2.8	1.5	1.5	1.7	1.1	1.2	-15.0	NA
Western	2.7	1.1	2.2	1.4	3.7	3.3	4.7	3.1
Italy	3.8	1.4	2.9	3.1	4.1	3.0	2.0	1.4
United Kingdom	1.9	1.9	3.9	4.8	4.2	2.3	0.8	-2.2
Eastern Europe								
Former USSR*	2.4	1.7	4.1	1.3	2.1	1.5	-2.4 to -5.0	NA†
Bulgaria	2.8	0.9	2.7	0.2	0.7	-1.9	-11.0	-21.7
Czechoslovakia	2.8	1.2	2.0	0.9	2.2	0.8	-2.3	-16.0
Hungary	2.7	0.7	2.2	1.7	1.7	-1.8	-6.5	-8.9
Poland	3.6	0.6	3.3	-1.5	2.3	-1.6	-9.7	-5.7
Romania	4.7	0.5	1.6	-2.0	-0.3	-3.4	-10.0	-13.7
Former Yugoslavia	5.0	1.3	4.2	-1.2	-1.4	-1.3	-7.3	-15.0
Other								
China	5.8	9.2	7.8	10.3	10.6	3.8	5.0	7.0

Notes:

* At factor cost, figures shown for 1990 are preliminary and subject to greater uncertainty than usual. The estimated decline of −2.4 per cent is based on the routine application of standard CIA estimating methods. Corrections for two measurement problems that worsened sharply in 1990 would change this figure to about −4 to −5 per cent. The first measurement problem is that we estimate year-to-year changes in GDP from data on gross output (the total value of output in a given sector), while the standard definition of GDP includes only the value added by primary inputs of labour and capital. We believe that this simplification usually does not lead to substantial errors in our estimates, but, given the breakdown in transportation and distribution that occurred in 1990, when materials were tied up in freight cars and warehouses, value added almost certainly fell more than total output. Data reported by an official of the Soviet State Planning Committee suggest that a rough correction for this problem might lower our estimate of the change in 1990 GDP by 1 or 2 percentage points. Second, we use Soviet data on rouble values of output in supposedly constant prices to calculate the change in some components of GDP. Almost all Western experts believe that these data overstate output growth – and understate inflation – because new products are introduced at prices that include overly generous allowances for improvements in quality that are often illusory. We believe that these data have not had a severe impact on our estimates in the past, but price controls weakened seriously in 1990, and inflation accelerated sharply. Our estimate of the change in GDP might be reduced by roughly one-half of a percentage point on this count. The above corrections for overestimation might be partly offset, however, by an adjustment for underreporting of output in physical units. In the past, production managers had incentives to overstate the output they reported to the statistical authorities because a considerable share of their incomes – and that of their workers – depended on reported output. Incentives for underreporting may have increased in 1990, partly because acute shortages made barter deals between factories more attractive than deliveries to the central supply system. Unfortunately, the impact of such a change in reporting cannot be quantified at this time.

† Estimates of GDP comparable to those through 1990 are not available at this time for 1991. According to official statistics for the former Soviet Union, GDP fell by 17 per cent in 1991 on the territory of the new Commonwealth of Independent States (which was not joined by Georgia, Estonia, Latvia, and Lithuania). This drop in output is too steep to be consistent with official statistics for Russia, which reported decreases in GDP of 9 per cent and 10 per cent, respectively. Reasons for the discrepancy probably include inconsistencies in adjusting for inflation and accounting for changes in foreign trade.

Source: CIA, *Handbook of International Economic Statistics*, CPAS 92-10005, September 1992, Table 8, p. 26.

CIA per capita GNP growth statistics displayed in Table 11.4 illustrate the remarkable similarity between the performance of capitalist and communist countries on this score over the period 1970–89, and it should be remembered that official Soviet growth statistics are much higher because they do not deflate the military and civilian machine-building sectors for hidden inflation, as was the agency's contestable practice (Rosefielde, 1988). Should it therefore be conceded that the proportional growth of outputs, hidden inflation aside, ensures that Soviet production potential increased 51 per cent in the 1970s and 1980s despite all Gorbachev's complaints about stagnation (*zastoi*)?

No, because the characteristics of the physical goods in question do not have any obvious connection with demand and utility. The amassing of machines to produce more useless goods, according to Marx's famous extended reproduction paradigm, does not increase the economy's production potential for manufacturing competitively valuable things. The Soviet Union's capital stock may well have grown rapidly during the Brezhnev and Gorbachev years, but this did not enhance the nation's ability to manufacture goods with commensurately enhanced international worth.

Hyperdepression

Soviet Russia's production potential reached its maximum in 1989 at 15,642 dollars per capita expressed in 1991 American prices using the agency's dollar index sizing methodology. The CIA's published figure, misleadingly labeled dollars, but actually derived from the geometric mean of its rouble and dollar comparative size indices was 11,672 dollars per capita.[4]

The hyper-depression which subsequently overtook the east reduced Russia's GDP 39 per cent by the end of 1993, according to Economic Commission for Europe (see Table 11.5). Other things being equal, production potential measured by the Russia's per capita GDP fell respectively to 9,375 and 6,997 dollars. But these figures, low as they are, falsely imply that the Russia's products were competitive on the global market. Although, an accurate assessment of the real competitive value of its GDP in 1995 is impossible because of residual controls, an estimate at or below 1,327 dollars per capita (in 1991

4. The geometric comparative GDP size ratio in 1989 was approximately 0.50. The Agency's corresponding per capita GDP figure for 1989 valued in 1991 prices therefore is $(0.50/0.67)$ $(\$15,642) = 11,672$ pseudo dollars. See note 1, and CIA, 'The Soviet Economy Stumbles Badly in 1989', paper presented to the Joint Economic Committee, US Congress, Washington, DC, 20 April 1990, p. A5.

Table 11.5 *European transition countries: economic activity, 1990–93 (percentage change over same period of preceding year)*

	NMP* or GDP[a]					Gross Industrial Output							
	1990	1991	1992	1993	1994 Forecast	1990	1991	1992	1993 Jan.-March	Jan.-June	Jan.-Sept.	Jan.-Dec.	1994 Forecast
Albania	-13.1	-29.4	-6.0	11.0*	8.0	-7.8	-30.0	–	–	–	–	-1.0*	–
Bulgaria[a]	-9.1	-11.7	-7.7	-6.0*	–	-17.2	-22.2	-16.2	-10.9	-8.2	-8.5	-9.3*	–
Bosnia–Herzegovina	1.6	–	–	–	–	0.9	-10.5	-25.0	–	–	–	–	–
Croatia[b]	-8.5	-29.0	-8.0	-8.0*	–	-11.0	-28.5	-14.6	-1.1	-1.5	-3.7	-6.0*	–
Czech Republic[a]	-1.2	-14.2	-7.1	-0.5	1.5-2.5	-3.3	-24.4	-10.6	-7.3[c]	-6.7[c]	-7.4	-7.1[c]	-(0.2)
Hungary[a]	-3.3	-11.9	-5.0	-2.0*	4.5	-4.5	-19.1	-9.8	0.1	2.4	4.2	3.8	–
Poland[a]	-11.6	-7.6	1.5	4.0	4.5	-24.2	-11.9	4.2	7.1	9.3	8.3	7.4	–
Romania[a]	-8.2	-13.7	-15.4	1.0	1.5	-19.0	-18.7	-22.1	-16.0	-6.7	-1.2	1.3	2.0
Slovakia[a]	-2.5	-14.5	-7.0	-4.7	–	-4.0	-25.4	-12.9	-26.2	-18.2	-14.7	-15.4	–
Slovenia[a]	-4.7	-9.3	-6.0	1.0	1.0	-10.5	-12.4	-13.2	-7.4	-6.7	-4.8	-2.8	-2.0
The FYR of Macedonia[b]	-10.2	-12.1	-13.4	-15.0*	-8.0	-11.0	-17.4	-15.8	-2.3	-7.5	-12.4	-15.0*	-12.0
Yugoslavia (FR)[b]	-8.4	-11.2	-26.1	-30.3	-10.0	-11.7	-17.6	-22.4	-39.8	-41.1	-38.7	-37.4	–
Eastern Europe	-7.9	-12.3	-7.4	-3.0	1.0*	-15.1	-18.1	-10.0	-7.6	-4.6	-3.6	-4.0*	–
CETE-4	-7.5	-10.2	-2.2	1.0	3.0*	-15.3	-16.8	-2.4	0.2	2.2	2.1	2.0*	–
SETE-8	8.6	-15.0	-14.5	-8.0	-2.0*	-15.0	-19.6	-19.2	-16.7	-12.9	-10.5	-10.0*	–

Armenia	-8.2	-11.4	-46.0	-9.9	–	-7.5	-7.7	-52.5	-58.4	-51.4	-39.9	-11.1	–
Azerbaijan	-11.3	-0.4	-28.1	-13.3	–	-6.3	4.7	-24.0	-20.4	-12.4	-11.6	-6.8	–
Belarus	-3.2	-1.9	-10.6	-10.0	–	2.1	-1.0	-9.4	-16.5	-16.3	-14.9	-10.9	–
Georgia	-4.3	–	-43.4	-35.0	–	-5.7	–	-45.8	–	–	–	-26.6	–
Kazakhstan	-0.9	-10.3	-14.2	-12.8	–	-0.8	-0.9	-14.8	-11.3	-10.7	-11.8	-16.1	–
Kyrgyzstan	4.8	-5.2	-19.0	-17.4	–	-0.6	-0.3	-26.8	-22.4	-24.6	-26.0	-24.2	–
Moldova	-0.5	-18.0	-21.3	-4.0	–	3.2	-11.1	-21.7	0.2	0.9	7.0	-10.0[d]	–
Russia	-4.0	-14.3	-22.0	-13.0	–	-0.1	-8.0	-18.0	-19.3	-18.0	-16.7	-16.2	-12.0
Russia[a]	-2.0	-12.9	-18.5	-12.0	(8.0–10.0)	–	–	–	–	–	–	–	–
Tajikistan	0.2	-8.4	-31.0	-21.0	–	1.2	-3.6	-24.3	-28.2	-30.5	-24.5	-19.5	–
Turkmenistan	1.8	-4.7	–	7.8	–	3.2	4.8	-16.7	5.1	16.9	15.9	5.3	–
Ukraine	-3.6	-11.2	-16.0	-16.0	–	-0.1	-4.8	-9.0	-15.0[d]	-18.0[d]	-18.0[d]	-22.4[d]	–
Uzbekistan	4.3	-2.4	-12.9	-3.5	–	1.8	1.5	-6.2	-3.5	-1.9	4.7	-7.0[d]	–
CIS	-3.4	-12.2	-19.9	-13	-10*	-1.1	-7.	-18.2	-17.5	-16.1	-14.9	-14.6	–
Estonia[a]	-8.1	-10.0	-14.4	-2.0*	–	-5.6	-9.0	-38.9	-39.8	-34.9	-31.8	-26.6	–
Latvia[a]	2.7	-8.3	-33.8	-19.9	–	-0.2	-0.6	-35.1	-41.9	-40.9	-38.4	-34.6	–
Lithuania[a]	-6.9	-13.1	-37.7	-17.0*	–	-2.8	-4.9	-51.6	-52.0	-51.9	-48.5	-46.0	–
Baltic States	-3.9	-10.8	-31.5	-14.8*	-2.0*	-2.5	-4.2	-43.3	-45.2*	-44.7	-41.7	-38.2	–
Total Transition Economies	-4.8	-12.3	-16.9	-10.0	-6.0*	-3.6	-8.8	-15.7	-16.3	-15.0	-13.8	-13.8	–
Ex-GDR Länder[a]	-15.5	-29.1	9.7	7.0	6-7	-27.3	-49.1	-6.2	-2.3	2.2	4.4	5.5*	–

Sources: *Economic Survey of Europe in 1993-94*, Economic Commission for Europe, United Nations Publication, New York and Geneva, 1994; national statistical publications and statistical office communications to ECE; IMF estimates for Albania; non-governmental forecasts. Aggregates for eastern Europe, the Baltic states and total transition economies are ECE secretariat computations based on 1992 weights and some estimates for missing components. Forecasts for 1994 are generally end-1993 forecasts of national conjunctural institutes.

Notes to Table 11.5

*   Net material product (produced) unless otherwise noted.

a   Gross domestic product.

b   Gross material product (value added of the material sphere including depreciation).

c   Enterprises with 25 or more employees.

d   Sample of physical output indicators. Since March 1993, the Russian Ministry of Statistics has published two industrial output indicators: one based on deflated gross output value analogous to those shown for other CIS countries, and one based on an aggregation of physical indicators. The former shows much more moderate rates of output contraction in 1993 (5 per cent for January–June, 8 per cent for January–September, 7.4 per cent for January–December), but may be affected by inadequate deflation procedures during a period of rapidly accelerating inflation. Similar physical indicator measures of industrial output for the full year 1993 were also published for Moldova (–10 per cent, vs. 4.2 per cent growth in deflated output value) and Uzbekistan (–7 per cent, vs 4.1 per cent growth). The physical indicator values are recorded in the table.

Aggregates are *Eastern Europe* (the 12 countries above that line in the table), with sub-aggregates *CETE–4* ('Central European Transition Economies': Czech Republic, Hungary, Poland, Slovakia) and *SETE–8* ('South European Transition Economies': Albania, Bulgaria, Romania, and the five Yugoslav successor states); *CIS* (12 member countries of the Commonwealth of Independent States); *Baltic states* (Estonia, Latvia, Lithuania), and *total transition countries*.

prices) is hardly unthinkable and puts Russia's plight in a more realistic perspective,[5] even without further consideration of the West's growth after 1989,[6] or its environmental liabilities.

Paupers' Paradise

The inability of the Soviet Union to keep pace with the West's continuously improving capacity to satisfy the economic demands of the global community, despite massive investments and steadily rising volumes of physical output, provides profound insight into the source of its failure. Experience has revealed that although administrative-command planning did not bring production to a grinding halt as predicted by Mises, Hayek and Robbins in the 1930s, neither did it work in the no-frills sense described by Bergson, Nove and the CIA, or in the visionary fashion claimed by Dobb. Instead, the command economy was epitomised by its inefficiencies. It worked to the extent that things were produced which crudely satisfied minimal human requirements for food, shelter, clothing, health, transportation, education and leisure, but at exorbitant cost in terms of capital, labour and personal liberty. The characteristics of the goods produced were inferior, and even when they met some high engineering standard they were discordant with demand. The assortment of goods likewise was both macro- and micro-economically deficient. Too many guns – and capital durables to produce them – were manufactured, while there were omnipresent shortages of things people wanted, and gluts of goods they did not need.

5. According to Oxford Analytic Reports, Russian GDP in the first quarter of 1995 was 55 billion dollars, and 220 billion annualised through year's end. The implied per capita GDP in current dollars, extrapolating the 1991 population at 1.004 per annum (149.5 million), is $1,472 dollars. Adjusted for inflation, current per capita GDP in 1991 prices is approximately 1,327 dollars: see 'The Russian Economy – Stabilization at Last?', in World Bank, *Transition*, Vol. 6, No. 5–6 (May–June 1995), p. 20.

6. Ibid. GDP fell at an annualised rate of 5 per cent in the first quarter of 1995. Industrial output in May was unchanged compared with May 1994. Steel, chemical and petrochemical industries raised output by 10 per cent in the first five months of 1995, compared with the same period of the preceding year. The budget deficit in the first four months of 1995 dropped to 3.3 per cent of GDP instead of 8 per cent. In 1994 inflation was 200 per cent and was running at 170 per cent through mid-1995.

This no doubt is what Gorbachev really meant when he spoke of stagnation, official growth statistics to the contrary notwithstanding. The Soviet Union, as became painfully clear, was on the fast track to nowhere, either requiring urgent radical reform (*perestroika*), or the adoption of a new system (*perekhod*).

According to Gorbachev and his Western advisers, radical reform and transition were the Soviet Union's only options. Administrative command planning must be debugged, or it would have to be rejected and replaced by competitive markets which would purge the economy of all its inefficiencies. This 'either/or' problematic, however, raised the fundamental question of whether past inefficiencies might survive the contemplated institutional changes. Did it really follow that the abolition of administrative–command planning would initiate a rapid capitalist market transition, unconstrained by a communist legacy steering the system on a different path?

Infungibility, Socialism and Post-Communist Inefficiency

The case for rapid transition rests on the assumption that Soviet inefficiencies were endemic to its command institutions, and can be discarded with them by rescinding Gosplan's authority to issue legally binding directives and contracts, revoking various state monopolies, including the domestic material technical supply system (Gossnab), partially decontrolling prices and denationalising some of the means of production, with property rights transferred to collective and in some cases individual private owners. Once proprietors are free to design their own goods, set prices, acquire inputs and distribute outputs in competition with other former state enterprises without government direction, it would seem that demand-driven market processes should eradicate Soviet inefficiencies. But one should not jump to conclusions.

First, even if markets were perfect, the characteristics embodied in Soviet manufactured capital and consumer goods cannot be easily altered. In order to adapt old embodied technologies to new uses, the design of capital durables must endogenise flexibility. This ran counter to command culture because in a planned order adaptivity was superfluous and costly. As a consequence, having inefficiently foreseen present needs, Soviet-embodied technologies are extremely infungible, and cannot be used to switch from inferior goods to those desired by the market. Although Russia has an immense physical capital stock, its production potential remains severely constrained by the dead hand of the communist past.

Similarly, while enterprises are described as being free, socialist culture persists. Housing, education, medicine, municipal transport, communications and public recreation are mostly provided collectively by the government at token cost. Private ownership is inversely correlated with size and national priority. The government continues to control key prices such as electricity and regulates in detail all aspects of business. The old monopolies continue to reign in their respective markets and the state pursues egalitarian objectives with nearly confiscatory profit taxes. And of course, the government determines macro-economic policy by printing money, coercing banks to grant credit, and managing foreign trade. Constraints may be softer than before, but they still pervasively impair economic efficiency.

The deleterious effect of governmental socialist regulation is compounded, moreover, by new institutions and coteries primarily interested in looting state assets and restricting market competition. Some of these are kleptocrats, state officials seeking to privatise society's wealth for themselves, and living passively off their assets, or incomes generated by influence-peddling. Others are managers and criminals more concerned with building monopolies and extortion than competitively maximising wealth through investment and improved efficiency (Intriligator, 1994; Kleiner, 1994; Rosefielde and Pfouts, 1988; Åslund, 1995b; Cohen, 1995). Each operates in its own distinct fashion, but has the common effect of suppressing the kind of textbook entrepreneurship essential if Russia is to transition into competitive market capitalism, instead of some destructively exotic variant of kleptocratic market socialism.

Rehabilitation, Recovery and Modernisation

It is premature to judge whether Russian reconstruction, to the extent it occurs, will be governed by some mutated form of its communist legacy, or by entrepreneurial capitalism. None the less, the foregoing analysis illuminates the alternatives and their determining factors. First, as already explained, the Russian hyper-depression is the inevitable consequence of past communist inefficiencies that could only have been papered over by preserving administrative–command planning, although sounder policies could have mitigated much pain. Second, the level of production can be quickly increased by reactivating idle capacities and putting redundant factors to alternative use through sundry public works projects, but only if the leadership is prepared to rehabilitate a system already shown to be on a treadmill to nowhere. Third, if Russia is to acquire a production potential capable of serving the global market, its leaders must empower competitive entrepreneurship by eradicating kleptocracy, graft, corruption, excessive socialist regulation and all critical non-state barriers to market entry. Playing at capitalist transition will not suffice, and muddling through is unlikely to be any better because the heritage of communism is too deeply encoded in the nation's physical environment, institutions and culture.

Conclusion

Russia's recovery potential to the year 2000 is clouded by the physical, institutional and cultural vestiges of Soviet communism. Although disparities between the performance during and after the Soviet period: the dismantling of command planning, the dissolution of the state distribution network, the decontrol of price, the partial denationalisation of the means of production, and the emergence of some market forces might seem to refute this assertion, close analysis has shown otherwise. Russia's shockingly low capacity to produce goods competitively in the international market is a direct consequence of past Soviet failures disguised by authoritative misinterpretations of the data, made explicit by the revocation of assured state demand for unwanted goods and services. Its inability to rectify the situation is likewise explained by the infungibility of its Soviet capital stock, socialist survivals, and new and transmuted institutions steeped in anti-competitive attitudes, none of which is likely to fade away of its own accord. As a consequence, Russia's prospects for capitalist transition depend crucially on incorruptible and resolute leadership empowering entrepreneurship by eradicating barriers to market entry. If it is forthcoming, recovery and modernisation will be swift; if not, the inefficiencies of Soviet socialism will combine with new anti-competitive institutions to thwart and distort Russia's production potential, even if there is a resumption in the physical growth of unwanted things.

References

Afanas'ev, Mikhail (1996), 'Command Constrained Efficiency in Soviet Cotton-Refining and the Kaunasskoi Candy Factory,' in Steven Rosefielde (ed.), *Efficiency and the Economic Recovery Potential of Russia.*

Åslund, Anders (1995a), *How Russia Became a Market Economy* (Washington, DC: Brookings Institute).

—— (1995b), 'Russia's Sleaze Sector', *The New York Times*, 11 July.

—— (1994), 'Lessons of the First Four Years of Systemic Change in Eastern Europe', *Journal of Comparative Economics*, Vol. 19, pp. 22–38.

—— (1988), 'How Small Is Soviet National Income?', in Henry Rowen and Charles Wolf, Jr (eds), *The Impoverished Superpower: Perestroika and the Soviet Military Burden* (San Francisco, CA: ICS Press), pp. 13–62.

Bergson, Abram (1953), *Soviet National Income and Product in 1937* (New York: Columbia University Press).

—— (1963), 'National Income', in Abram Bergson and Simon Kuznets (eds), *Economic Trends in the Soviet Union* (Cambridge, MA: Harvard University Press), pp. 1–37.

—— (1978a), *Productivity and the Social System: The USSR and the West* (Cambridge, MA: Harvard University Press).

—— (1978b), *Soviet Postwar Economic Development* (Stockholm Almqvist & Wiksell).

—— (1987), 'Comparative Productivity: The USSR, Eastern Europe and the West', *American Economic Review*, Vol. 77, No. 3, pp. 342–57.

—— (1989), *Planning and Performance in Socialist Economies* (Boston, MA: Unwin Hyman).

—— (1994), 'The Communist Efficiency Gap: Alternative Measures', *Comparative Economic Studies*, Vol. 36, No. 1, pp. 1–12.

Birman, Igor (1983), *Ekonomika nedostach* (New York: Chalidze Publishers).

Campbell, Robert W. (1994), *The Postcommunist Economic Transformation: Essays in Honor of Gregory Grossman* (Boulder, CO: Westview).

CIA (1982), *USSR: Measures of Economic Growth and Development, 1950–80*, Joint Economic Committee of Congress, 175–250 (8 December).

—— (1988), *Handbook of International Economic Statistics*, CPAS 88-10001 (September).

—— (1990a), *Measuring Soviet GNP: Problems and Solutions*, SOV90-10038 (September).

—— (1990b), 'The Soviet Economy Stumbles Badly in 1989', paper presented to the Joint Economic Committee, US Congress (20 April).

—— (1992), *Handbook of International Economic Statistics*, CPAS 92-10005 (September).

Cohen, Ariel (1995), 'Crime and Corruption in Eurasia: A Threat to Democracy and International Security', *Transition*, Vol. 6, No. 5–6, pp. 7–10.

Edwards, Imogene, Margaret Hughes and James Noren (1979), 'U.S. and U.S.S.R.: Comparisons of GNP', in *Soviet Economy in a Time of Change*, Joint Economic Committee, US Congress (Washington, DC), Vol. 1, pp. 369–401.

—— (1981), *Consumption in the USSR: An International Comparison*, Joint Economic Committee, US Congress (Washington, DC).

Intriligator, M. (1994), 'Privatization in Russia Has Led to Criminalisation', *The Australian Economic Review*, No. 106, pp. 4–14.

Kleiner, George (1994), 'Russian Management: A Test for Incomplete Profit Maximization', *Comparative Economic Studies*, Vol. 36, No. 4, pp. 101–18.

Murrell, Peter (1995), 'The Transition According to Cambridge, Mass.', *Journal of Economic Literature*, Vol. 33, No. 1, pp. 164–78.

Nowakowski, Joseph (1994), 'Efficiency at Different Stages of Production in the Soviet Union', *Comparative Economic Studies*, Vol. 26, No. 4, pp. 79–100.

Rosefielde, Steven (1990), 'Comparative Productivity: The USSR, Eastern Europe and the West: Comment', *American Economic*

Review, Vol. 80, No. 4, pp. 45–54.

—— (1994), 'Russia's Economic Recovery Potential: Optimizing the Residual Productivity of the Soviet Capital Stock', *Comparative Economic Studies*, Vol. 36, No. 4, pp. 119–42.

—— (1995a), 'Eastern Economic Reform: Transition or Mutation?', review of Christopher Clague and Gordon C. Rausser (eds), *The Emergence of Market Economies in Eastern Europe*, *Atlantic Economic Journal*, Vol. 23, No. 4, pp. 323–32.

—— (1995b), 'Review of Robert Campbell (ed.), *The Postcommunist Economic Transformation: Essays in Honor of Gregory Grossman*', *Journal of Economic Literature*, Vol. 33, No. 4, pp. 2023–4.

—— (1996), *Efficiency and The Economic Recovery Potential of Russia*.

—— and R.W. Pfouts (1995), 'Neoclassical Norms and the Valuation of National Product in the Soviet Union and Its Postcommunist Successor States', *Journal of Comparative Economics*, Vol. 21, No. 3, pp. 375–89.

—— (1988), 'Economic Optimization and Technical Efficiency in Soviet Enterprises Jointly Regulated by Plans and Incentives, *European Economic Review*, Vol. 32, No. 6, pp. 1285–99.

Sachs, Jeffrey D. (1994), 'Prospects for Monetary Stabilization in Russia', in Anders Åslund (ed.), *Economic Transformation in Russia* (London: Pinter).

Van Selm, Gijsbertus and E. Dölle (1993), 'Soviet Interrepublican Capital Transfers and the Republics' Level of Development, 1966–91', *MOST, Economic Journal on Eastern Europe and the Former Soviet Union*, No. 1, pp. 133–49.

Van Selm, Gijsbertus and H.J. Wagener (1993), 'Soviet Republics' Economic Interdependence', *Osteuropa Wirtschaft*, No. 1, pp. 23–39.

Winiecki, Jan (1991), 'The Inevitability of a Fall in Output in the Early Stages of Transition to the Market: Theoretical Underpinning', *Soviet Studies*, Vol. 43, No. 4, pp. 669–76.

World Bank (1995), 'The Russian Economy – Stabilization at Last?', *Transition*, Vol. 6, No. 5–6.

Appendix 11 A

Gross National Product, by end use, in the US and the USSR, 1987[a]

	Billion 1982 Roubles			Billion 1982 US $			Geometric mean of the comparisons in dollars and roubles
	USSR[b]	US	USSR as percentage of US	USSR	US	USSR as percentage of US	USSR as percentage of US
GNP	766	1,857	41	2,608	3,797	69	53
of which: consumption	408	1,536	27	1,253	2,637	48	36
New fixed investment	217	233	93	928	776	120	106

Source: CIA, *Handbook for Economics Statistics, 1988*, CPAS 88-10001 (September 1988), p. 32, Table 8.

Notes:

[a] The preferred procedure for making international economic comparisons is to convert each country's GNP to the currency of the other. Two comparisons can then be made, one in roubles and one in dollars. The two comparisons will yield different answers. This phenomenon is commonly known as the 'index number problem', and it results from differences in the relative price and quantity structures found in each country. Goods produced in relatively large quantities in either country tend to sell at relatively low prices in the country, and vice versa. Soviet GNP is, therefore, a large share of US GNP when comparisons are made in dollars since dollars place a greater weight than rouble prices do on investment and defence goods, which account for larger shares of output in the Soviet Union than in the United States.

The important point about index numbers is that valuations in either roubles or dollars are equally correct. When a single comparison of US and Soviet GNP is required, economists by convention often use the geometric mean of the rouble and dollar comparisons as a reasonable compromise that falls between the two.

The geometric mean comparison is presented here, although the reader is warned that it is used for its presentational convenience and does not, strictly speaking, represent a more valid result than that presented in either currency.

The estimate of Soviet GNP in dollars presented here is different from that given in Table 11.7, which uses the geometric mean of the comparisons for consistency with the other data in that table. The approach used in this table, however, is theoretically preferable.

[b] The above Soviet GNP data in established prices should not be used in conjunction

with Soviet foreign trade data appearing in Tables 138–40 of the CIA *Handbook*. The latter tables use official foreign exchange rates to derive dollar values for trade; we have yet to estimate the value of Soviet foreign trade in terms of actual purchasing power, which would allow for an estimate of the share of foreign trade in Soviet national income.

The magnitudes for the Soviet end-use components were calculated to measure value of output compared with the United States but not the cost in resources. The share of total economic resources devoted to particular end use (such as defence) or the share of total output originating in an individual sector (for example, agriculture or industry) in the USSR should be measured in internal rouble prices and costs.

The identified end uses of GNP are defined as follows: (1) Consumption includes personal expenditures for goods and services for all purposes and noninvestment outlays by government for goods and services for health and education. (2) New fixed investment is defined as the sum of expenditures for gross private domestic investment net of inventories for public construction other than that for military facilities; and for equipment purchased by the government except that for defence. Since part of Soviet capital repair is considered new investment in the Western sense, a portion of Soviet expenditures on capital repair is included in Soviet new fixed investment.

Other uses of GNP include defence, space, research and development, inventory change, administration, net exports, and a statistical discrepancy. The total value for these expenditures cannot be derived for the USSR by subtraction, however.

12 Georgian Economy: Main Directions and Initial Results of Reforms
From 'Shock Therapy' to 'Social Promotion'

Vladimer Papava

Georgia before 'Shock Therapy'

The question is often posed of when the economic reform started in Georgia. In my opinion the period from 1989, when the idea of national independence embraced the whole society, should be considered as its starting-point. It became a turning-point for both economists and those claiming to know economies, resulting in the creation of a number of interesting new concepts linked to the idea of economic independence (Papava, 1990). This first stage can conventionally be called *the stage of naïve comprehension*.

The second stage of economic reform started after the election of the Supreme Council in the autumn of 1990. At that time several very important laws on economic reform were issued, though they were unfortunately not implemented effectively. This stage of reform can therefore be considered *the stage of reform stagnation*.

After the coup d'état of December 1991–January 1992 there began *the stage of populist economic reform*. At that time the government transferred land and dwellings to people without compensation in order to enlist the 'easy' support of the population. These redistributive policies caused substantial damage to the agricultural sector and house-building. In particular, land privatisation was carried out mechanically and it practically ruined the necessary infrastructure for agricultural production (the system of supply of machinery, fertilisers and other resources); and without a legal basis for private ownership of land the efficiency of land tenure is very low. If differentiation of rental payments for dwellings had been made according to location and amenities, the money thus received could have been accumulated for further housing development. This became impossible because of the over-hasty, free distribution of dwellings (Papava, 1992, pp. 97–101).

During this populist stage of economic reform the method of 'shock therapy' was used in Georgia at almost at the same time as in Russia and in accordance with the Russian scenario. Was Georgia ready to apply this well-known approach to economic reform?

In order to answer this question, an important distinction of principle should be pointed out, concerning the nature of the state. Thus, it turned out to matter a great deal whether countries were with or without their own independent statehood at the beginning of their reforms. To the first type belong the countries of Eastern Europe, such as Poland, Hungary, Bulgaria, and so on, and to the second – the newly created countries following the disintegration of the former Soviet Union and Yugoslavia (and also Czechoslovakia). Among the latter countries, the legal successors of the original larger states are the only exceptions because they preserved almost all the attributes of statehood. Thus, after the disintegration of the Soviet Union, Russia was recognised as the legal successor of the USSR, retained Moscow as its capital and preserved all the attributes of statehood, inheriting the institutions of the former Soviet Union. Hence Russia can be classified with the group of post-communist countries already possessing statehood. All other countries had to build up their own state institutions, often from almost nothing (to a certain extent, Ukraine and Belorussia can be considered exceptions, since, although formally lacking independent statehood, they were already members of the United Nations). Georgia was one of the countries facing this situation. It therefore had to manage two major tasks simultaneously: the need to build up the institutions of a new state, and the process of transition from central planning to a market-type economy.

As is well known, the 'shock therapy' method of economic reform was developed and used first in West Germany after the Second World

War. New life was breathed into it in post-communist Poland with the introduction of the Balcerowicz Plan in 1990 (Balcerowicz, 1994; Schaffer, 1992). The implementation of this approach to macro-economic stabilisation requires the active involvement of several different governmental institutions. To apply the method of 'shock therapy' in the absence of these crucial institutions is impossible and any attempt to do so is doomed to failure. The experience of Georgia also supports the validity of this view. It is not difficult to demonstrate this. It is enough to elaborate what 'shock therapy' means according to the so-called 'Balcerowicz Plan' (considered today as the modern and already classical scheme of 'shock therapy') and then to study the defects in the implementation of 'shock therapy' when it was applied in Georgia, blindly imitating the reflections in the Russian 'mirror'.

The Method of 'Shock-Therapy' and its Defective Georgian Modification

The method of 'shock therapy' generally assumes that a strict fiscal policy is being implemented. It entails the simultaneous adoption of measures concerned with price liberalisation, a considerable reduction of the state budget deficit by cancelling budgetary subsidies, and stringent control over the money supply and income of the population. The plan developed by the former Polish finance minister, Leszek Balcerowicz, is considered to be an excellent, modern example of the method of 'shock therapy', and is frequently referred to favourably by other transition economies. According to this plan, the following measures were simultaneously implemented in Poland from the very start:

1. Multiple increases of all types of prices; a deliberate, though it was hoped temporary, increase in inflation aimed at ensuring and then maintaining market equilibrium;
2. Tough restrictions on the (real) incomes of the population;
3. A substantial increase in (nominal) interest rates and restrictions on the money supply in circulation;
4. Increases in the interest rates on cash and other deposits, aimed at stimulating the population to save;
5. Sharp cuts in state budget expenses by reducing government

investments and by refusing to subsidise unprofitable enterprises any longer;

6. Using issues of government bonds to help cover the state budget deficit;
7. Regulating the tax system and moving towards a more uniform, western-type tax structure;
8. Introducing a common rate of exchange of the zloty to the dollar (involving a substantial initial devaluation) and ensuring zloty convertibility in the domestic market;
9. Introducing a common customs tariff in order to restrict imports and stimulate exports;
10. Providing social assistance to the population within the limits of government possibilities;
11. The elimination of monopoly positions and a substantial withdrawal of administrative intervention in enterprise activities.

The use of the 'shock therapy' method began in Russia on 2 January 1992. A month later it began in Georgia. To explain how the 'shock therapy' approach used in Georgia deviated from the Polish approach it is helpful to compare each step taken in Georgia with the corresponding item in the 'Balcerowicz Plan' (which is a classical scheme of the 'shock therapy' approach in post-communist countries), as listed above.

1. The reform of price formation started in Georgia as early as spring 1991 when free prices on some types of goods were introduced. If in 1991 these changes were still of an exceptional character, by February 1992 (that is a month later than in Russia) there were radical changes in the price-formation system in Georgia. Thus, the prices of one group of goods and services were liberalised, while the regulated prices of another group increased considerably. All this was aimed at balancing the market. If in 1991 the consumer price index stood at 1.8, in 1992 it rose to 25. At the same time it is noteworthy that the regulated consumer prices increased 68 times in 1992 in comparison with those of 1991 (for bread, the main food product in Georgia, 100 times). We can say that the first item of the 'Balcerowicz plan' was on the whole fulfilled in Georgia.

2. From 1992 indexation of minimum wages and social security benefits began to be used in Georgia. In 1991 this indexation was

carried out only once, but in 1992, in the process of liberalising price formation, income indexation was performed six times. In 1991 the minimum wage and the average wage of employees increased in comparison with the previous year by 1.85 times and 1.26 times, respectively, and in 1992 compared with 1991 – by 13.14 times and 17.94 times, respectively. True, there were no strict regulatory measures in Georgia to control increases in the wage fund (as was done in Poland, when in the case of a 2 per cent overspending of the wage fund the penalty imposed on an enterprise was equal to 200 per cent of this sum; and if the overspending was more than 2 per cent the penalty was 300–500 per cent of the corresponding sum), but the increases in wages and social security benefits lagged behind price increases. Thus, it can be considered that item two of the 'Balcerowicz Plan' was also, to a certain extent, more or less fulfilled in Georgia.

3 and 4. In 1992 in comparison with 1991, the interest rate on deposits increased from 2 per cent to 5 per cent per annum and for ten-year deposits the interest rate increased from 9 per cent to 80 per cent. Such an increase of the interest rate was still far from reflecting the actual inflation rate [with the result that real interest rates remained strongly negative – Ed.]. It should also be noted that it was generally impossible to restrict the money supply in circulation in Georgia in those days by increasing the interest rate, because the country had no monetary system of its own; there were in circulation in Georgia only the rouble of the already disintegrated USSR, and the newly issued Russian rouble.

In summer 1992 it was decided to double cash deposits on a deferred withrawal basis. In particular, on 25 July the decision was taken to double cash deposits devalued by inflation on 1 August. The population immediately responded by depositing more money in cash deposits. On 1 August, a new decision was made to prolong until 10 August the time available for placing money in cash deposits for doubling. After doubling the additional money could be withdrawn after only a year, unless the money was to be used in the process of privatisation (which was, however, suspended at that period in Georgia). As it became rather difficult to receive the necessary quantity of bank-notes from Russia in a timely way in the second half of 1992, the money accumulated in this way was paid out as wages and pensions, and this practically prevented the government from restricting the money supply. As a result, we can conclude that items three and four of the 'Balcerowicz Plan' were not carried out in Georgia.

5. In 1992 the share of government investment in the total expenditure of the state budget was not reduced, and up to that year it varied in the range 20–25 per cent. The nominal amount of subsidies in 1992 compared with 1991 increased by about 5.1 times. However, in 1991 the share of subsidies in budget expenditure amounted to the remarkably high level of 47 per cent, and in 1992 this was cut back to 30.1 per cent. Even so, this does not enable us to suggest that item five of the 'Balcerowicz Plan' was realised in Georgia.

6. Government internal bonds were formally issued in 1992. But they were offered for sale only in autumn 1993 and mainly in order to convert bonds of the former Soviet Union into new Georgian bonds. As for the use of government bonds to meet the state budget deficit, it should be noted that this has not yet proved feasible in Georgia. It is clear that item six of the 'Balcerowicz Plan' was not implemented either.

7. Comprehensive reform of the tax system in accordance with the requirements of a market economy started as early as the spring of 1991. For this reason item seven of the 'Balcerowicz Plan' should mainly be considered as fulfilled in Georgia at that time, although it should also be noted that further reform of the tax system is continuing constantly, as in many other countries of the world.

8. In 1992 there was no national currency in Georgia, and so it was practically impossible to fulfil item eight of the 'Balcerowicz Plan'.

9. In 1992, general customs tariffs were introduced at rates of 2 per cent on imports and 8 per cent on exports. Obviously, this policy did not favour either import restrictions or export stimulation, so that item nine of the 'Balcerowicz Plan' was clearly not fulfilled in Georgia either.

10. It was already mentioned above that in 1992, as in 1991, there was income indexation, albeit imperfectly applied, and subject to lags. At that time any type of assistance to families with small incomes was disregarded. That is to say, the social protection system did not differentiate by income level in a way that supported those with low real incomes. As a result, the real minimum wage in 1992 amounted to only 86 per cent of that of 1991. Since, despite the income indexation in

1992, targeted assistance to the families most in need was inadequate, item ten of the 'Balcerowicz Plan' was unfortunately not fulfilled.

11. In 1992, for the first time in Georgia, legal and government resolutions and decrees restricting monopolistic institutions and practices and promoting competition were issued, although their effective implementation was significantly delayed. True, as early as 1991, the Soviet procedures for the centralised supply of resources to enterprises and final customers were disrupted and gradually abandoned, but many elements of the system of state administrative interference in enterprise activity were still preserved. For instance, the mechanism of state orders continued to be widely used. Hence item eleven of the 'Balcerowicz Plan' was also not carried out at that time.

Thus, in 1992 in Georgia eight out of eleven items of the 'Balcerowicz Plan' (that is, all except items one, two and seven) were not fulfilled.

Also neglected were such important measures as the cancelling or at least serious restriction of budgetary subsidies and tough restriction of the money supply. Many of those items were actually doomed to failure, above all because there was no independent monetary system at that time in Georgia.[1] In these conditions, implementing a defective variant of the 'shock therapy' method based only on price liberalisation could hardly be expected to succeed. In other words, in the absence of corresponding governmental institutions, the transition to a market economy using the 'shock therapy' approach was practically impossible. In this situation it might have been much more effective to choose the step-by-step approach to the transition to a market economy, which could have been based on the successive creation of the various institutions necessary both for pursuing reforms and for constructing the Georgian state.

The populist stage of economic reform ended with the inevitable failure of the defective Georgian modification of the 'shock therapy' approach, and this then gave rise to serious delays to economic reform process.

1. It is not clear that such a negative conclusion is justifed in principle, since the Georgian authorities could have imposed far more extensive and effective monetary control than they chose to do. However, one effect of the lack of an independent currency might well have been an absence of clarity concerning the real locus of responsibility for monetary control, together with serious lack of experience regarding the means for exercising such control [Editor's note].

The Stage of Delayed Economic Reform

The stage of delayed economic reform includes 1993 and the first half of 1994 (Georgia, 1995). One factor resulting in delayed reforms was outside the economic sphere, while another factor explained delays in terms of basic mistakes of economic policy. The economy of Georgia (and not only the economy) was not prepared for the full-scale military operations that started in Abkhazia in summer 1992, nor for the civil war that intensified in autumn 1993. These events seriously strained the state budget, and in 1993–94 it proved impossible to get the budget approved in advance in the normal manner. To cover the resulting deficits, the only possible source was money emissions. The gap between state expenditures and revenues was 1.118 billion coupons in 1993, and in 1994 the corresponding deficit amounted to 28.293 billion coupons.

Both in consequence of a general amnesty announced in the winter of 1992, and later on through its participation in military operations (as a country without an army), the crime situation in Georgia worsened so much that it became too dangerous to conduct most economic activity. As a result, many businessmen left their native land, and this accelerated the outflow of capital. At the same time undisguised robbery was replaced by racketeering, which is also not conducive to successful business development. These criminal elements could not usually manage to accumulate wealth (had they done so, it might in the future have put them in a position where they needed a stable situation to protect their new wealth). The reason for this is that the overwhelming majority of these people were drug addicts or had links with the drug trade, and so there was substantial leakage of stolen property to the neighbouring countries from where the drugs illegally penetrated into Georgia.

In late 1992 and early 1993 the most important policy mistake occurred. The government, for some reason, did not expect that it would receive additional banknotes from Moscow, and it therefore brought into circulation the temporary banknotes of Georgia – the coupon of the National Bank of the Republic of Georgia. Unfortunately, representatives of the different levels of authority in Georgia were unable to take the new currency seriously, sometimes revealing contemptuous attitudes towards it. This had a decisive impact on the already serious devaluation process under way. Basically, the nature of the mistake was the illusion that it was economically expedient for Georgia to remain temporarily or even permanently within the proposed 'rouble zone'. As a result of this unfortunate illusion, the coupon became the sole legal tender of payment only in July–August 1993, when Russia carried out a partial currency reform of its own and withdrew the rouble of the former Soviet Union from circulation. This act made it clear that Georgia would be obliged to introduce its own currency.

Uncontrolled credit emissions were the foundation of the inflationary process in Georgia. Attempts to solve agricultural problems (for example, the procurement of agricultural products in autumn 1993 and carrying out essential agricultural work in spring 1994), from a budget that had been practically non-existent since the autumn of 1993, resulted in initially unreported budgetary emissions which finally ruined the financial system of the country. Georgia developed a hyperinflationary spiral, with the inflation rate from 1993 until autumn 1994 proceeding at some 60–70 per cent per month. In the long run this money was not, unfortunately, used for agricultural purposes. In conditions of such high inflation, the coupon could not perform the normal function of sustaining commercial turnover, because the real value of the coupon supply was constantly falling. Other things being equal, this promoted wider use of the rouble instead of the coupon as means of payment.

In 1991–92 the foundations of the system of informal relations which is characteristic of low-income counries were laid down in Georgia (Adams and Fitchett, 1992).

The incorrect policy of the National Bank towards restricting cash circulation (which gave rise, contrary to common sense, to restrictions on the withdrawal of coupons from the banking system) resulted in sunstantial discrepancies between cash and non-cash monetary values. This further restricted the circulation of the coupon. Also, state commercial banks tolerated excessive overdrafts, which promoted hidden credit emission. Subsidised prices on bread, gas, electricity and transport gave the budget an additional 'loading' and also promoted budgetary emissions.

A serious error was perpertrated in Georgia's foreign trade policy, which allowed the 'unique Georgian' clearing system to be consolidated. Barter was considered the only way to receive gas from

Turkmenistan. The prices of both Turkmen gas and a lot of poor-quality goods produced in Georgia were artificially overcharged. According to the 'innovators' of such an approach, this would result in the creation of an environment for Georgian enterprises that stimulated their activity. It should be mentioned that such an environment for producing goods of poor quality has really been created. At the same time this production had to be purchased by government. In the absence of a proper budget, however, this operation could be only partially carried out, and even then only by means of money emission (which also promoted inflation). Most of this production was taken from enterprises by the government using a form of the state order system,[2] with guarantees to pay the corresponding price in the future. Needless to say, this put these enterprises in a difficult financial situation and resulted in the formation of a non-payment 'network' within the country, which was difficult to stop. For the government it became impossible to collect the full volume of goods within the country to fulfil the barter commodity exchange agreed with Turkmenistan. In recent years the existing difficulties with the Azerbaijan transport route, first the blocking of the railway line passing through Abkhazia and then through Chechnya, at first complicated and then made impossible the normal transportation of goods, assembled by the government, to Turkmenistan. As a result of these difficulties and mistakes, Georgia's debt to Turkmenistan amounted to about half a billion US dollars over two years. The country's total external debt rose to one billion US dollars.

Ignoring the interests of enterprise workers and employees effectively impeded the privatisation process in 1992–93 and held up the restructuring of enterprises into joint-stock companies.

Much of this lay behind the energy crisis, associated with the use of credits for purposes other than the intended ones; non-payment of the real cost of power resources (in other words, absurdly low domestic prices); chronic irresponsibility in regard to technical norms that made it impossible to carry out not only capital renewal, but even routine repairs and maintenance; constant theft of power equipment containing

2. Using the system of state orders required a complicated system of quotas and licensing. When receiving debts from different foreign countries and international organisations, in some cases the interest rates and prices on goods bought with the help of credits were artificially increased, and the credits received were partly used in less important directions.

copper (including wire) to sell in Turkey. All the above-mentioned factors, including the energy crisis, gave rise to an unprecendented collapse of production.

Moreover, given the general state of disarray in both national and enterprise-level accounting, it became impossible to obtain full information on firms and their activities. This, in its turn, artificially exaggerated the already apparent decline in the major macro-economic indicators and, at enterprise level, facilitated firms' efforts to hide their tax liabilities.

This stage of economic reform was characterised by extremely imperfect recording of foreign economic activities, inefficient customs procedures, extensive waste of commodity stocks, uncontrolled transfers of state property to foreign countries, a decline in the economic role of normal wages, unrecorded expansion of the shadow economy, and uses of humanitarian aid for purposes other than those intended. Overall, the picture of the Georgian economy was exceedingly bleak.

The Stage of Correction of Errors

At the beginning of 1994 the head of state of the Republic of Georgia, Eduard Shevardnadze, initiated the preparation of an anti-crisis programme of macro-economic stabilisation and systemic change. In spring 1994 the programme was initiated, and this made a good start to *the stage of correction of errors* committed during the earlier stages of the process of economic reforms.

This new stage of economic reform was also characterised by problems of a non-economic nature. By spring 1994 the hostilities in Abkhazia had already come to an end. True, this fact had a positive influence on the economy as a whole, but it also gave rise to a new problem: social protection of refugees and displaced people, which was a heavy burden on the government budget. Until the refugees and displaced people return to their homes these social (and not only social) problems will not be solved.

Law-enforcment institutions intensified the fight against criminals in order to improve the situation. Definite positive results were achieved, but the country still has a long way to go to solve the problem. Many enterprises, for instance, are afraid to undertake high levels of production for fear of being robbed by organised (including semi-official) and other criminal elements.

From spring 1994 the government gradually changed its attitude towards the coupon. According to the standard policy of the International Monetary Fund (IMF) it is ready to assist any country that has its own currency and whose government does its best to strengthen it. If Georgia stayed within the 'rouble zone' the IMF would undoubtedly prefer to work with Russia – the country issuing the rouble. This fact undermined the positions of those in power supporting the 'rouble zone' since they would have had to advocate openly the requirement to regard the Russian rouble as the sole legal tender. Conversely, it assisted those in power who, from the very beginning, realised that the Georgian economy had no prospects without its own national currency. Interestingly, in 1994 a noble but perhaps hopeless experiment was already going on in Kutaisi, where the city authorities were supporting the coupon – the one region of Georgia to do so. All this, together with the relative stabilisation of the Georgian coupon and worsening depreciation of the rouble, encouraged the population to take the coupon more seriously.

Uncontrolled monetary emissions became impossible owing to the increasing firmness of the authorities of the national bank of Georgia. In autumn 1994 the Bank cancelled the prevailing restrictions on the withdrawal of cash from the banks, under obvious pressure of the IMF. As a result cash and non-cash money values drew considerably closer to each other.

From late 1994, on the advice of the IMF, the national bank started regulating the banking system using the classical methods widely used elsewhere in the world. Apart from solving other problems, this prevented the state-commercial banks from continuing to work in overdraft conditions. Also, from the second half of 1994 the process of corporatisation of the state-commercial banks started.

According to the programme worked out with the IMF in September 1994, the prices of gas and electricity were raised to world levels, the price of bread increased 285 times (!), metro fares increased greatly, and so did tariffs on other municipal services. There was a wage increase for those employed in activities financed by the budget, pensions and social welfare payments were also increased, but these increases lagged considerably behind the price rises. This enabled a great reduction in the budgetary subsidies needed to cover the discrepancies between consumer and producer prices or between producer prices and actual costs. It was followed by a substantial strengthening of the rate of the Georgian coupon. If before the price rise on bread one dollar was worth 5.3 million coupons, after the price rise one dollar was already valued at 2.4 million coupons. This process continued; at the end of 1994 the price of bread increased again by 40 per cent and as a result a stable coupon exchange rate was established (at one dollar = 1.3 million coupons).

Unfortunately, Georgia could not manage a full recovery of money either for gas and electricity, or even for bread. However, if enterprises and the population did not pay for their gas and electricity supplies, or paid only negligible sums, the price of bread was almost fully paid by the population. Delays in enforcing these payments encouraged a more sceptical attitude to the coupon by economic agents: trade organisations, enterprises and banks delayed corresponding money transfers and conducted speculative operations in the currency market, sustaining significant losses in the process. Starting from 1995, when the coupon rate became stable, timely withdrawal of these sums was prevented not only by the sluggishness of the banks, but also by some local authorities using these sums temporarily in order to settle the problems of their local budgets.

Also, the pseudo-protection of enterprises by some representatives of government, and the often groundless fears of the population about interruptions of supply, meant that enforcement of payments by cessation of deliveries – the normal method in market-type economies – was not achieved. Gas supply to the population of Tbilisi stopped only in January 1995. Carrying out a stricter policy to recover the cost of bread was achieved step by step in the first and second quarters of 1995.

The impossibility of collecting the full cost of gas and electricity also meant that the government could not revise the corresponding prices, because of the general commitments on reform. The dollar prices of gas and electricity increased every month as a result of the strengthening of the coupon. This led to an artificial increase in the product cost, having an adverse affect, first of all, on industrial enterprises. Following a review of its commitments to the IMF, the Georgian government revised coupon prices downwards. In particular, since April 1995 the cost of gas was reduced by 35 per cent and the cost of electricity by 25 per cent. At the same time, the government of Georgia refused to purchase gas after June 1995. Instead, purchases had to be undertaken by the immediate consumers, namely by 'Sakenergo' (Georgian state energy company), big industrial enterprises and municipalities. To enable these direct purchases of gas by consumers to take place, the above-mentioned Georgian clearing system was, in effect, annulled.

All this put on the agenda the requirement to terminate quotas and simplify licensing. This process soon started: the system of quotas was completely annulled with effect from 1 June 1995, and licensing was preserved for only a limited list of goods. Order was also re-established in borrowing and using debts, building on the practices established in connection with Georgia's first loans from the IMF and the World Bank. In December 1994, Georgia received from the IMF the first tranche of a Systemic Transformation Facility (STF) (approximately 39 million US dollars). In July and November 1994 and March 1995, Georgia received an Institutional Building Loan from the World Bank (approximately 10 million US dollars), a Rehabilitation Loan on Municipal Infrastructure (approximately 18 million US dollars) and an Economic Rehabilitation Loan (75 million US dollars). The STF is used by the national bank to stabilise the rate of the Georgian coupon by means of credit allocation to support particular approved activities. The Institutional Building Loan is used to improve the material and technical base of government structures. As for the Rehabilitation Loan, it is used to finance a part of budget expenditures on a temporary basis.

Approval of the republican budget by parliament at the beginning of 1995, after a two-year interval, can be considered a very important step towards establishing order in the financial system of Georgia. The real significance of this budget is that emissions of credit and also monetary emissions themselves were not used to balance budgetary income and expenditure. In 1995, only 47 per cent of the expenditures of the state budget were covered by taxes and the remaining 53 per cent had to be covered through the monetisation of wheat and flour received as humanitarian aid (mobilising proceeds of sales in the state budget). In that way, an unbalanced budget could be balanced without monetary emission. It was achieved through the help of donor countries and organisations promoting reforms in Georgia. Unfortunately, the planned financial indicators for the first two quarters were not achieved, though the actual results were improving considerably month by month.

With the support and efforts of the IMF, the majority of the countries to which Georgia's debt of approximately one billion US dollars was owed agreed to debt rescheduling. This allowed the IMF to allocate the second credit tranche of the STF at the end of June 1995 (approximately 44 million US dollars) and the stand-by credit (approximately 113 million US dollars). All this was expected to create the conditions for Georgia to preserve financial stability, to carry out currency reform and to place the *lari* (national currency) into circulation, avoiding the errors previously commited by the government in connection with the coupon.

The exchange rate of the national currency was expected to remain unaltered until the end of 1995. If the inflation rate in the first half of 1995 averaged 2–3 per cent per month, then in the second half of 1995 it was expected to fall to just 1 per cent per month [in the event, Georgia's consumer prices rose by 65 per cent in 1995 as a whole - Ed.]. In fact, after July 1995 the price of bread increased by 7 per cent on average, while the wages of budget sector employees increased by 50 per cent on average. In autumn 1995 the liberalisation of bread prices was planned. This was expected to become possible as a result of the planned dissolution of the government monopoly in this sphere.

From 1 July 1995 the minimum monthly wage of those employed in the budget sector was just US$2.69 and the maximum US$12.69. These figures are, of course, very low, though one should recall that at the beginning of September 1994 the minimum wage was less than ten cents, and the maximum a little more than a dollar (all evaluated using the then prevailing exchange rate, without adjustment for purchasing power parity).

From the point of view of sectoral development, the reforms in Georgia are being implemented most vigorously in the health-care system, where the project for reform was elaborated in close co-operation with experts of the World Bank. In the health-care sphere there is a gradual transition to paid medical service and establishing a system of medical insurance. Reforms in the education sphere are also making gradual progress.

In May 1994 the head of state issued a decree according to which enterprise personnel were given precedence in the process of corporatisation. This speeded up the process. At the same time the process of privatisation, by means of direct purchases, was also encouraged. In 1995 in Georgia, as in many other former communist countries, the process of using vouchers in privatisation began: part of the social property is distributed to people free of charge. The approach is justified by the necessity to give everyone a fair chance to acquire assets in the course of privatisation (Papava, 1992, pp. 92–7).

Method of 'Social Promotion' of Economic Reform

Putting right the mistakes made due to the deficient modification of 'shock therapy' as applied in Georgia and those due to delayed or blocked economic reforms will be difficult enough. This then places on the agenda the rather complicated question of how, and using what methods, the reforms in Georgia should be continued.

Unfortunately, there is no satisfactory or comprehensive answer to this question in economic theory. It is not uncommon for economists to continue to debate how the transition to the market economy should be carried out – by means of 'shock therapy' or by more gradual reform. At this time, however, they forget that we are no longer at the start of the transition period to the market economy: the choice has already been made, which is why to speak about gradual reform (striking examples of which are provided by the experience of communist Hungary in its final period, and China, which is still under a communist regime) is, at least, rather late.

To learn how best to continue reforms for a country in Georgia's situation, it is useful to determine the *main indicator* for assessing the maturity of the market system. A human being who himself creates the market system and for whom it is created can be considered as the best indicator of this kind.

In the classical market system, in order to describe a man working successfully, the notion *homo economicus* was long ago defined in economic theory. This is the person whose activity is guided by his or her private interests to gain the maximum profit. Of course, *homo economicus* is an abstract notion, but still, in a sense, it captures well the typical behaviour of a private-sector manufacturer.

During the last period of the existence of the USSR, referred to as *perestroika*, *homo sovieticus* was a rather popular notion to describe a Soviet man. This is a person afraid of and subordinated to the state 'machinery', who depends on the good will of the powerful to improve his or her well-being. Naturally, *homo sovieticus* is also an abstract notion, but it also reflects the type of person created for decades by communist power.

At the present stage of economic reform, there are many who, on the one hand, try to act on their own initiative and according to their own interests, and on the other still regard the government with fear, but also in the hope of charity and expecting to be protected. Voucher privatisation might be considered as an instance of such confused thinking, when principles of social justice are introduced as a foreign body into the economic interests associated with privatisation (Papava, 1992, pp. 92–7; 1995, pp. 34–7). Another example to illustrate the above characterisation is given by the urgent pleas from depositors in bankrupt commercial and industrial trust companies which functioned on the principle of a 'pyramid' (when to cover old debts new debts at high interest are taken on). They begged the government to provide them with financial assistance. True, the government had not undertaken any preliminary obligations with respect to those companies or corresponding depositors, but the social and political pressure was so great that the government of Georgia had to intervene as requested. For a period of one year it exempted from all taxes all stock companies set up on the basis of these bankrupt ones, and the depositors were also given vouchers as compensation (each depositor was provided with a block of vouchers, with nominal price of US$200).

Thus, at the present stage of transition to a market economy, the type of a person in whom the qualities of *homo economicus* are steadily developing is formed, although he is not yet liberated from qualities more characteristic of *homo sovieticus*. Such an individual can conventionally be called *homo transformaticus*, which is the same abstraction as the similar notions mentioned above. Many entrepreneurs today can be considered as striking examples of *homo transformaticus*. They operate their enterprises sufficiently to satisfy their personal needs, the needs of their family members and a small number of workers employed at their enterprises. This type of entrepreneur is not interested in operating his enterprise at a higher level, because *homo economicus* has only partly developed in him.

Proceeding from such an approach to contemporary man, we can conclude that the sooner *homo transformaticus* is transformed into *homo economicus* the sooner and more completely the market economy will become firmly established. It determines the specificity of a new stage of economic reform (due to start in Georgia in 1996). In particular, the market stratification of society is bound to take place, that is the formation of social strata corresponding to the market system. The whole spectrum of social stratification is meant here, including economic, political and professional stratification (Sorokin, 1959).

All this seeks to create a stratum of entrepreneurs strongly supported both politically and professionally, and to provide the basis for improving the economic situation of the 'middle stratum' (representatives of middle and small business, physicians, teachers, scientists, and so on). From this point of view, the formation of democratic society helps to strengthen the institutions of political support to entrepreneurs; and the creation of a strong stratum of entrepreneurs is itself a guarantor of the existence of democratic society.

One aspect of the transition to a market economy is the urgent need for new professions (managers, brokers, dealers, and the like), which are especially necessary in post-communist countries for the development and formation of entrepreneurship and its supporting institutional framework. At the same time, it is important to provide targeted assistance to the poorer segments of society, especially those losing badly in the early stages of transition. To do this, it is necessary to identify the stratum of the population whose income does not meet the living standards and subsistence minimum.

To summarise the above, we can conclude that in 1996 Georgia was entering a new phase of economic reform, that is, the *stage of target-oriented social market formation.*

During the process of social market formation, special attention is paid to the aspect of target-orientation, because otherwise the period of time needed to bring about the transformation of *homo transformaticus* into *homo economicus* will be greatly extended. And this, in its turn, will create a situation where we would have neither a developed stratum of entrepreneurs nor the means to improve social assistance to the poor. So in the process of social market formation, the aspect of target-orientation acquires a special meaning. In order to avoid a very sluggish transition to a market economy, the government must participate in the process of formation of entrepreneurs and in the process of market stratification of the society as a whole. In other words, to continue economic reforms in Georgia (and in other post-communist countries in a similar situation) we suggest that the government should adopt the method of 'social selection', which can be called the method of *'social promotion'* of economic reform. The essence of the approach is that the government should create conditions to promote the rapid expansion of a strong stratum of entrepreneurs. At the same time, it is necessary to render targeted assistance to the most needy social groups so that they should not block the reforms.

The method of social promotion of economic reform includes three types of measures:

- considerable improvements in the crime situation, to relieve widespread fears associated with various types of military group, including bandit-type militias. If this problem is not settled, it will place serious obstacles in the path of both domestic and foreign entrepreneurs. In particular, few foreign investors would come to Georgia;
- stimulating the development of entrepreneurial activity, without which the process of creating a solid layer of entrepreneurs mostly takes place in the 'shadow economy'; this also creates fertile soil for reinforcing illegal actions, and thus impedes the process of creating sound, legally-based entrepreneurial activity;
- directing social assistance towards the most needy strata in society, in a targeted manner, enabling them to overcome the difficulties brought about by the reforms. At the same time this targeted social policy facilitates the reform process by widening the social basis of support for reforms.

These three problem areas are closely interwoven. The difficult crime situation prevents the development of entrepreneurial activity, new goods are not produced and this in turn makes it impossible to assist the poor social stratum; and the representatives of the poor, other things being equal, are drawn into the criminal world because of this hardship. An initial improvement in the crime situation was already mentioned above. It is necessary, however, to continue the struggle being waged by the government against the criminal world.

To develop entrepreneurship it is necessary to create a social environment in which the entrepreneur can have the possibility of free choice. In such an environment he or she will have an interest in transferring from the 'shadow economy' into a legal state, and will also direct part of his or her profits to support the expansion of production. At the same time, against a background of financial stabilisation, once there is a reduction of interest rates, it will be important to promote the wider use of savings to expand production; that is, a favourable investment environment must be created. In other words, it is necessary to stimulate the domestic supply side. In general, during the period of transition to a market economy, special attention must be paid to the problems of supply (see Tanzi, 1993, Ch.1).

Early discussions of supply-side economics focused on the need for a liberal system of taxation (Canto, Joines and Laffer, 1988). One of the theory's proponents, Laffer, gave his name to the *Laffer curve*, which shows the connection between average (effective) tax rates and budget revenues. According to the Laffer curve, at low tax rates an increase in taxes increases the budget revenues, but after a definite limit any further increase in average tax rates leads to a reduction in budget revenues. Thus, with comparatively low tax rates, one group of entrepreneurs would be encouraged to start production, a second group would transfer from illegal activity into legal production, and a third group would even expand production considerably.

These findings of the theory have been applied more or less successfully in some of the developing countries. Generally, in these countries arguments based on the Laffer curve were used to justify reducing income tax rates (Gandhi, 1987). However, in present-day Georgia the maximum income tax rate is just 20 per cent. Nevertheless, a further reduction in this tax is not out of the question, although it is not at present under consideration. Much more important is the reduction of tax rates associated with corporate activity. According to supply-side economics, in order to stimulate production, the total amount of taxes should not normally exceed one-third of the income of entrepreneurs and the general population. In that case, as indicated by empirical work on developed countries, tax revenues into the state budget would reach their maximum level. Various tax allowances should be avoided where possible, since they complicate the tax system and reduce its efficiency (Tanzi, 1993,

Ch.5). It is more effective to use a general approach based on supply-side economics.

A well-known model for the practical implementation of the supply-side theory is 'Reaganomics' (named after its popularity during the presidency of US President Reagan), when the reduction of tax rates is not confined to the income tax, and spending cuts go far enough to threaten the vital interests of large corporations. Together with the reduction of tax rates, 'Reaganomics' assumed an increase in military expenditure and accompanying sharp reductions in the budget financing of social programmes. In Georgia, it is clearly impossible to adopt fully the principles of 'Reaganomics', and in any case it could not be justified because of the unfavourable distributional impact of such a programme. The third group of measures to implement the method of social promotion of economic reform pays special attention to the social protection of the population, and this makes it impossible and unjustifiable in Georgian conditions to adopt the system of 'Reaganomics' without alteration.

According to supply-side economics, the government should assume a completely new role. In particular, 'a state based on social welfare and insurance principles' should be formed, which will not restrict the impact of market forces on the expansion of production and the creation of the basis for economic growth (Kristol, 1979). In this case, poverty is perceived not as a relative value but as an absolutely low level of welfare. And it implies that to overcome poverty it is necessary to increase the total wealth accumulated by the society, which is achieved by stimulating the supply.

Until a transition from 'galloping' to 'creeping' inflation is achieved in Georgia the bank interest rate is bound to be high. This also limits the possibility of using commercial credit in order to establish the current assets of enterprises. That is why, in order to stimulate the supply, it is not enough to be guided by the recommendations of supply-side economics alone, since these are mainly derived from the principles of liberal taxation. Alongside the latter it is necessary to conduct a strict financial policy to reduce inflation and to improve the banking system. It will then be possible to reduce the bank rate. At the same time it should be borne in mind that the reduction in tax rates will then make it possible for enterprises to use accumulated funds to restore their current assets.

Eliminating barter from the normal practice of foreign trade and using straightforward currency transactions will also contribute to the stimulation of supply. The reduction of tax rates not only stimulates an expansion of supply, but it also creates an indispensable condition for stimulating demand; this results from the fact that lower taxes result in incresed disposable income which can then be spent on consumer goods and investments. True, according to the Keynesian approach, in order to stimulate demand attention must be paid to government expenditure, but this approach does not exclude reducing taxes in order to stimulate demand. However, this indirect way of stimulating demand is usually less popular in the Keynesian theory.

For a country in Georgia's situation, increasing government expenditures in order to stimulate demand is practically impossible, since the state budget can be balanced only with difficulty, with the help of external aid. Additional spending would disturb the balance and, consequently, it would be impossible to preserve financial stability.

By reducing tax rates, the stimulation of demand should seek to contribute to the solution of social problems as far as possible, notably the problem of employment. Reducing taxes in any case raises consumption, which can have a negative effect in a developed market system. In particular, with existing stocks of productive assets, output capacity is essentially fixed in the short run, and with no change in public expenditure a growth in consumption will be accompanied by a fall in savings and an increase in the interest rate. This will decrease investment and production in the future (see, for example, Mankiw, 1992, Ch.3). This unfavourable effect is not present in the countries in transition, as the real stocks of productive assets are far from fully utilised in a situation where production has already declined markedly. This gives incentives for expanding production as consumption grows, while saving is not reduced either (and in some cases may actually be raised).

Thus, the theoretical foundations for the method of 'social promotion', proceeding from the above, lead to a form of *Laffer–Keynesian synthesis*, which might seem contradictory. To illustrate this Laffer-Keynesian synthesis let us consider a relatively simple version of the integration of the Laffer curve and the Keynesian expenditure multiplier. Let the 'Laffer curve' be described by the function:

$$T = N.t.lnt \qquad (1)$$

where

> T is the total tax revenue of government;
> N *is* the value of gross national product (GNP), corresponding to maximum total tax revenues;

and t is the tax rate $(0<<t<<1)$.

Clearly, $T = 0$, when $t = 0$ and $t=1$.

If we take into consideration that the link between the total tax revenues (T) and the actual volume of GNP (Y) is:

$$T = tY \qquad (2)$$

the dependence between Y and t on the basis of (1) will be:

$$Y = N.lnt \qquad (3)$$

Graphically (1) and (3) can be described by the following curves (Figure 12.1):

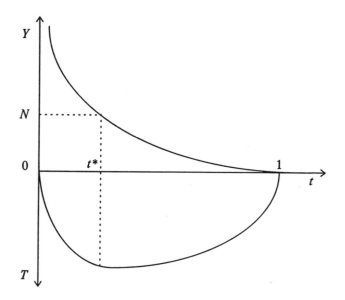

Figure 12.1   The Laffer curve and relation of tax rates to output

Figure 12.1 reflects the notion of the Laffer curve, roughly corresponding to similar curves by writers on supply-side economics (Canto, Joines and Laffer, 1983, p.76). $t*$ is the tax rate which corresponds to the maximum value of total tax revenue, T. Equating the derivative of the function T to zero and solving the resulting equation for t, we find that $t* = 1/e$ (where e is the base of natural logarithms). According to (3), while t grows, the Y is reduced. This statement fully corresponds to the Keynesian views (for example, Stoleru, 1969, Ch.5).

In order to combine the Laffer curve and the Keynesian multiplier, let us consider the standard Keynesian formula of the aggregate demand:

$$Y = c(Y - T) + G + I + X - M \qquad (4)$$

where

c is marginal propensity to consume $(0 < c < 1)$;

G is government expenditure;

I is private investment;

X is exports; and

M is imports.

Under conditions of market equilibrium the total supply (3) is equal to the total demand (4), that is

$$N.lnt - c.(N.lnt - N.t.lnt) = G + I + X - M \qquad (5)$$

In (5), equations (1) and (2) are taken into account. Now we solve (5) for N. According to the 'Laffer curve', $Y=N$, when $t=1/e$. Using this in (5) we find that:

$$N = (G + I + X - M)/(1 - (1-1/e)c) \qquad (6)$$

Thus, under the 'Laffer–Keynesian synthesis' the volume of GNP when total tax revenues reach their maximum level is determined using equation (6).

As mentioned above, a liberal tax policy not only stimulates supply, but also demand. Given this, the whole society, including entrepreneurs, are being 'medically treated' with both supply and demand stimuli. The resulting economic policy based on the 'Laffer–Keynesian synthesis' can be referred to as *tax therapy* for short.

One of the main ways of stimulating an expansion of production is through the accelerated depreciation of fixed capital. In this case, depreciation allowances reduce the portion of profit liable to taxation, and hence reduce taxation. The sums released in that way, as a rule, are used for investment. Thus, the method of accelerated depreciation is an integral part of 'tax therapy'.

After the decrease of tax rates the simplification of the system itself should follow, which will have to promote the formation of a culture of taxation in the society. Disbursement of taxation must be easier and more convenient than attempts to avoid it. This will create in the public a very important and necessary attitude (or 'set', to use the terminology of Uznadze, 1966) towards the due and complete payment of taxes, seriously deficient in early forms of *homo transformaticus*.

When carrying out *tax therapy* it is necessary to use maximum possibilities of the state budget to solve the problems of social protection. At the same time, the above-mentioned principle of the 'state of social insurance' must be protected, whereby the problem of poverty can be addressed most effectively using the collective resources accumulated by the government. Thus, sums from the state budget should be targeted to render assistance to those most in need (Tanzi, 1993, Chs 14,15), rather than increasing the total amount of state budget expenditure allocated for social protection (these sums are of a productive nature [see Papava, 1993, pp. 58–60; 1994, pp. 39–40), which must be taken into account in determining the directions of their usage).

To achieve this, it is first of all necessary to free the budgetary sector from 'superfluous' burdens. For instance, today, that part of the population of Georgia employed in the budgetary sector is, in many cases, engaged in private activities. True, the wage received by each citizen from the budgetary sources is extremely small, but on the whole it is nevertheless a heavy burden for the budget. Hence those people who earn their living in the non-budgetary sphere, and who in reality are not occupied in their state offices, should no longer be employed in the budgetary sphere. It is possible to solve this problem by reorganising the health care, education, science, culture and state management spheres. The budgetary resources released in this way will be of greater value to those who receive money only from the budget.

One of the most important tasks of the 'state of social insurance' is to create the most encouraging conditions for setting up and developing private institutions of social protection (for example, private pension and insurance funds). [Experience elsewhere, however, suggests that this is extremely difficult, since it requires parallel developments in the financial structure of private sector firms, the market for government debt, and the development of a variety of financial institutions – Ed.]

The 'Laffer–Keynesian synthesis' provides a perfect opportunity to apply different (but not incompatible or mutually exclusive) approaches to macro-economic regulation which stimulate economic growth and further develop the country. Let us take, for example, programmes for the renovation of cities in the US, justified by the Keynesian approach, according to which, in particular, for every dollar invested by the US federal government, private investments of 5–7 dollars would follow (Hansen, 1964, pp. 643–4). For Georgia, given its objective of developing a federalised state model, this type of effect could assume great importance, for instance in connection with regional budgets used to help develop regional city capitals. It should also be mentioned here that, in the process of federalisation of Georgia, other countries' extensive practical experience with budgetary federalism (Tanzi, 1993, Ch.16) should be taken into consideration.

And finally, there is no real alternative to the continuation of economic reform by means of the *social stimulation* method, as there is no shorter or more effective way to implement the market sociogenesis. At the same time, *tax therapy* creates all the conditions for the simultaneous stimulation of supply and demand in the Georgian economy.

References

Adams, D. W. and D. A. Fitchett (eds) (1992), *Informal Finance in Low-Income Countries* (Boulder, CO: Westview).

Balcerowicz, Leszek (1994), 'Poland, 1989–92', in *Political Economy of Economic Reform* (Washington, DC: Institute for International Economics).

Canto, V. A., D. H. Joines and A. B. Laffer (1983), *Foundations of Supply-Side Economics, Theory and Evidence* (New York: Academic Press.

Gandhi, V. P. et al. (1987), *Supply-Side Tax Policy: Its Relevance to*

Developing Contries (Washington, DC: International Monetary Fund).

'Georgia' (1995), *IMF Economic Reviews*, 1994, No. 15 (March), (Washington, DC: International Monetary Fund).

Hansen, A. (1964), *Business Cycles and National Income* (New York).

Kristol, I. (1979), 'Confession of a True, Self-Confessed – Perhaps the Only – 'Neoconservative', *Public Opinion*, October–November.

Mankiw, N. G. (1992), *Macroeconomics* (New York: Worth).

Papava V. (1990), 'On the Concepts of Economic Reform in the USSR', *Ekonomika i matematicheskie metody*, Vol. 26, No. 6.

—— (1992), 'Privatisation of Major Production Factors', *Fair Play, Problems of Management*, No. 3.

—— (1993), 'A New View of the Economic Ability of the Government, Egalitarian Goods and GNP', *International Journal of Social Economics*, Vol. 20, No. 8, pp. 56–62.

—— (1994), 'The Role of the State in the Modern Economic System', *Problems of Economic Transition*, Vol. 37, No. 5, pp. 35–48.

—— (1995), 'Marxist Points of View on the Soviet Communist Economic System and the Manifestation of Egalitarianism in Post-Communist Economic Reform', *International Journal of Social Economics,* Vol. 22, No. 6, pp. 29–37.

Schaffer, M. (1992), *The Economy of Poland,* Centre for Economic Performance, Working Paper No. 67 (London: London School of Economics).

Sorokin, P. A. (1959), *Social and Cultural Mobility* (New York).

Stoleru, L. (1969), *L'equilibre et la croissance economiques* (Paris: Dunod).

Tanzi, V. (1993), *Fiscal Policies in Economies in Transition* (Washington, DC: International Monetary Fund).

Uznadze, D. N. (1966), *The Psychology of Set* (New York: Consultants Bureau).

Index